ECONOMETRIC MODELS OF PERSONAL SAVING

To My Father,
S. H. El-Mokadem
the source of my inspiration
and the one I am endeavouring to model

ECONOMETRIC MODELS OF PERSONAL SAVING
The United Kingdom
1948-1966

A. M. EL-MOKADEM
Battelle Institute, Columbus, Ohio, U.S.A.
and University of Lancaster, U.K.

with a foreword by Professor R. J. Ball
London Graduate School of Business

LONDON   BUTTERWORTHS

THE BUTTERWORTH GROUP

ENGLAND
Butterworth & Co (Publishers) Ltd
London: 88 Kingsway, WC2B 6AB

AUSTRALIA
Butterworths Pty Ltd
Sydney: 586 Pacific Highway, NSW 2067
Melbourne: 343 Little Collins Street, 3000
Brisbane: 240 Queen Street, 4000

CANADA
Butterworth & Co (Canada) Ltd
Toronto: 14 Curity Avenue, 374

NEW ZEALAND
Butterworths of New Zealand Ltd
Wellington: 26—28 Waring Taylor Street, 1

SOUTH AFRICA
Butterworth & Co (South Africa) (Pty) Ltd
Durban: 152—154 Gale Street

First published in 1973

ISBN 0 408 70436 5

Text set in 10/11 pt. IBM Press Roman, printed by photolithography,
and bound in Great Britain at The Pitman Press, Bath

Foreword

A great deal of work has been conducted since the second world war with regard to the determinants of personal savings and customers' expenditure. The Keynesian consumption function lay at the heart of Keynes theory of the determination of economic activity and the level of employment. It was, therefore, natural that many researchers should have devoted a great deal of time to establishing the empirical validity of the underlying hypothesis that the level of saving depended essentially on the level of income. Since the early post-war days the basic hypotheses about overall savings behaviour have become more sophisticated in the hands of Milton Friedman, Franco Modigliani, the late Richard Brumberg, Albert Ando and many other scholars.

At the present time it is difficult to forecast that any major new insights with regard to aggregate savings behaviour will be forthcoming in the next decade. Research work has also been undertaken on the theory of asset choices, deriving initially from theories of portfolio selection, but relatively less work on the allocation of savings between alternative assets has been undertaken by comparison with the work on aggregate savings.

This volume by Dr. El-Mokadem is, therefore, to be welcomed as a first step towards quantifying the influence of various economic activities on the allocation of the flow of personal saving.

The data with which he has worked have been improving but there are still many gaps in our information about the allocation of saving between alternative assets as indicated by the large unidentified item that appears in the personal financial transactions account of the National Income Blue Book. Nevertheless, despite the incompleteness of the data and the relatively short time span for which more adequate data is available, Dr. El-Mokadem has succeeded in establishing the framework of analysis that others will no doubt be able to build on.

R. J. Ball
Professor of Economics
London Graduate School of
Business Studies

Preface

Ever since the publication of Keynes' *General Theory*, the study of personal saving has occupied a prominent place both in economic theory and practical economic policy. Many theories have been developed since. What Keynes meant by the 'psychological law' which 'leads individuals to refrain from spending out of their income' is now subject to several interpretations and in its original form is hardly mentioned, except in textbooks and in survey articles. Not only do the new theories of consumption and saving attract great interest, but so do the mathematical formulations and the statistical estimations of the so-called Statistical Saving Function.

True, nearly forty years after Keynes' revolution, great advances have been achieved and new knowledge has come into the open; nevertheless, certain aspects of the overall problem have been neglected and a number of questions have remained unanswered. Three groups may be distinguished.

What determines the level of aggregate personal saving? Is it only the level of income? If so, does this provide an adequate explanation of why people save? Does the rate (or rates) of interest play any role in determining the amount a community saves out of a given income? Is the saving—income relationship stable or does it shift? And if it does, what causes such shifts? Is it a wealth effect? If so, is it total or some component of wealth that matters?

What determines the composition of aggregate personal saving? Does it matter in which form one saves? To what extent can one regard the various forms of saving as homogeneous? How do individuals allocate their portfolios? What factors do they take into account in deciding whether to save in the form of, say, cash, or bonds, or life assurance, etc.?

What is the optimum rate of saving? How can this rate be sustained? What course of action should the Government adopt? Should they, for instance, reduce taxation? Which tax, or taxes, should be reduced and by how much? Or is it more effective to rely on monetary measures? Or both? etc.

These questions and the like represent the subject matter of this study, which is based on my PhD thesis at Manchester University in 1969. In this connection, I should like to express my sincere thanks to my supervisor Mr. W. Peters of Manchester University who suggested the topic for this research. He devoted much of his time to the work and was always most patient, encouraging and willing to offer useful advice. My debt to him is, indeed, great. Many thanks are also due to Professor R. J. Ball of the London Graduate School of Business who, in my opinion, has inspired many of the economists of my generation. The penetrating comments he made as the external examiner for my PhD, and later on in the preparation of this book have been most constructive. I am also grateful to: Professor A. R. Prest of the London School of Economics for his help and guidance during my graduate years, Professor A. D. Bain of the University of Stirling who read parts of the first draft and made valuable suggestions, and Professor M. J. Parkin of Manchester University for his helpful comments on parts of this book.

During the course of this study I have benefited from the help of several members of the Econometric Department at Manchester University; particularly the late Mr. D. Bugg, also Mr. K. Holden and Mr. J. Stewart. Some of my colleagues at the University of Lancaster have been most helpful. Special thanks are due to: Professor A. I. MacBean for his help and encouragement, Mr. A. D. Airth and Mr. D. T. Nguyen for designing special computer programs which facilitated the work significantly, and Mr. J. V. Hillard for reading the final draft and making a number of corrections. I must mention in particular my colleague, Mr. R. A. Whittaker, without whose help life would have been much more difficult.

I wish to express my appreciation to the staffs of the computer units at Manchester University, Stirling University and Lancaster University. Also to their library staffs who were most co-operative. I am also thankful to Miss P. Townley for typing the final manuscript and to Mr. T. Myers for proof reading.

Finally, my debt to my wife, Ann, is considerable. Her contribution was of immense importance. She painstakingly edited every page of this manuscript, and assisted me in every phase of this undertaking.

A. M. El-Mokadem

Contents

Contents

Contents

List of Tables

List of Tables

1

Introduction

Extensive work has been undertaken dealing with total personal saving, with particular emphasis on the short-run and long-run propensities to save out of personal disposable income. Excellent surveys of the literature on this subject are available[56c] and duplication seems unnecessary. Considerably less attention has been devoted to the study of the factors which determine the components of personal saving. As noted by Friend,[65] the comparative neglect of the latter type of study may be attributed to a variety of reasons: partly to the difficulties of isolating meaningful demand functions for many items of financial and real assets from time series data, partly to the limitations of cross-section data and to the idea that different forms of saving are competitive with, or substitutable for, one another, rather than with items of consumption, so that it is easier to predict total saving rather than its components.

In recent years there have been an increasing number of studies in the United States, and to some extent in the United Kingdom, of consumers' saving in real assets, with motor cars receiving most attention, then financial assets in money and near money, and fewer studies of consumers' saving in other types of financial assets. Moreover, only very few have attempted to analyse the entire structure of consumer real and financial assets. Probably one of the most comprehensive attempts in this respect was made by Watts and Tobin,[211] based on single cross-section data. They estimated linear relationships of the stocks of automobiles, other consumer durables, mortgage debt, instalment debt, cash balances and insurance. The basic hypothesis underlying their empirical work was that households endeavour to maintain a certain equilibrium, or balance amongst the various items of the capital account. The desired structure, so they add, will be different for different households, depending on factors varying from the desire to obtain direct services, to maintain a degree of liquidity, and to undertake a degree of risk. One implication of their hypothesis is the possibility of an imbalance in the actual asset and debt structure of households, and given the imperfection of asset markets and illiquidity of many assets, the structure cannot be changed overnight. They therefore concluded that: 'the capital account adjustments of a household are necessarily a continuing dynamic process; the appropriate amount and composition of wealth varies over the life-cycle . . . the hypothesis implies that the change in each stock will be negatively related to the initial level of the stock itself, but positively related to the initial level of other stocks.'[211]

Another cross-section study was carried out by Claycamp in 1963.[29] He analysed the substitutability between thirteen different types of assets by means of a regression analysis. Two most interesting findings were reached: that households 'give far more consideration to the specific needs each asset fulfils, than to the effect the asset has on the total portfolio', and that total assets, but not income, were a major determinant of the composition of the total portfolio, as measured by the proportion of variable dollar assets. Using continuous cross-section information for a very small sample of families in the Philadelphia area, Taubman[201] examined the effects of permanent and transitory income on the various components of saving. Consumer durables and indebtedness were found to be the only items of saving significantly affected by transitory income. Crockett and Friend[35] considerably extended Taubman's analysis and applied it to different and significantly larger samples. They showed that the influence of transitory income on changes in liquid assets was somewhat greater than that of normal income but the reverse was true for contractual saving and for total assets. There was conflicting evidence with respect to the speed at which individuals adjust their actual stocks towards the desired level, though the stock-adjustment model was found to give better performance than the static model.

Using time-series data, Hamburger[82b] investigated the household demand for four financial assets: marketable bonds, time and saving deposits at the commercial banks, life insurance reserves and savings accounts at other financial institutions such as credit unions, savings and loan associations and mutual saving banks. He focused attention on the substitution relationships among liquid assets, and between these assets and marketable securities. His results suggested that, for the period 1952–62, the principal arguments in the demand functions for these assets were interest rates and total financial non-human wealth, with income showing a negligible contribution. The adjustment of the household portfolio, in response to changes in wealth or interest rates, was found to be distributed over a number of time periods. In many instances, he pointed out, 'very little adjustment seems to occur until three to six months after the changes in the exogenous variables.' De Leeuw, in his model of financial behaviour,[40c] estimated equations for household holdings of United States securities, household borrowing, and saving deposits and insurance. His estimates were based on a stock adjustment model. In addition, there are numerous recent studies of the demand for money in the United States. Some of these will be discussed in the course of our analysis in Chapter 3.

In the United Kingdom the study of the composition of personal saving has received very little attention, to say the least. Apart from attempts by the Oxford Institute of Statistics in the 1950s,[165] there does not seem to be any empirical study – to the best of our knowledge – of the entire structure of consumer assets in the United Kingdom. Scattered articles which study one form or another of personal saving do exist, though they are very scarce. Lydall,[129c] has examined the factors which influence the holding of liquid assets by British households. Using the Oxford Survey data, his analysis indicates that total wealth (measured as net worth) rather than income level is the primary determinant of such holdings. Demand for consumer durables was given careful attention in the joint work of Stone and Rowe. Their articles in this field have virtually become 'classics'[195] and since then a number of articles on similar lines have been appearing in the economics journals.[162b, 163] Recently some attempts were made at the National Institute of Economic and Social Research to estimate the demand by the personal sector for motor cars, other consumer durables, and dwellings. With regard to the demand for financial assets, there are a number of studies of money holdings,[105, 57a] and only one study by Norton[160] of the demand for National Savings. However, none of these studies dealt with the personal sector as such.

Owing to the highly aggregative procedure which is commonly adopted in studying the aggregate saving function, with no attention being given to the composition of saving, studies of the effects of taxation and monetary policy on saving have been partial and inconclusive. For instance, with respect to taxation, most of the available evidence refers to the incidental effects of taxation via its influence on the level and distribution of income, and only in one study by Balopoulos[8] has an econometric investigation of the discriminatory effects of fiscal policy instruments been carried out. With respect to the effects of taxation on the incentives to save, although there are an increasing number of theoretical studies — mostly dealing with the effects of taxation on holding of risky assets[149, 207a, 175] — much less empirical work exists. This may be attributed partly to measurement problems, e.g. lack of data and difficulties in formulating expectational indices, but mainly to the controversy regarding the incorporation of financial variables, notably interest rates, in saving functions. Moreover, very few empirical attempts have been made[106] to study the effects of any tax discriminations,* which exist in the tax laws of a number of countries, on the favoured saving item as well as on aggregate personal saving.

In the United Kingdom's system of taxation there are some forms of tax discrimination. Minor tax privileges are given on interest on Savings Bank deposits, Building Society shares and deposits, and Savings Certificates. The first £15 of interest on Savings Bank deposits is disregarded for income tax purposes. In the case of Building Society shares and deposits, income tax is deducted at source at a somewhat reduced rate. In the case of Savings Certificates, the excess of the maturity value over the initial value is exempt from both income tax and surtax. There are, however, some restrictions on individual holdings of any one issue of Savings Certificates. In addition, there are two important forms of tax discrimination in favour of life assurance and super-annuation saving, as well as in investment in owner-occupied dwellings. The extent to which such tax discriminations have influenced aggregate personal

---

*There are several forms which tax discrimination may take. It may take the form of a deduction from personal income allowed with respect to amounts saved in a specific form, or of an exemption from personal taxes of the return which individuals receive on saving made in particular forms, or of differential tax treatment of institutions at the receiving end of the saving process . . . etc.[106]

saving and its composition in post-war Britain will become clear in the course of this study.

With respect to the influence of monetary policy, although there is sufficient evidence in the United Kingdom that the composition of personal saving is significantly affected by changes in relative interest rates, the debate is still highly unsettled where the effect of the absolute level of the rate of interest on total personal saving is concerned. This is due to a considerable extent, as will be shown later on, to the aggregate approach adopted in the majority of personal saving studies. On the other hand, there seems to be a consensus of opinion that changes in the terms of credit could have a substantial impact on purchases of motor cars and other consumer durables, and that the flow of mortgage funds might have a considerable effect on the volume of residential construction.[131] Our empirical results subscribe to this view.

1.1 THE PURPOSE AND ORGANISATION OF THE STUDY

The purpose of this study is to construct econometric models of aggregate personal saving and its composition in the United Kingdom, for the period 1948–66. Three characteristic features will be noted. Firstly, particular emphasis is given to the composition of personal saving and an aggregate saving function is derived from a number of equations, each of which describes the determinants of one form or component of personal saving. Secondly, an attempt is made to account for the (incidental, incentives and switching) effects of taxation and monetary policy on aggregate personal saving and its composition. Thirdly, the empirical investigation of personal saving, in relation to the instruments of economic policy, is carried out within the framework of a general, rather than partial, econometric model. In this model incomes, prices and most of the rates of interest are determined within the system.

In Chapter 2, personal saving is measured as a residue from the income account of the personal sector, and an aggregate structural model, based on the Friedman–Modigliani–Brumberg–Ando hypothesis, is derived and estimated. A number of related problems are also examined, e.g. the choice between a narrow and broad definition of saving, the effects of changes in the functional distribution of income, etc. This is followed, in Chapters 3, 4 and 5, by an econometric study of the composition of personal saving. A financial model is developed first, and a number of equations – describing the personal sector's demand for financial assets – are estimated. The relationship between the markets for real and financial assets is then discussed, and a circular flow model based on the Radcliffe views is chosen to explain the personal sector's demand for real assets. In Chapter 5 the determinants of life assurance and superannuation saving are analysed, and accordingly a disaggregate model is set up and estimated. By focusing attention on the net worth definition of personal saving, combining together all the estimated equations (selected in Chapters 3, 4 and 5), and supplementing them by a number of additional equations and identities, an alternative aggregate model is derived in Chapter 6. Finally, the conditional and unconditional forecasting performance of the models are verified in Chapter 7.

2

An Aggregate Model of Personal Saving: The Income Account Approach

In this chapter, attention is focused on the personal sector's income account, and an attempt is made to explain the determinants of aggregate personal saving in the United Kingdom. We begin, in section 2.1, by the specification of the model. This is followed, in section 2.2, by a discussion of some statistical and econometric considerations. In section 2.3, the model is estimated on annual data for the period 1949–66, and the results obtained are discussed.

2.1 THE MODEL

The model specified in this chapter is based on the permanent income hypothesis, as first put forward by Friedman,[62a] and by Modigliani, Brumberg and Ando.[142b] Hence this section begins with a brief account of this hypothesis and is then followed by the specification of the model.

2.1.1 THE PERMANENT INCOME HYPOTHESIS

This hypothesis represents an important modification of Keynes' theory of consumer behaviour. It emerged as a result of rising concern regarding the adequacy of current incomes as the most appropriate determinant of consumption and saving. In its simplest form it is based on three fundamental propositions:

1. The permanent level of consumption, or in Modigliani's terminology 'the scale of living', is a function of current and prospective resources:

$$\tilde{C} = f(x)$$

According to Friedman, the variable x is defined in relation to an array of assets from which the consumer expects to receive streams of income. Thus:

$$x = \sum_j i_j \sum_{\tau=1}^{\infty} \frac{Y_\tau^j}{(1 + i_j)^{\tau-1}}$$

where Y_τ^j is the expected return from the jth asset during the τth future period and i_j is the subjective discount rate appropriate for the jth asset. According to Modigliani, x is the expected sum of the household's net worth at the beginning of the period, denoted by a, plus the present value of its non-property income w, minus the present value of planned bequests q. By assuming that the value of planned bequests, q, is of negligible magnitude as compared with $(w + a)$, Modigliani–Ando define the present value of non-property income for a household at age t as:

$$w = \sum_{\tau=t}^{n} \frac{Y_\tau^l}{(1 + i)^{\tau+1-t}}$$

where Y_τ^l is the expected non-property income at age τ, n is the expected retirement age, and i is again a measure of the yield of assets.

2. The actual consumption expenditure, or measured consumption, is determined by the permanent level of consumption up to a stochastic component. The specific properties of such a component depend to an important extent on the length of the measurement period, as well as the definition of consumption expenditure:

$$C = \tilde{C} + \text{stochastic component}$$

3. The income received over some arbitrary interval of time is related to the overall level of resources up to a stochastic component:

$$y = G(x) + \text{stochastic component}$$

where y denotes current measured income. Since both income and consumption are related to the underlying level of resources one would expect these two variables to be systematically related; though such a relationship is unavoidably subject to a considerable margin of error as current measured income is only an indirect measure of the true determinants of consumption.

In addition to the three previous propositions, a fourth controversial one assigns a specific form to the function $f(x)$:

$$f(x) = kx$$

where k is a proportionality factor depending on various characteristics, but independent of x. These taken together suggest a model of the form:

$$C = kx + \text{stochastic component}$$

Despite great similarities between Friedman's hypothesis on the one hand and the Modigliani, Brumberg and Ando on the other, they differ in certain respects. In the first place, while in the former C and x are flows and hence k

is a pure number, in the latter x is a stock and hence k, denoted by k^*, has a dimension (1/time); its value depends on the length of time covered by variable C. To this extent the Modigliani–Brumberg–Ando formulation is essentially a 'Permanent Wealth Hypothesis' rather than a 'Permanent Income Hypothesis', though in practice the two approaches converge. In the second place, k^* is assumed to vary explicitly with the age of the consumer unit, as is x, and possibly with other factors, such as family size. This association with age results from the fact that the household's choice of a consumption plan, over the balance of life, is limited by the budget constraint. In the Friedman formulation k is a constant for the same consumer over time, though k may vary among consumer units. Finally, the fundamental difference is to be found in the assumption regarding the properties of the stochastic components of both income and consumption. Friedman assumes that the correlations between transitory and permanent income, transitory and permanent consumption, and transitory consumption and transitory income are strictly zero. The Modigliani–Brumberg–Ando formulation is more flexible in that it is possible for transitory income and transitory consumption to be related to each other. In that event Modigliani and Ando show that the essence of the Permanent Income Theory is not affected. The estimated equation would be slightly altered in that consumption is determined by both current and permanent income.

The objections raised to the Permanent Income Hypothesis are at least as impressive as the argument in its favour. They are directed at the specific formulation of the theory, rather than at the basic proposition that behaviour must be studied in terms of a time period, longer than a year. More specifically, the assumption that k is independent of the level of income and the lack of correlation between transitory income and transitory consumption, in Friedman's formulation in particular, were subject to most of the criticism.

To test the zero-propensity to consume out of transitory income, Bodkin[12a] analysed the extent to which consumption was made out of unexpected dividends paid in early 1950 from the National Service Life Insurance. His empirical analysis showed not only a statistically significant propensity to consume out of these incomes, but it was much higher than out of regular income. In reply to Bodkin's criticism, Friedman[62c] asserted that these dividend payments might be regarded as a proxy for permanent income and hence merely reflect the effects from permanent income in disguise. He based his argument on some *a priori* knowledge of the circumstances surrounding the payment of the dividends and a significant correlation between dividend income and other income. Bodkin,[12b] in a rejoinder, came even more firmly in support of his previous conclusions to the extent of questioning the validity of the Permanent Income Hypothesis. Kreinin[116] obtained a low marginal propensity to consume out of restitution payments made by Germany to former citizens of Israel. Further econometric work[94, 194b] cast doubt on the validity of this assumption, especially in relation to expenditure in consumer durables. It should also be noted that this is not a necessary assumption in the Modigliani–Brumberg–Ando version.[142b]

Nevertheless, the Permanent Income Hypothesis is analytically very rich and lends itself to a number of significant inferences regarding individual and aggregate behaviour. This is not the place to develop these inferences, particularly since they have been developed elsewhere.[62a, 142b] It suffices to say that in its more dynamic formulations it provided the link between the short-run and long-run consumption function.

With this brief theoretical background we now turn to the specification of the behavioural model of aggregate personal saving.

2.1.2 SPECIFICATION OF THE AGGREGATE MODEL

The model described in this sub-section consists of two behavioural equations and a number of definitions. It has been formulated first in terms of consumption expenditure, and then transformed into an aggregate personal saving model. This means that although the reduced form is estimated directly for the latter, the structural parameters refer to consumption expenditure. By defining aggregate personal saving S_t, as the difference between aggregate disposable income, Y_t^d, and consumers' expenditure, C_t,

$$S_t = Y_t^d - C_t \tag{1}$$

attention is therefore focused on the determinants of C.

Observed income and consumption at any point in time, Y_t^d and C_t, are segregated into 'permanent' and 'transitory' components. Thus:

$$Y_t^d = Y_t^P + Y_t^T \tag{2}$$

$$C_t = C_t^P + C_t^T \tag{3}$$

According to the Permanent Income Hypothesis, the permanent level of consumption, or 'scale of living', is a function of current and prospective resources. This suggests a functional relationship between C_t^P and Y_t^P. In addition, recent theoretical and econometric work[194b, 216] gives support to the view that wealth (either total or some components of wealth particularly liquid assets) should enter the consumption function explicitly. Denoting a wealth variable (to be defined later on) by W_t, permanent consumption is determined by permanent income and wealth:

$$C_t^P = a_1 Y_t^P + a_2 W_t + u_{1t} \tag{4}$$

Equation (4) is the first behavioural relationship of this model, and is assumed to be a linear homogeneous function in Y_t^P and W_t. u_1 is a stochastic term obeying the following assumptions:

$$E(u) = 0$$
$$E(uu') = \sigma^2 I$$

It is further assumed that transitory consumption C^T is a linear homogeneous function of transitory income up to a stochastic component u_2. The term u_2 holds the same statistical properties as u_1 in (4). Thus:

$$C_t^T = a_3 Y_t^T + u_2 \tag{5}$$

Although equation (5) is strictly contradictory to Friedman's formulation, it does not represent a serious defiance of the fundamental propositions of the permanent income hypothesis adopted in this study. As mentioned earlier, Modigliani and Ando[142b] showed that when transitory consumption is correlated with transitory income this only leads to a slight alteration in the reduced form, without affecting the basic essence of the theory. Empirical evidence provided by Bodkin[12a] and Kreinin[116] in their respective studies (cited previously), showed a highly significant marginal propensity to consume out of transitory income.

From equations (2–5) the consumption function takes the form:

$$C_t = (a_1 - a_3)\, Y_t^P + a_3\, Y_t^d + a_2\, W_t + u_{3t} \tag{6}$$

where u_3 is a new disturbance term assumed to hold the same statistical properties as u_1 and u_2. Current observed consumption is determined by both current observed and permanent income plus a wealth variable. It is worth noting that equation (6) is very similar to one suggested by Modigliani and Ando[142b] when the assumption regarding transitory income was relaxed. The only difference is that a wealth variable appears explicitly in (6).

Since permanent income Y_t^P, is a theoretical magnitude which is not directly observable, a linear distributed lag function, relating permanent and observed income, is added. It takes the following form:

$$Y_t^P = B \sum_{\tau=0}^{\infty} (1 - B)^\tau\, Y_{t-\tau}^d \qquad 0 \leqslant B \leqslant 1 \tag{7}$$

where B is a numerical coefficient describing the way in which the concept of permanent income is formed.

Inserting (7) in (6) leads to:

$$C_t = (a_1 - a_3) \sum_{\tau=0}^{\infty} B(1 - B)^\tau\, Y_{t-\tau}^d + a_3\, Y_t^d + a_2\, W_t + u_{3t} \tag{8}$$

By lagging (8) one period, multiplying by $(1 - B)$, then subtracting from (8), and rearranging terms, the derived consumption function takes the following form:

$$C_t = \{a_1 B + a_3(1 - B)\}\, Y_t^d - a_3(1 - B)\, Y_{t-1}^d + a_2\, W_t - a_2(1 - B)\, W_{t-1}$$
$$+ (1 - B)\, C_{t-1} + [u_{3t} - (1 - B)u_{3t-1}] \tag{9}$$

which might be put in the form:

$$C_t = (a_1 B)\, Y_t^d + a_3(1 - B)\,\Delta Y_t^d - a_2(1 - B)\, W_{t-1} + a_2\, W_t + (1 - B)C_{t-1} + u_{4t} \tag{10}$$

where $u_{4t} = [u_{3t} - (1 - B)u_{3t-1}]$.

By virtue of (1), (10) is transformed in terms of aggregate personal saving.

$$S_t = (1 - a_1 B)\, Y_t^d - a_3(1 - B)\,\Delta Y_t^d - a_2\, W_t$$
$$+ a_2(1 - B)\, W_{t-1} - (1 - B)C_{t-1} + u_{4t} \tag{11}$$

Equation (11) is expressed in the form:

$$S_t = \gamma_0 Y_t^d - \gamma_1 \Delta Y_t^d + \gamma_2 W_t + \gamma_3 W_{t-1} + \gamma_4 C_{t-1} + u_{4t} \tag{12}$$

where

$$\gamma_0 = (1 - a_1 B) \qquad \gamma_1 = a_3(1 - B) \qquad \gamma_2 = -a_2$$

$$\gamma_3 = a_2(1 - B) \qquad \gamma_4 = -(1 - B) \tag{12a}$$

From the estimation of equation (12) the reduced form coefficients $\gamma_0, \gamma_1, \gamma_2,$ $\gamma_3,$ and γ_4 can be obtained directly. Given the values of these coefficients, an estimate (or estimates) of the structural parameters $a_1, a_2, a_3,$ and B can be derived by virtue of (12a).

2.1.3 DISAGGREGATION OF INCOME

In this sub-section, we take account of the functional distribution of income, in an attempt to study the saving behaviour of different economic groups. This approach has been preferred to the use of a measure of inequality or specifying a non-linear saving function. On the one hand, studies which used the Gini coefficient or similar measures of dispersion did not find this factor to be statistically significant.[172, 206a, 191] A non-linear saving function has not been chosen for mathematical simplicity. On the other hand, taking functional distribution into account might allow for any curvature in the aggregate saving function, since functional shares vary with income.

Let $Y_{1.t}^d$ and $Y_{2.t}^d$ stand for disposable wage and non-wage income respectively, where

$$Y_t^d = Y_{1:t}^d + Y_{2.t}^d \tag{13}$$

Wage income includes income from employment plus transfers, while non-wage income covers income from self-employment plus property income. The division is arbitrary since mixed incomes cannot be identified in the National Income Accounts. Property Income is combined with self-employment because no separate tax figures are available.

Both disposable wage and non-wage income are, then, divided into two components: permanent and transitory.

$$Y_{1.t}^d = Y_{1.t}^P + Y_{1.t}^T \tag{14}$$

$$Y_{2.t}^d = Y_{2.t}^P + Y_{2.t}^T \tag{15}$$

Defining the permanent component in relation to the total observed by a Koyck-type distributed lag function, we have:

$$(Y_{1.t}^P - Y_{1.t-1}^P) = B_1(Y_{1.t}^d - Y_{1.t-1}^P) \tag{16}$$

$$(Y_{2.t}^P - Y_{2.t-1}^P) = B_2(Y_{2.t}^d - Y_{2.t-1}^P) \tag{17}$$

Saving of each income group is explained by the model described previously.

Thus, the aggregate personal saving function is given by:

$$S_t = (1 - a_{01}B_1) Y_{1.t}^d + (1 - a_{02}B_2)Y_{2.t}^d - a_{31}(1 - B_1) \Delta Y_{1.t}^d - a_{32}(1 - B_2)\Delta Y_{2.t}^d$$
$$- (d_1 + d_2)L_t + \{(d_1 + d_2) - (d_1 B_1 + d_2 B_2)\} L_{t-1} - (1 - B_1) C_{1.t-1}$$
$$- (1 - B_2)C_{2.t-1} + \text{a stochastic term} \tag{18}$$

Equation (18) is then put in the following form:

$$S_t = \gamma_{01} Y_{1.t}^d + \gamma_{02} Y_{2.t}^d - \gamma_{11}\Delta Y_{1.t}^d = \gamma_{12}\Delta Y_{2.t}^d + \phi_1 L_t + (\phi - \phi_2)L_{t-1}$$
$$- (1 - B_1)C_{1.t-1} - (1 - B_2)C_{2.t-1} + \text{a stochastic term} \tag{19}$$

where

$$\gamma_{01} = (1 - a_{01}B_1) \qquad\qquad \gamma_{02} = (1 - a_{02}B_2)$$
$$\gamma_{11} = a_{31}(1 - B_1) \qquad\qquad \gamma_{12} = a_{32}(1 - B_2)$$
$$\phi_1 = -(d_1 + d_2) \qquad\qquad \phi_2 = -(d_1 B_1 + d_2 B_2) \tag{20}$$

2.2 SOME STATISTICAL AND ECONOMETRIC CONSIDERATIONS

2.2.1 VARIABLES AND DATA

In this sub-section a brief discussion is made of the variables and data used in the estimation of Models (12) and (19).

Personal Income, Consumers' Expenditure and Personal Saving

Personal saving covers the savings of the personal sector. The latter, as defined in the *National Accounts Statistics: Sources and Methods*[153] (p. 99) is composed mainly of households and individuals resident in the United Kingdom. The sector also includes: unincorporated private enterprises of sole traders and partnerships, private non-profit making bodies serving persons, private trusts and Life Insurance and Superannuation funds. It should be noted that while the personal sector is extended to include 'collective persons', no separate accounts are available in the published statistics regarding the transactions of these bodies; with the exception of the Life Insurance and Superannuation Funds. Of course, in a study of saving behaviour, it would be preferable to separate the transactions of unincorporated businesses from the purely personal transactions of proprietors, but this has proved impossible in practice. Also, it would be more useful to treat non-profit making bodies serving persons as a separate sector, but the necessary information is not available.

Total personal saving is measured in two ways in this study. Firstly, using a National Income Flow measure as the difference between the estimate of total personal income on the one hand and the total of consumers' expenditure, transfers abroad, income tax accruals and National Insurance contributions on the other. Secondly, using a stock measure as the rate of change in personal wealth. This is equivalent to the change in personal or private non-corporate assets less changes in liabilities.

Based on the flow measure, the figure of total personal saving is obtained as the residual. Its accuracy, therefore, depends on the relative reliability of total personal income and expenditure. In the *National Income and Expenditure* 'Blue Book', these two aggregates are classified in the *A* category, and thus regarded as highly reliable with a margin of error of less than ±3%. However, in addition to the problem of aggregating non-homogeneous items arising mainly from the broad definition of the personal sector, there are other problems related to the Central Statistical Office estimates of income and expenditure. One example is the treatment of employers' contributions to superannuation schemes. These are treated as supplements to wages and salaries, and hence as saving out of employees' current income. This raises the problem that personal income includes elements of income accruing to persons which are not received currently in cash and over which individuals have no direct control. In the case of non-contributory pensions, sums actually paid to past employees are included in employment income instead of the currently accruing liability to pay pensions to present employees in the future. This results in an underestimation of personal income in view of the marked growth in the numbers and average pay of civil servants. Another serious problem is the failure to separate the distributed and undistributed profits of unincorporated businesses, or to distinguish between what should be considered as capital gain and as an item of trading income in estimating the incomes of jobbers. Also, profits of companies engaged in farming are included, for 'statistical convenience',[153] (p. 99) in income of farmers, rather than in the appropriation account of the company sector. All farms are treated as though they are tenanted and therefore rented, and an imputed rental value of land and buildings is considered as costs. Personal income from rent, dividends and net interest appears as a combined item in National Income Accounts and it is obtained as a residual. Like all figures obtained as residues, the estimate of the combined figure cannot be regarded as accurate. For example, there is no direct estimate of personal receipts from company dividends, or of income — in this form — from overseas investment. Rent estimates are not very reliable, especially before 1964. Incomes of concerns owning and letting property as a business, that is the 'real estate' industry, are included in rent income. The reliability of the 'Blue Book' estimate of income of professional people is relatively poor, especially for the more recent years. Current transfers to charities from companies are thought to be underestimated. Estimates of these transfers are obtained from Inland Revenue Data and cover only contributions that are not allowed as a business expense. No information is available about contributions included in business expenses. This could be a significant omission, especially at present when many services are undertaken by non-profit making bodies for the company sector, e.g. from Universities for the use of computers.[11]

On the expenditure side, estimates are based on a wide variety of sources; consequently there is less assurance of internal consistency than in the case of income estimates. Three general points have been mentioned in the *National Accounts Statistics*[153] regarding the estimates of consumers' expenditure and are meant to serve as a warning. Firstly, it was suggested that the data used 'do not all refer strictly to expenditure by consumers — that is, generally, to retail sales. Some series for food and the series for alcoholic drink relate to supplies coming at some earlier stage . . . Thus changes in the series used may sometimes reflect changes in the stocks held in the distributive chain beyond the point of recording, rather than genuine changes in consumers' expenditure, and there may be "errors of timing". Secondly, a proportion of many classes of consumer goods and services is bought on business accounts, and must not be included in consumers' expenditure. The basis for an accurate estimate of these business purchases rarely exists. Thirdly, the use of a variety of independent sources increases the risk of overlapping or of omissions; errors in one item are not necessarily compensated in other items as they are when an overall measure of total expenditure is used.'

Since personal saving is a comparatively small difference between two large aggregates, any small error in the latter results in a significant error in the former, providing that the errors in income and expenditure are not fully compensatory. This is illustrated in the following example by using the system of reliability gradings applied by the Central Statistical Office. For simplicity,* let us assume that: (1) estimates of personal income taxes as well as National Insurance Contributions may be regarded, for the present purpose, as error free; (2) errors in the estimate of personal income are independent from those implied in the estimate of consumers' expenditure; (3) errors in the components are likely, at least in part, to affect each other, with the resulting effect that the proportionate error attached to the aggregates is likely to be less than the weighted mean of the proportionate errors attached to the components, and (4) grades A, B and C imply error percentages of the order ±2, ±7 and ±12 respectively. If the margin in the estimates of both aggregate personal income and consumers' expenditure lies within the range of category A (±2% − assumption 4) as suggested by the Central Statistical Office, the effect on the figure of personal saving for the year 1966 is shown in *Table 2.1* (cases 1 and 2):

Table 2.1

Case	Income adjustment (£m)	Consumption adjustment (£m)	Saving adjustment (£m)	Saving adjustment (%)
Case 1	±630·16	±482·32	±147·84	±8·01
Case 2	±630·16	∓482·32	±1 112·48	±60·33
Case 3	±2 088·11	±1 777·72	±310·39	±16·83
Case 4	±2 088·11	∓1 777·72	±3 865·83	±209·64

By assuming that both income and consumers' expenditure are to be adjusted in the same direction (case 1), other things being equal, this results in approximately an 8% change in the 1966 figure of personal saving. In the case of opposite direction adjustment (case 2) nearly 60% adjustment is required. If, however, one (or more) of assumptions (1) to (4) is relaxed, the size of adjustment becomes a few times larger (±) than the aggregate figure of personal saving. For instance, if assumption (3) is dropped, the estimated margin of error in aggregate personal income and consumers' expenditure becomes approximately ±6·63% and 7·37% respectively (*Tables Agg. 1* and *Agg. 2*). Assuming a one-direction adjustment (case 3), this results in approximately ±17% change, while in the case of

* This example is meant for illustration only.

Table Agg. 1 PERSONAL INCOME 1966

(1) Form of Income	(2) Total Income by type (£m)	Reliability grade allocation (%)			Estimated margin of error (£m)				Percent- age of (9) to (2)
		(3) A	(4) B	(5) C	(6) ±A	(7) ±B	(8) ±C	(9) Total	
1. Income from employment	22 437	21·31	66·75	11·94	95·64	1 048·39	321·36	1 465·39	± 6·53
2. Income from self-employment	2 470	0	100·00	0	0	172·90	0	1 72·90	± 7·00
3. Other incomes	3 598	0	24·18	75·82	0	60·90	327·36	388·26	±10·79
4. Current transfers	30	0	100·00	0	0	2·1	0	2·10	± 0·07
5. N. Insurance benefits and other current grants	2 973	100·00	0	0	59·46	0	0	59·46	± 0·02
Grand total	31 508	–	–	–	155·10	1 284·29	648·72	2 088·11	± 6·63

opposite direction adjustment in income and expenditure the estimate of personal saving needs to be adjusted substantially – nearly ±210% (case 4).

Comparing the two estimates of personal saving – as a residual and as the rate of change in net worth – casts more doubt on the reliability of the available official figures. Personal saving estimated as a residual and adjusted for certain capital transfers (additions to tax reserves, capital transfers received and capital taxes paid) should theoretically be equal to net changes in assets, providing that gains (or losses) from revaluation are excluded. However, in practice, the two estimates are not equal and, despite great improvements in the United Kingdom official *National Accounts Statistics*, the discrepancy is still surprisingly large. As shown in *Table Agg. 3*, the unidentified item has varied over the period under review, reaching its maximum in 1955 exceeding £900 million with a mean around £648 million. An attempt has been made to provide an explanation of the discrepancy by subjecting the unidentified item to several statistical tests. The analysis carried out in this respect has thrown some light on areas where possible explanations may be found. A statistical relationship has

Table Agg. 2 CONSUMERS' EXPENDITURE 1966

(1) Total (£m)	Reliability grade allocation (%)			Estimated margin of error (£m)				Percentage of (8) to (1)
	(2) A	(3) B	(4) C	(5) ±A	(6) ±B	(7) ±C	(8) Total	
24 116	14·70	63·17	22·13	70·88	1 066·52	640·32	1 777·72	±7·37

been found between the unidentified item of the personal sector on the one hand and the residual error in the *National Income Accounts* and the unidentified items of some of the other sectors — particularly that of the company sector — on the other hand. The residual error, in turn, has shown some correlation with personal income, a price index and a time trend. In general, the results obtained seem to indicate that to the extent that the residual error reflects errors in the

Table Agg. 3 THE UNIDENTIFIED ITEM OF THE PERSONAL SECTOR (£m)

Year	$Y_t^d - C_t$	$+ATR_t$	$+CTR_t$	$-CTX_t$	$= S_{1t} -$	$S_{2t}(= \sum\limits_{i=1}^{N} \Delta A_{it})$	$= UNIP_t$
1952	380	− 14	62	159	269	958	−689
1953	431	+ 9	49	165	324	907	−583
1954	382	+ 33	39	183	271	884	−613
1955	490	+ 35	67	184	408	1 389	−981
1956	769	+ 20	60	166	683	1 345	−662
1957	766	0	51	176	641	1 221	−580
1958	605	+ 50	54	182	527	1 434	−907
1959	802	+ 15	57	212	662	1 296	−634
1960	1 195	+ 95	64	236	1 118	1 871	−753
1961	1 649	+ 20	74	259	1 484	1 862	−378
1962	1 503	− 30	93	266	1 300	1 958	−658
1963	1 504	+ 17	102	308	1 315	1 930	−615
1964	1 731	+ 95	125	308	1 643	2 104	−461
1965	1 745	+150	151	290	1 756	2 365	−609
1966	1 844	+ 35	155	317	1 717	2 322	−605

Notes

ATR Additions to tax reserves
CTR Capital transfers
CTX Capital taxes
S_1 Personal saving as a residual before depreciation and stock appreciation, but adjusted for *ATR, CTR* and *CTX*
S_2 Personal saving as measured from the balance sheet
ΔA_1 Transactions in assets and liabilities
UNIP Unidentified item of the personal sector.

'real' magnitudes, these are only responsible for a very small proportion of the unidentified item of the personal sector, while errors in the estimation of transactions in assets and liabilities may be responsible for a large proportion of the discrepancy. On the basis of the statistical analysis alternative estimates have been calculated for personal income, consumers' expenditure and personal

saving and are shown in *Table Agg. 4.* They suggest an upward adjustment of
12% and 16% in the published figures of personal income and consumers'
expenditure. The effect on personal saving varied; a cyclical pattern for the
period 1952–59 and a downward trend since 1960. However, the quality of
these estimates is open to question in view of the exploratory nature of the
analysis and the arbitrary and weak assumptions which form the basis of the
derived figures.

Table Agg. 4 PERSONAL INCOME, CONSUMPTION AND PERSONAL SAVING:
ALTERNATIVE ESTIMATES

Year	Personal income		Consumption		Personal saving		
	Published (£m)	*Estimated* (£m)	*Published* (£m)	*Estimated* (£m)	*Published* (£m)	*Estimated* (£m)	*Adjustment* (%)
1952	12 793	14 416	10 766	12 487	269	285	+ 5·95
1953	13 568	15 432	11 475	13 219	324	554	+70·99
1954	14 343	16 192	12 164	14 042	371	382	+ 2·60
1955	15 571	17 577	13 113	15 274	408	379	− 7·11
1956	16 738	18 902	13 829	15 956	683	852	+24·74
1957	17 652	19 960	14 599	16 761	641	940	+46·65
1958	18 600	21 052	15 386	17 642	527	855	+62·24
1959	19 694	22 240	16 196	18 679	662	888	+34·14
1960	21 205	23 870	17 006	20 046	1 118	920	−17·71
1961	22 908	25 704	17 917	20 812	1 484	1 571	+ 5·86
1962	24 102	27 043	18 966	22 027	1 300	1 361	+ 4·69
1963	25 497	28 569	20 141	23 443	1 315	1 313	+ 0·15
1964	27 594	30 798	21 492	25 017	1 643	1 536	− 6·51
1965	29 846	33 313	22 851	26 794	1 756	1 461	−16·80
1966	31 508	35 050	24 116	28 050	1 717	1 547	− 9·90

Since the estimates of aggregate personal income, consumers' expenditure
and, to some extent, personal saving (estimated as a residual) prepared by the
Central Statistical Office appear to be the best available, and in view of the
failure of the statistical analysis attempted in this study to provide alternative
estimates, we are left with little option but to use these figures in estimating
equations (12) and (19). However, in the interpretation of the estimated parameters, the deficiencies, discussed in this sub-section, should be borne in mind.

Personal Wealth

In the model described previously, total or some components of personal wealth
are assumed to enter the aggregate personal saving function explicitly. However,

empirical work has been, and continues to be, hampered by the lack of highly accurate data on personal wealth. This is particularly true in the case of the United Kingdom. On the basis of the Estate Duty Statistics, some estimates are now made and published regularly by the Board of Inland Revenue. Estimates obtained from these statistics are biased. One source of the bias arises from the possible unrepresentativeness of a sample consisting only of those who die in a particular year. Matching the statistics of deaths with those of Estate Duty is another problem. By supplementing the Estate Duty Statistics with information from other sources, J. Revell[174] and his associates compiled a different series for the period 1957—61, and it is being brought up to date by them. For the pre-1957 period, Morgan[146a] made an estimate for the year 1955, and for the period 1948—54 no complete series is available. In sum, no statistics of total personal wealth are readily available, for the whole period under review, which are consistent and fairly accurate.

One way of dealing with this problem is to attempt an indirect estimation of the wealth coefficient in equation (12). This can be achieved by specifying an additional relationship in which wealth is to be expressed in terms of an observable variable. Suppose, for example, that in addition to the two behavioural equations (4) and (5), another functional relationship is added, specifying wealth as a proportion of permanent income:

$$W_t = a_4 Y_t^P + v \tag{21}$$

Therefore, equation (6) is reduced to:

$$C_t = (a_1 + a_2 a_4 - a_3) Y_t^P + a_3 Y_t^d + \ddot{u}_3 \tag{$\overline{6}$}$$

By using (7) and (8), equations (9) and (10) take the form:

$$C_t = \{B(a_1 + a_2 a_4) + a_3(1 - B)\} Y_t^d - a_3(1 - B) Y_{t-1}^d + (1 - B)C_{t-1} + \ddot{u}_3 \tag{$\overline{9}$}$$

$$C_t = B(a_1 + a_2 a_4) Y_t^d + a_3(1 - B) \Delta Y_t^d + (1 - B)C_{t-1} + \ddot{u}_3 \tag{$\overline{10}$}$$

By virtue of (1) equation (12) takes the form:

$$S = \dot{\gamma}_0 Y_t^d - \gamma_1 \Delta Y_t^d + \gamma_4 C_{t-1} + \dot{u}_4 \tag{$\overline{12}$}$$

where γ_1 and γ_4 are defined as in (12a) but $\dot{\gamma}_0$ is now defined as:

$$\dot{\gamma}_0 = \{B(a_1 + a_2 a_4)\}.$$

Comparing equations ($\overline{12}$) and (12) it can be noted that the wealth variable has now been eliminated while its coefficient is included in $\dot{\gamma}_0$. However, no separate estimates of the structural coefficients $a_1, a_2,$ and a_4 can be derived from the estimation of the composite coefficients $\dot{\gamma}_0, \gamma_1$ and γ_4. In addition, assumption (21) is theoretically unsatisfactory since the logic of introducing a wealth variable in equation (4) is that non-human capital has characteristics (realisability, availability, security, etc.) which human capital lacks.

Another alternative is to use some components of personal wealth, instead of the aggregate, which can be supported on theoretical grounds and for which there is reliable statistical data. Accumulation of wealth in the form of liquid assets has been chosen in a growing number of empirical studies,[111,216] and its relevance to consumption and saving has been recognised in the theoretical literature for some time. Liquid assets are a strategic form of wealth, as far as consumer behaviour is concerned. Other consumer assets are not so easy to convert into a spendable form, although this remark applies differently amongst the various assets held by spending units. At individual level, liquid assets are highly correlated with total wealth, and thus serve as a good wealth indicator. Evidence, from the Oxford Surveys[59] indicates that for a certain group of income earners, liquid assets were found to represent an important ingredient of their total assets. Fortunately, information is available for the major items that constitute this group of assets. For the period under review, statistical data exist for the total personal sector's acquisition of non-marketable Government debt. Personal holding of Building Societies' shares and deposits can be derived from the latter's published Balance Sheets. In the estimation of equations (12) and (19) liquid assets (denoted by L), comprising acquisition of non-marketable Government debt, plus Building Societies' shares and deposits, has been used instead of W_t and W_{t-1}. However, it should be noted that the use of Building Societies' Balance Sheet figures might lead to a timing problem. These figures relate to accounting years ending on any date between 1 February of that year and 31 January of the following year.

Net Investment in Consumer Durables

Two alternative concepts of aggregate personal saving are used in the estimation of equation (12): a narrow one which excludes purchases of consumer durables, and a broader one which treats net investment in consumer durables as an act of personal saving. However, no figures are available for net investment in consumer durables. Estimates are derived from the published figures of total expenditure on consumer durables using a method suggested by Stone and Rowe.[195] A brief summary of this method follows.

1. For any durable commodity, the purchases at time t, denoted by G, may be regarded as the sum of two components representing an amount, CD, of consumption during the period and an amount, ID, of net investment:

$$G = CD + ID \tag{22}$$

2. Net investment, ID, is by definition the net addition made to the opening stock, Q, during the period. Thus

$$EQ = Q + ID \tag{23}$$

where E is an operator, such that $E^\theta Q(t) = Q(t + \theta)$.

3. The amount used up, CD, can be expressed by a reducing balance depreciation formula, with a depreciation rate per period of $1/n$. Thus, in a period $1/n$th of the opening stock will be used up plus an equal or smaller proportion $1/m$ of the purchases during the period, so that:

$$CD = Q/n + G/m$$
$$= \{m/n(m-1)\}Q + \{1/(m-1)\}ID \tag{24}$$

4. From (22), (23) and (24), it follows that:

$$EQ = (m - 1)/m \sum_{\theta}^{\infty} \{(n - 1)/n\}^{\theta} E^{-\theta} G \qquad (25)$$

or

$$Q = \{n(m - 1)/m(n - 1)\} \sum_{\theta}^{\infty} \{(n - 1)/n\}^{\theta} E^{-\theta} G \qquad (26)$$

5. Assuming that purchases are spread evenly through the period, and given n, m is calculated from the following expression:

$$1/m = 1 - [1/n \log\{n/(n - 1)\}] \qquad (27)$$

6. Given n, m and G, Q is calculated from (26). This in turn makes it possible to estimate CD and ID from (24) and (22).

The Disaggregated Model

In order to proceed with the estimation of equation (19), data for $Y^d_{1.t}$, $Y^d_{2.t}$, $\Delta Y^d_{1.t}$, $\Delta Y^d_{2.t}$, $C_{1.t-1}$ and $C_{2.t-1}$ are needed. Income data are available from official publications, but no disaggregated figures of consumption can be obtained.

One way of dealing with this problem is to define C_1 and C_2 in terms of C. A simple proportional relationship of the following form: $C_{1.t} = \delta C_t$ and $C_{2.t} = (1 - \delta)C_t$ is not acceptable on theoretical grounds. This is so, since a change in the functional distribution of income might be expected to vary the division of the total of consumers' expenditure. It also implies that almost invariably the marginal propensity to save out of observed income change will be greater for entrepreneurs and property owners, as their incomes fluctuate more than employee incomes.

Alternatively B_1 and B_2 may be assumed equal, and in this case $C_{1.t-1}$ and $C_{2.t-1}$ will be replaced by C_{t-1}. However, there is no *a priori* reason why the two groups should have the same horizon. Available evidence from survey data[59] gives support to the view that non-wage income groups have a relatively longer horizon. While recognising this possibility, in the absence of any data for consumption by income groups there is little option but to use figures for total consumption, C_{t-1}, with a reduced form parameter $\phi_3 = (1 - B)$. With this modification, no estimate of the structural parameters of equation (19) can be obtained.

It should also be noted that in the derivation of equation (19) we have assumed that there is a simple proportional relationship of the form $L_{1.t} = \delta_2 L_t$ and $L_{2.t} = (1 - \delta_2)L_t$, where $L_{1.t}$ and $L_{2.t}$ are the stocks of liquid assets held by wage and non-wage income groups respectively. This is because there are no available data for L_1 and L_2.

2.2.2 METHOD OF ESTIMATION

Examination of the model reveals that equation (12) is over-identified. This is so since one estimate of B is derived from γ_2 and γ_3, while another independent estimate is obtained from γ_4. For the two estimates of B to be identical, the following condition must hold:

$$\gamma_3 = \gamma_2 \gamma_4 \tag{28}$$

In practice, this will not necessarily be the case, and it is highly probable that two different estimates will be obtained not only of B but also of the rest of the structural parameters a_1, a_2 and a_3 if Unrestricted Least Squares is used in the estimation. Moreover, it is obvious that equation (28) is a non-linear restriction and hence equation (12), though linear in the variables, is non-linear in the parameters. An Iterative Maximum Likelihood (IML) method, first suggested by M. Nerlove[157a] using an Ordinary Least Squares programme is used in the estimation. As shown by Nerlove, the IML method provides maximum likelihood estimates of the parameters. The procedure for estimating equation (12) is described as follows:

1. Assume different values of B and compute the variables X_1, Z_1, and Z_2 for each value of B where:

$$X_{1t} = [S_t + (1 - B)C_{t-1}]$$
$$Z_{1t} = [(1 - B)\Delta Y_t^d] \qquad Z_{2t} = [L_t - (1 - B)L_{t-1}]$$

2. For each assumed value of B compute the Least Squares regression of

$$X_{1t} = \gamma_0 Y_t^d - a_3 Z_{1t} - a_2 Z_{2t}$$

and determine the coefficient of determination R^2 as a function of B.

3. Find the maximum of R^2 with respect to B. The value of B associated with the maximum of R^2 is its maximum likelihood estimate, as are the values of the coefficients a_1, a_2, and a_3 given the value of B.

This method produces unique estimates of all the parameters, and its applicability does not depend on the observations of $S_t, C_{t-1}, \Delta Y_t^d, L_t$ and L_{t-1} entering the variables X_{1t}, Z_{1t} and Z_{2t} linearly.

With respect to the disaggregated model, estimates of the reduced form parameters of equation (19) should be consistent with the estimates obtained of the reduced form parameters of equation (12). $\gamma_{01}, \gamma_{02}, \gamma_{11}$ and γ_{12} are estimated subject to the following two linear constraints:

$$\gamma_0 = \theta_0 \gamma_{01} + (1 - \theta_0)\gamma_{02} \tag{29}$$
$$\gamma_1 = \theta_1 \gamma_{11} + (1 - \theta_1)\gamma_{12} \tag{30}$$

Given (29) and (30), equation (19) is estimated by means of two alternative methods, for reasons which will be discussed later on. These methods are: the Iterative Maximum Likelihood (IML) which has been described earlier on, and the Limited Information (Single Equation) Maximum Likelihood (LIML). For the sake of simplifying the estimation, we have assumed that $\theta_0 = \theta_1 = 0.5$

instead of attempting to obtain, possibly by iteration, a direct estimate of these parameters. This assumption; which defines γ_0 and γ_1 as simple arithmetic means of γ_{01} and γ_{02} and γ_{11} and γ_{12} respectively; may be unrealistic and hence considerable care is required in the interpretation of the estimates of equation (19).

2.3 RESULTS

This section begins with *Table Agg. 5* which gives a statistical summary of variables used in the estimation.

TABLE Agg. 5 VARIABLES USED IN THE ESTIMATION OF THE AGGREGATE MODEL

Index Variable	Min.	Max.	Mean	Quartile 1	Median	Quartile 3	Standard deviation
S_t†	184·2	1 620·2	893·494	477	799·7	1 387·8	511·497
Y_t^d	12 908	21 312	16 634·9	13 945	15 932·5	18 897	2 855·9
C_{t-1}	12 509	19 410	15 309·8	13 098	14 841	17 156	2 222·03
IDU_t	181·3	426·9	292·4	245·3	300·7	355·8	76·25
ΔY_t^d	35	1 240	498·111	225	363	730	346·11
$Y_{1.t}^d$	10 062	17 441	13 380·4	11 214	13 073·5	15 148	23 534·7
$Y_{2.t}^d$	2 603	3 955	3 169·78	2 754	2 927·5	3 595	465·07
$\Delta Y_{1.t}^d$	−7	543	376·22	302	378	487	133·24
$\Delta Y_{2.t}^d$	−246	322	51·5	−73	27	128	14·05
L_t	8 732·9	11 661·2	9 765·27	8 926·3	9 555·7	10 169·6	953·611
IDM_t	2·8	149·7	72·79	44·9	68·8	98·6	41·63

* All variables are deflated by the price index of consumers' expenditure
† Before providing for depreciation and stock appreciation, but adjusted for addition to tax reserves
IDU_t Investment in consumer durables
IDM_t Investment in motor cars

2.3.1 THE AGGREGATE MODEL: NARROW DEFINITION OF PERSONAL SAVING

Table Agg. 6 sets out the results of estimating equation (12) by means of the IML method for values of B. Parameter estimates are given with their standard errors in parenthesis, together with the (corrected) coefficient of determination, R^2, and the Von-Neumann Ratio, VN.

The best estimate obtained is equation 2.6.6. For B = 0·33, R^2 reaches its maximum. Comparing the size of the parameters with their corresponding standard errors, it is obvious that all parameters are highly significant. Judging by the Von-Neumann Ratio, there is no evidence of first order serial correlation. With 18 observations the theoretical Von-Neumann Ratio falls in the interval 1·3 to 2·9 for acceptance of the hypothesis of no first order serial correlation at 5% level of significance. In sum, given available evidence, equation 2.6.6 satisfies both the statistical and econometric criteria.

Table Agg. 6 ESTIMATION OF THE AGGREGATE MODEL: NARROW DEFINITION OF SAVING (£m) 1949–66

Equation number	B	Dependent variable	Y_t^d	Z_{1t}	Z_{2t}	Structural parameters $a_{1s}=1-a_1$	$a_{3s}=1-a_3$	a_{2s}	R^2	VN
2.1.6	0·9	X_{1t}	0·290 (0·025)	−0·594 (1·324)	−0·267 (0·046)	0·211	0·406	−0·267	0·9410	0·71
2.2.6	0·8	X_{1t}	0·375 (0·025)	−0·767 (0·652)	−0·279 (0·052)	0·218	0·233	−0·279	0·9680	0·75
2.3.6	0·7	X'_{1t}	0·454 (0·025)	−0·728 (0·413)	−0·283 (0·058)	0·220	0·272	−0·283	0·9810	0·86
2.4.6	0·6	X_{1t}	0·534 (0·024)	−0·695 (0·295)	−0·288 (0·067)	0·223	0·305	−0·288	0·9870	1·00
2.5.6	0·5	X_{1t}	0·612 (0·024)	−0·672 (0·227)	−0·293 (0·081)	0·224	0·328	−0·293	0·9910	1·16
2.6.6	0·33	X_{1t}	0·733 (0·019)	−0·467 (0·125)	−0·269 (0·100)	0·191	0·533	−0·269	0·9967	1·44
2.7.6	0·2	X_{1t}	0·830 (0·024)	−0·671 (0·155)	−0·182 (0·208)	0·150	0·329	−0·182	0·9958	1·67

$$X_{1t} = [S_t + (1 - B)C_{t-1}]$$
$$Z_{1t} = [(1 - B)\Delta Y_t^d]$$
$$Z_{2t} = [L_t - (1 - B)L_{t-1}]$$

Notes
1. All variables are deflated by the price index of consumers' expenditures
2. Personal saving parameters are denoted by a subscript(s); i.e. a_{1s}, a_{3s} and a_{2s} refer to propensities to save out of permanent income, transitory income and liquid assets respectively

Turning to the economic criteria, all the estimated parameters have the correct *a priori* signs, and they are of plausible magnitudes. Further examination of equation 2.6.6 reveals some interesting findings. (1) Firstly, it is important to note that the value of B which has led to the best fit, i.e. B = 0·33, is of identical magnitude to the value suggested by Friedman. It implies a 3 years planning horizon. (2) Secondly, the sizeable magnitude and the highly significant parameter for the liquid asset variable should be noted. This result, in our opinion, is of particular importance in view of its policy implications and the existing confusion regarding the liquid asset effect on consumption and saving. Estimates of the propensity to save out of liquid assets have varied rather widely. The Klein–Goldberger[111] consumption function, covering the period 1929–52 in the United States, provides an estimate of the propensity to save out of liquid assets of the order 0·024, while Friend[65] (p. 662) estimates 0·11. Zellner,[216] in more recent studies, reports even larger negative values ranging between 0·22 and 0·79. Using the Oxford Sample Survey data[165] Fisher[59] gives a smaller estimate of the order 0·05.

Further tests show that estimates of both the adjustment coefficient B and the liquid assets coefficients are relatively sensitive to the specification of the model and the method used in the estimation. Equation (12) is re-estimated by means of Unrestricted Least Squares (ULS), Limited Information (Single Equation) Maximum Likelihood (LIML), and Two Stages Least Squares (TSLS). The results obtained are shown in *Table Agg. 7*, and a comparison is made with equation 2.6.6. First of all, consider equations 2.1.7, 2.2.7, and 2.3.7. Two estimates of B are obtained; one from γ_4 and the other from γ_2 and γ_3; though in the three equations they do not seem to differ significantly. However, the ULS, TSLS and LIML estimates of B are smaller in size than the estimate obtained in 2.6.6, or what would theoretically be expected. Compared with B = 0·33 in 2.6.6, it ranges between 0·11 and 0·13 in 2.1.7, 2.2.7 and 2.3.7, and thus implies a longer horizon of the range 7–10 years, rather than 2·5–3 years as originally suggested by Friedman. Moreover, available evidence suggests that they are not only smaller in size than the IML estimate, but also statistically insignificant. Since Var (B) = Var (1 − B), it follows that the standard error of γ_4 equals the standard error of B. Comparing the size of B with the standard error of γ_4, it becomes clear that B is statistically insignificant. Turning to the rest of the structural parameters, it is possible to conclude that estimates of a_{1s} and a_{3s} have shown relatively less sensitivity to the method of estimation than a_{2s}. In addition, with the exception of γ_2 in equation 2.1.7, γ_2 and γ_3 are statistically insignificant in all equations 2.1.7, 2.2.7, and 2.3.7. Secondly, altering the specification by dropping L_{t-1}, as shown in equations 2.4.7, 2.5.7 and 2.6.7, adds another shred of evidence in support of the conclusions previously reached regarding the uncertainty of the liquid asset effect. a_{2s} has been reduced from 0·269 as in equation 2.6.6 to an average of 0·06 in equations 2.4.7, 2.5.7 and 2.6.7.

Next, equation 2.6.6 is compared with a recent estimate of the personal saving function in the United Kingdom, which was developed a few years ago by Stone and Rowe.[194b] Although both models are based on the same theoretical considerations, namely the Friedman–Modigliani–Brumberg–Ando hypothesis, and are both estimated on United Kingdom aggregate annual data, nevertheless

Table Agg. 7 SENSITIVITY OF THE ESTIMATES TO THE METHOD OF ESTIMATION (£m) 1949–66

Equation number	Method of estimation	Dependent variable	Y_t^d	ΔY_t^d	Z_{1t}	L_t	L_{t-1}	Z_{2t}	C_{t-1}	Structural parameters				R^2	VN
										a_{1s}	a_{3s}	a_{2s}	B		
2.6.6	IML	X_{1t}	0·733 (0·019)		−0·467 (0·125)			−0·269 (0·100)	−0·67	0·191	0·533	−0·269	0·33	0·9967	1·4
2.1.7	ULS	S_t	0·914 (0·158)	−0·362 (0·117)		−0·435 (0·199)	0·385 (0·205)		−0·891 (0·192)	0·210	0·593	−0·435	0·109* 0·107†	0·9887	1·5
2.2.7	LIML	S_t	0·877 (0·188)	−0·368 (0·118)		−0·362 (0·284)	0·313 (0·288)		−0·851 (0·221)	0·174	0·568	−0·362	0·149* 0·133†	0·9886	1·5
2.3.7	TSLS	S_t	0·897 (0·187)	−0·365 (0·117)		−0·402 (0·283)	0·354 (0·287)		−0·873 (0·220)	0·189	0·582	−0·402	0·127* 0·119†	0·9887	1·5
2.4.7	ULS	S_t	0·683 (0·109)	−0·365 (0·127)		−0·069 (0·054)			−0·627 (0·143)	0·150	0·418	−0·069	0·37	0·986	1·5
2.5.7	LIML	S_t	0·711 (0·110)	−0·384 (0·128)		−0·052 (0·053)			−0·669 (0·146)	0·127	0·426	−0·052	0·33	0·985	1·6
2.6.7	TSLS	S_t	0·702 (0·109)	−0·378 (0·127)		−0·056 (0·055)			−0·656 (0·142)	0·134	0·424	−0·056	0·34	0·985	1·6

* An estimate of B from γ_4
† An estimate of B from γ_2 and γ_3

Notes

1. All variables are deflated by the price index of consumers' expenditure on goods and services
2. Personal saving, S_t, is measured before providing for depreciation and stock appreciation, but adjusted for additions to tax reserves

estimates obtained of the reduced form and the structural parameters seem to differ greatly. This can easily be observed from *Table Agg. 8*. In the Stone and Rowe model, the lagged income and the lagged consumption parameters γ_1 and

Table Agg. 8 COMPARISON WITH THE STONE AND ROWE MODEL

	$(\gamma_0 - \gamma_1)$	γ_1	γ_2	γ_3	γ_4	a_{1s}	a_{3s}	a_{2s}	B
Equation 2.6.6	0·420	0·313	−0·269 (0·100)	0·180	−0·67	0·191	0·533	−0·269	0·330
Stone and Rowe	0·413 (0·084)	0·130 (0·157)	−0·046 (0·017)		−0·366 (0·210)	0·279	0·645	−0·073	0·634

γ_4 are not statistically significant. With respect to the size of the parameters, while the reduced form parameters are larger in equation 2.6.6 than those of Stone and Rowe, the opposite is true regarding the structural parameters, with the exception of a_{2s}. However, the two models are not strictly comparable. Firstly, the method used in the estimation is not the same; Stone and Rowe's model is estimated by means of ULS, while the IML method is used in the estimation of equation 2.6.6. Secondly, only one form of wealth; namely the stock of liquid assets; has been used in this study, while Stone and Rowe constructed a series of total personal wealth based on V. Morgan's 1954 estimate.[146a] Thirdly, the data used in both models are not the same. The present study covers a longer period and is based on a revised* series of income, consumption and saving.

2.3.2 THE AGGREGATE MODEL: BROAD DEFINITION OF PERSONAL SAVING

In the preceding analysis, as well as in the United Kingdom National Income Accounts, an arbitrary line has been drawn between consumption expenditure and personal saving. The purchases of land and dwellings, and all the expenses incurred with the transfer of their ownership, have been regarded as acts of personal saving, which are automatically offset by capital formation. On the other hand, purchases of consumer durable goods have been treated as consumer expenditure, rather than personal saving.

It has often been suggested that the arbitrary line between consumption and saving should be shifted so as to make outlay on durables, like outlay on property, a part of personal saving. It may be argued that consumer durables are fairly tangible and sizeable assets rendering a stream of services and therefore should be classified as investment (and consequently included in saving) rather than consumption. Others maintain the view that consumers do not consider net expenditure on consumer durables as saving, and thus in a behavioural sense they should not be so treated. In this sub-section, an attempt is made to examine the effects of broadening the concept of personal saving on the stability and the estimated parameters of the personal saving function. Thus, net investment in consumer

---

* National Income statistics have recently been subject to a number of revisions. The effect of these revisions, as noted by Odling—Smee[162a] has been 'to lower the saving ratio and more so for the more recent years'.

durables is added to the figures of personal saving (C_{t-1} is adjusted accordingly) and equation (12) is re-estimated under the constraint that B = 0·33.

From *Table Agg. 9* some interesting results can be observed. By comparing equation 2.6.6 with equations 2.1.9* and 2.2.9 it is clear that the broadening of the concept of saving to include net investment on durable goods results in a better fit. The standard errors of all the parameters are reduced significantly, and this is associated with an increase in R^2 from 0·9967 in equation 2.6.6 to 0·9973 in equation 2.1.9 to 0·9987 in equation 2.2.9. Turning to the structural parameters, two points are worth noting:

1. The propensity to save out of transitory income, a_{3s}, appears to be relatively sensitive to the concept of saving showing an increase of the range 15—20%. Similar results are reported in other studies. Ruth Mack's[130] incremental income elasticities point to a higher marginal propensity to acquire durables out of transitory income. Using the 1953 and 1954 Saving Surveys for Great Britain, Klein and Liviatan[113] found a distinct correlation between expenditure on durable goods and the receipt of windfalls. In the course of discussing the relationship between transitory income and transitory consumption, Friedman[62a] implicitly suggested that transitory income may have a strong effect on the purchase of consumer durable goods. He pointed out that the 'timing of the replacement of durable goods and of addition to the stock of such goods . . . is likely, to some extent, to be adjusted so as to coincide with windfalls'.

2. While the addition of only net investment on motor cars to the figures of saving has left the magnitudes of a_{1s} and a_{2s} more or less unchanged, by further broadening the concept of saving to include total (net) investment on consumer durables these parameters have been reduced, particularly a_{2s}. Comparing equations 2.6.6 and 2.2.9 shows that both a_{1s} and a_{2s} have fallen from 0·191 and −0·269 to 0·162 and −0·205. This implies that while net investment on consumer durables is positively correlated with the stock of liquid assets; which is expected *a priori*, it is negatively correlated with permanent income; which does not seem very plausible. This point is discussed again in Chapter 4.

What conclusions can be reached with regard to the narrow and broad definitions of personal saving? On the basis of the statistical criteria, there is no doubt that the broad concept of personal saving results in a more stable (in the statistical sense) saving function. Similar conclusions have been reached in other studies. Based on cross-section data, Friend and Jones[66] used the standard error of the income coefficients in two linear saving functions and reached the conclusion that there is 'fairly strong evidence in favour of combining durable expenditure with saving, rather than with consumption'. Other findings by Goldsmith[76] and to a lesser extent by Klein and Morgan[145a] seem to support this view.

However, in discussing Friend and Jones' paper, Okun[164a] has expressed some reservations regarding the use of only the statistical criteria in making a choice between the two concepts of saving. He argued that 'if the income total may be divided arbitrarily into saving and consumption components, it should be obvious that we can choose our division to make the saving or consumption function fit

---

* In estimating net investment in motor cars (see equations 24—27) a value of $n = 2$ has been used. This value was found by O'Herlihy[163] to provide the best estimate of a demand function for cars in Great Britain. This value of n is certainly implausible, and for this reason equation 2.1.9 should be interpreted with caution.

Table Agg. 9 ESTIMATION OF THE AGGREGATE MODEL: BROAD DEFINITION OF SAVING (£m) 1949–66

Equation number	B	Dependent variable	Y_t^d	Z_{1t}	Z_{2t}	Structural parameters			R^2	VN
						$a_{1s} = 1 - a_1$	$a_{3s} = 1 - a_3$	a_{2s}		
2.6.6	0.33	X_{1t}	0.733 (0.019)	−0.467 (0.125)	−0.269 (0.100)	0.191	0.533	−0.269	0.9967	1.44
2.1.9	0.33	X_{2t}	0.733 (0.017)	−0.393 (0.113)	−0.273 (0.090)	0.191	0.607	−0.273	0.9973	1.79
2.2.9	0.33	X_{3t}	0.723 (0.012)	−0.360 (0.077)	−0.205 (0.062)	0.162	0.640	−0.205	0.9987	1.76

Notes

1. All variables are deflated by the price index of consumers' expenditure
2. IDM and IDU are net investment in motor cars and motor cycles, and total consumer durables respectively

$X_{1t} = [S_t + 0.67C_{t-1}]$

$X_{2t} = [S_t + 0.67C_{t-1} + 0.33IDM]$

$X_{3t} = [S_t + 0.67C_{t-1} + 0.33IDU]$

just as well as we wish. If we absurdly limit the definition of saving to the accumulation of pennies, and labelled as consumption all other uses of total disposable income, we should get an exceedingly small standard error of estimate in a regression of saving on income.' Nevertheless, Okun has not suggested any alternative criteria. After specifying two plausible models of consumer behaviour, it is quite reasonable to choose between them on the basis of statistical tests of stability, particularly if the choice on theoretical grounds is not clear. Given the theoretical framework of the model specified in this chapter and to the extent that the linear approximation of the relationships holds true, the relative (statistical) superiority of equation 2.2.9 over equation 2.6.6 suggests that for the purpose of studying the short-run saving behaviour the inclusive concept of personal saving may be preferred.

2.3.3 THE DISAGGREGATED MODEL

We have encountered great difficulties in the estimation of equation (19). It has been estimated under various assumptions, by imposing one or more of the following constraints:

$$B_1 = B_2$$
$$B_1 = B_2 = B = 0.33$$
$$\gamma_0 = 0.5\gamma_{01} + 0.5\gamma_{02}$$
$$\gamma_1 = 0.5\gamma_{11} + 0.5\gamma_{12}$$
$$\phi_2 = 0$$
$$\gamma_{01} = 0$$

The best estimate obtained is shown below:

$$S_t = 0.560Y^d_{1.t} + 0.862Y^d_{2.t} - 0.837\Delta Y^d_{2.t} - 0.178L_t - 0.495C_{t-1} \qquad (\overline{19})$$
$$\quad\; (0.180) \qquad\qquad\quad (0.244) \qquad\quad (0.108) \quad\;\; (0.187)$$

$$R^2 = 0.999, \text{VN} = 1.71$$

Equation $(\overline{19})$ has been estimated by means of the LIML method under the constraints that: $B_1 = B_2$, $\gamma_{01} = \phi_2 = 0$, $2\gamma_0 = \gamma_{01} + \gamma_{02}$ and $\gamma_0 = 0.711$. This value of $\gamma_0 (=0.711)$ is the one obtained by estimating equation (12) by means of the LIML, as shown in 2.5.7.

Equation $(\overline{19})$ satisfies the statistical* and econometric criteria and shows that the non-wage income earners have both a higher short-term propensity to save and a greater response to income variability than wage income earners. Several reasons have been put forward to explain this group's higher propensity to save. In Klein's[109n] opinion the most important one is the need and desire of entrepreneurs to reinvest their unspent business earnings in further business expansion. He adds that 'to some extent they have an inherent preference for using thier own funds and to some extent the nature of today's capital market forces them into this avenue of finance'. Friedman[109n] argues that entrepreneurs find a higher rate of return from investment in their own firms than in the general

---

* No estimate of the standard error of γ_{02} is given because γ_{02} is estimated indirectly from the constraint $2\gamma_0 = \gamma_{01} + \gamma_{02}$ given γ_0 and γ_{01}.

capital market, and hence prefer internal over external financing. More important is the desire to retain control over their business affairs. In seeking external equity funds, the small businessman definitely sacrifices control and in seeking loan funds he may put personal control in jeopardy. Another reason may be difficulties in obtaining credit by small businessmen. However, little evidence exists of discrimination against smaller firms in the extension of credit facilities. Lydall[129b] emphasised that, although there was not a great discriminatory pressure on small manufacturing firms in 1957 in the United Kingdom they were worried about sources of finance as opposed to the state of sales during the credit squeeze. In a later survey of credit availability in Britain[109n] covering the six months from September 1957 to March 1958, the Association of British Chamber of Commerce found some evidence of relatively strong adverse effects of stringent monetary measures on smaller businesses. Friedman and Modigliani pointed out the importance of income variability on savings behaviour. Entrepreneurs, it is argued, have more frequent and violent income movements over time than do other groups in the economy, and this high variability accounts for their high savings. Klein asserted, on the other hand, that this is not a very significant factor, since by subtracting retained earnings from saving and income the Engel curve is brought nearer to that of the non-entrepreneurial group, using British data. He concluded that the main reason is reinvesting in their businesses. However, results obtained in this study support the view that to the extent that income changes is a proxy for income variability, it is surely an important factor. Not only is the coefficient of income change large, but it is also highly significant. In another study, J. Crockett[34] reached similar conclusions using Time Series Data.

3

Composition of Personal Saving: Financial Assets

This chapter is concerned with the personal sector's saving in the form of financial assets. The identified items of this group of assets include notes and coins, bank deposits, deposits with financial institutions other than banks, marketable and non-marketable Government and local authority securities, marketable and non-marketable company and overseas securities, as well as unit trust units. Financial liabilities of the personal sector to the other sectors of the economy, though being negative financial assets which ideally should be analysed in this chapter, are discussed in the next chapter in conjunction with the demand for real assets, for reasons which will become clear later on.

In section 3.1 the principal behavioural assumptions of the financial model are set out, where the typical portfolio equation is specified. A discussion of some of the statistical and econometric considerations follows in section 3.2, and in section 3.3 the financial assets equations are estimated and the results obtained are examined.

3.1 THE MODEL

3.1.1 THE THEORETICAL FOUNDATIONS OF THE MODEL

These are based on the theories of Friedman,[62b,63,64] Keynes,[108b] and Tobin[207a,207b] on the one hand, and on the other hand in De Leeuw's[40c] pioneering model of the Financial Sector in the United States. More specifically, the model may be regarded as:

1. Friedmanite, in the general theoretical framework adopted. The demand for any financial asset is determined by its characteristics subject to a wealth constraint.

2. Keynesian, in emphasising the importance of interest rates expectations in determining the desired demand for an asset. Also, Keynes' 'normal' rate of interest forms the base for the expectational mechanism which is used in the empirical work.
3. Tobinian, in the sense that it allows for diversification and makes room for both the speculator and the financial investor, and
4. De Leeuwian, in assuming that the 'actual' path of adjustment towards the 'desired' level of asset holding may be different from the 'planned' path, due to the existence of short-term constraints.

3.1.2 SPECIFICATION OF THE FINANCIAL SAVINGS MODEL

The model specified in this section resembles, to a great extent, De Leeuw's financial model of the United States,[40c] which has since been used by others, particularly in empirical studies of the demand for money.[52] It is derived from three behavioural assumptions: the first explains the factors which determine the desired stock of an asset, the second specifies a partial adjustment mechanism which relates the actual stock to the desired stock, while the third imposes a constraint on the path of adjustment to allow for short-run variations in the funds readily available to the personal sector.

To begin with, let A_{it}^*, W_t, $\underline{R}$ and E_t stand for the desired stock of the asset i, a measure of the size of the total portfolio in terms of wealth, a vector of current rates of return on the asset i and all other assets, and a measure of interest rates expectations respectively. As a first approximation, the desired stock of the asset i may be expressed as a function of W_t, $\underline{R}$ and E_t and hence we have:

$$A_{it}^* = \phi(W_t, \underline{R}, E_t) \tag{1}$$

The significance of the size of the total portfolio in determining the demand for an asset, and hence influencing the portfolio composition, stems from the fact that asset management is an activity with decreasing costs to scale. The cost in terms of cash and effort of choosing assets subject to risk is much smaller per £1 invested for a large portfolio, than for a smaller one. The net gain to be obtained from buying variable price securities, as opposed to saving deposits of one type or another, is not likely to be worth the trouble for the holder of a relatively small portfolio.[45d]

Given the size of the portfolio, the demand for a particular type of asset will depend on the comparative yield* of that asset (or inversely, on cost in the case of liability). A higher yield on saving deposits, for instance, relative to other yields is expected to increase the proportion of the portfolio held in the form of saving deposits. This is so, whether or not there has been an increase in the total funds available for investment, or in the size of the portfolio. However,

---

* What is meant by 'the yield' on an asset is not, however, simple and varies with the type of asset. For example, while the yield for non-marketable savings instruments bears a fixed (i.e. certain) return, for a marketable bond with time to maturity longer than the planning period it bears a fixed return and in addition has the possibility of yielding capital gain or loss. In the case of equities the yield consists of the expected dividend return and an uncertain capital gain or loss.

because of uncertainties about future yields, rational investors are not likely to hold the total of their portfolio in one form of assets.

Expectations about future interest rates also enter into the demand function for an asset, and thus influence the portfolio composition. For example, in deciding whether to hold bonds or money, investors are likely to take account of the prospective capital gains (or losses) from holding bonds, which in turn depend on interest rate expectations. However, specifying a theory of how expectations are formed, and attempting to formulate an operational concept, is an extremely difficult task. One widely held hypothesis has been suggested by Keynes[108b] which assumes that investors have in mind a 'normal' level of long-term interest rates, towards which current rates are expected to move. When current rates are above normal, investors expect rates to fall, and hence capital values to rise; when current rates are below normal investors expect capital losses. The difference between the current long-term rate and its normal level might, therefore, be regarded as a good approximation of capital gains or losses. A different hypothesis advanced by Duesenberry[45b] (p. 318) suggests that expectations might be extrapolative. He argued that 'on *priori* grounds, there is no reason why the [Keynesian] argument should not be turned the other way. In many fields, trend projection seems to be the dominant influence on expectation. It would not, therefore, be surprising if it turned out that a rise in rates led to an expectation of a further rise and vice-versa.' In the author's opinion, both mechanisms are plausible;* whether one or the other is more dominant is a matter of empirical testing. As will be shown later, the expectional variable E is formulated in relation to some 'interest' rate 'norm', which in turn, is assumed to be generated by a statistical model.

Since A_{it}^*, the desired stock of the asset i, is a theoretical magnitude which is not directly observable, an assumption is needed to explain the adjustment of the actual level of assets to their desired level. For this purpose, we assume an adjustment mechanism of the following form:†

$$A_{it} - A_{it-1} = \theta_0(A_{it}^* - A_{it-1}) + \theta_1 S_{t-j} \qquad \theta \leqslant \theta_0, \theta_1 \leqslant 1 \qquad (2)$$
$$+ \text{a stochastic term}$$

where S is aggregate personal saving, and j describes the lag duration. This mechanism consists of two components. The first is the partial adjustment mechanism, which is widely used in the demand for consumer durables, and its application in the case of money balances has recently been rationalized by Feige.[55b] The second component of the adjustment mechanism is based on the assumption that the 'actual' path of adjustment may be different from the 'planned' path, due to the existence of short-run constraints. The funds readily available to the personal sector vary from time to time, and it seems plausible in these circumstances to assume that the amount of these funds constricts changes

---

* Owing to the uncertainty regarding interest rates, investors expectations of how interest rates will change are very likely to differ: some might expect continuity, others might expect no change, and still others might expect a convergence.
† Equation (2) is almost identical to the adjustment mechanism which was suggested by Chow.[26a] However, Chow referred to θ_0 and θ_1 as weights and used total saving, S_t, as a proxy for the short-term constraints. By further specifying a 'stable' saving/income relationship S_t was eliminated from Chow's reduced form.

in the stock in the short-run, just as the size of the portfolio constricts the level
of stocks. To account for the possibility of a short-term constraint, the total
funds available for investment by the personal sector, measured by aggregate
personal saving S, are used in the empirical work. The choice of this variable,
rather than income which may appear in the first instance as the appropriate
candidate, may be justified on theoretical grounds. It is possible to assume,
indeed without loss of realism, that the personal sector is a multi-stage optimiser
following the Utility Tree approach in the portfolio decision-making process, and
thus attempting to maximise a 'separable utility function'.[198a] If this is the case
therefore it seems reasonable to assume that the short-run constraint is represented
more appropriately by the funds available for a *specific* bundle of goods, rather
than by the funds available for *all* bundles of goods. This possibility is considered
again in section 3.3.3.

A stochastic term is included in equation (2) to indicate functional mis-
specification. That is, it may be argued that, if the cost of portfolio change is a
function of S_t, then θ_0 should be specified as a function of S_t, and this in turn
would lead to a non-linear adjustment mechanism different from (2). For reasons
of mathematical simplicity, a stochastic term was introduced. Hence equation (2)
should be regarded as a linear approximation — with errors — of some non-linear
adjustment mechanism.

Now assuming that equation (1) is linear in the variables and the parameters,
and using (2), the following reduced form is derived:

$$\Delta A_{it} = a_i \theta_0 W_t + \theta_{0i} b\underline{R} + C_i \theta_{0i} E_t + \theta_{1i} S_{t-j} - \theta_{0i} A_{it-1} + u_i \qquad (3)$$

Equation (3) is estimated empirically for all the identified financial assets, and
results obtained are discussed in section 3.3.

3.2 SOME STATISTICAL AND ECONOMETRIC CONSIDERATIONS

3.2.1 VARIABLES AND DATA

A Measure of Interest Rate Expectations

As mentioned previously the interest rate expectational variable, E, is
formulated in this study in relation to some interest rate 'norm'. Thus, we assume
that at any point in time, the expectational variable E is derived as follows:

$$E_t = R_t - R_t^N \qquad (4)$$

$$R_t^N = [(1 - \lambda)/(1 - \lambda^F)] \sum_{i=1}^{F} \lambda^{i-1} R_{t-i} \qquad 0 \leqslant \lambda \leqslant 1 \qquad (5)$$

According to (4) the demand for an asset i depends not only on the absolute
level of the interest rate, but also on the degree of divergence from what is considered as a fairly safe level. A close examination of the definition and derivation
of E reveals the following points:

1. It is important to emphasise the dynamic definition of the normal rate of
interest adopted in this study, where R^N has a subscript t to indicate variability
with time. This is contrary to the static definition which was advocated by both
Hicks[32a] (p.154) and Harrod,[91b] who regarded a yield on consols of about 3%

as having some claim·historically to be regarded as the norm. In this study, the dynamic definition is preferred because it does not seem realistic to assume a static (constant over time) norm in a situation where there is a steady increase in government borrowing during peace time, associated with a continuing expectation of inflation, and an investment market which has become very competitive.

2. It is also important to note that in this study the normal rate of interest R^N is generated by a 'mechanical' model, using a distributed lag function, rather than, as should be, an economic model. Keynes himself did not provide any theoretical explanation of the factors which determine the norm; instead, it seems, he regarded the norm either as a necessary analytical tool or as a psychological concept (!). Indeed such a model is required.

3. With respect to (5) it is clear that if λ is close to unity this implies a market of a very strong memory in which rates in the more distant past have substantial weight in determining the level of the normal rate, and vice versa if λ is closer to zero. In the empirical work, E is estimated on quarterly data of two interest rates: the rates of interest on short-dated and long-dated government securities: with λ being given the values 0·9, 0·55 and 0·25.

The Size of the Total Portfolio

We now turn to the problem of specifying a variable to represent the size of the total portfolio. The lack of reliable figures of total personal wealth — particularly for the pre-1957 period — necessitates the use of a proxy variable. An income index, similar to the one suggested by Friedman, is chosen. To construct the required series from the sources of total personal income, formula (5) is used on quarterly data, with λ assuming the value 0·9. The use of permanent income may be criticised on the grounds that it is wealth times some rate of return which is proportional to income, rather than wealth. This suggests that the appropriate proxy should ideally be a weighted average of incomes divided by some interest rate. However, this raises the problem of deciding on the appropriate rate of return to be used in the calculation. If a market rate of interest is used, it would, therefore, be reflected in the model, since interest rates are excluded as explanatory variables in equation (3).

Financial Statistics

In the estimation of equation (3), the Bank of England annual figures for the personal sector's transactions in financial assets and liabilities[9b] are used. These figures are unreliable and may be subject to a considerable margin of errors. These arise either from the inaccurate recording of transactions between sectors or from incompleteness in the coverage due to the lack of information about certain transactions, or from both.*

Most of the figures of transactions in financial assets by the personal sector are obtained indirectly either from data provided by financial institutions and public authorities, or as residuals. Thus, any differences in the valuation or

---

* Analysis in this sub-section is based to a great extent on Berman.[11]

timing of the recording of transactions are likely to result in a sizeable margin of error. For example, the available figures for transactions in marketable government (and government guaranteed) securities by the personal sector are obtained as a residual. The difference between identified purchases and sales by the public sector, by the banking sector and financial institutions, and by non-residents, is equal to the purchases, less sales of the other two sectors. In the 'Blue Book', this residual is arbitrarily attributed to the personal sector, in the belief that net changes in the holdings of industrial and commercial companies are relatively small[153] (p. 421). In the Bank of England *Quarterly Bulletin* transactions by the company sector are roughly estimated from a variety of sources. In both cases the residual changes are attributed to the personal sector. Since sales and purchases of securities are not recorded on precisely the same basis, the resultant residual is necessarily subject to a large margin of error. Cash paid for a block of stock will exceed the cash received by the seller by the sum of the commission paid to the seller by the purchaser. The figures of the banking sector do not relate to cash transactions, while those for financial institutions and for non-residents are subject to errors of sampling and may not relate to precisely the same period of time.

Transactions in the financial accounts should be recorded on a consistent timing basis. This implies that the sale of an asset by a sector is recorded at the same point in time as its purchase by another sector on the one hand, and on the other hand that all transactions in the financial accounts of each sector are recorded at the same point of time as the estimate of personal saving (estimated as a residual). The shorter the period of time under review, the more important is the problem of timing. An obvious example of timing inconsistencies is related to transactions in company securities. They could be recorded when the contract was made, or when payments were settled. The latter could be several weeks later, after the signing of the contract. Transactions might be recorded in the company register only when the change of ownership took place. Even if the date of contract is taken as a base for all home transactions, there may be inconsistencies of timing between the figures for the domestic sectors and those of transactions taken from the Balance of Payments.

Differences in timing and valuations are not the only sources of errors in the transactions recorded in the Financial Accounts. There may be errors in the basic data provided by the various institutions, or from sampling. They can also arise because different sources record the same information on differing bases. An obvious example is the differences in reporting bank deposits and advances by the various sectors which give rise to the large unallocated item.

Until recently incompleteness was a serious problem. Before 1963 there was no data from which any kind of direct estimate could be made of personal transactions in securities: Government, company and overseas. Figures are now available, but, in addition to being unreliable, they are also incomplete. For example, the figures for company and overseas securities relate to companies whose shares are quoted on the Stock Exchange, and no comprehensive information is available for capital issues by non-quoted companies. Recently, some information has been made available by the Board of Trade from a sample of 500 non-quoted companies. Another important omission is borrowing from companies in the form of trade credit, often simply a delayed settlement of accounts. The Board of Trade figures for increases in gross trade credit extended by quoted non-manufacturing companies show a marked rise between 1951 and 1965, and fluctuations in the figures reveal some association with those of the unidentified item of the personal sector[9b] (Sept. 1966).

Despite these limitations, the Bank of England estimates of the personal sector's transactions in financial assets and liabilities are the best, and for some items are the only ones available, and hence are used in the estimation of equation (3). However, in the interpretation of the results, these limitations should be borne in mind. Figures for the stocks of assets are not readily available, and estimates are made from various sources.* Finally, figures are available for most of the interest rates required in the estimation.

3.2.2 ECONOMETRIC CONSIDERATIONS

Aggregation

Although the financial assets model, specified in section 3.1, is developed with respect to an asset (i) and for the individual, data for groups of assets and for the personal sector as a whole are used in empirical work. This results in aggregation bias and leads to difficulties in the definition of variables and the interpretation of the estimated parameters. Needless to say, the problem is less serious in the case of aggregation over individuals than over assets. For one asset (i), if the assumption of linearity holds true, the macro variables will simply be either arithmetic sums or weighted arithmetic averages of the micro variables. On the other hand, aggregation over types of assets raises various conceptional problems, e.g. the definition of the rate of return on an asset. This question will be investigated further in section 3.3.3 in the light of the results obtained.

The Selection of the Rate (or Rates) of Return

According to equation (3) the demand for an asset (i) depends, amongst other things, on its own rate of return and the rates of return on *all* other assets. However, in practice this is limited by the number of degrees of freedom provided by post-war annual data, and by the desire to avoid difficulties in the estimation, as well as in the interpretation of estimated parameters, which may result from the high degree of multicollinearity between the interest rates variables. Thus, in the estimation of equation (3) only *two* interest rates are used, and the choice between the various rates is made by comparing the estimated equations on economic, statistical and econometric criteria.

Method of Estimation

Equation (3) is estimated by means of Unrestricted (Ordinary) Least Squares (ULS), under the assumption that the stochastic term in every equation is

* See Data Appendix.

normally distributed, and serially independent with a zero mean and constant variance. It is also assumed that in each equation there exists one, and only one, endogenous variable, while the rest of the variables are defined as exogenous. Under these assumptions, two problems arise:

1. The fact that equation (3) is autoregressive, * including the lagged level of the dependent variable as an explanatory variable, suggests a violation of the ULS assumptions. As shown by Hurwicz,[97] the estimated coefficient of the lagged endogenous variable is likely to be biased in small samples; the expected value of θ is given, to the first order approximation in θ and $1/N$ by: $E(\theta) = \{1 - (2/N)\}$ where N is the size of the sample. Malinvaud[132b] (p. 456) investigated the statistical properties of a model containing a lagged endogenous variable, an exogenous variable and a constant term, for samples of 20 observations. He found that the ULS method led to biased estimates and that the distribution was clearly skewed with a considerable tail towards the small values. For this reason, limited emphasis is given to the coefficients of the lagged stock variable† θ, in equation (3), particularly when there is evidence of serial correlation.

2. The second problem concerns the definition of interest rates as exogenous variables. In several relationships this does not represent a serious problem. For instance, the rate of interest on National Savings Certificates is set by the authorities as a policy decision, and in this case one can reasonably assume that there is only a demand relation in this market. The rates of interest on Bank deposits and deposits with other financial institutions may also be regarded as exogenous. However, similar assumptions will be difficult to justify with respect to the rates of interest on marketable securities particularly in the case of company securities and long-dated government securities.

3.3 RESULTS

This section begins with *Table Fin. 1* which gives a statistical summary of the financial assets variables used in the estimation.

The best estimates obtained are shown in *Tables Fin. 2* and *Fin. 4*; the former is for Bank deposits, ΔFA_2, Cash, $\Delta FA_1 + \Delta FA_2$, and Deposits with Non-bank Financial Institutions, ΔFA_3, while the latter is for Securities, ΔFA_i $(i = 4 \ldots 9)$. Parameter estimates are given with their standard errors, together with the Coefficient of Determination corrected for the degrees of freedom, R^2, and the Von-Neumann Ratio. The implied values of the long-run coefficients are also calculated.

The results are, in general, satisfactory. Judging by reference to the overall fit, the values of R^2 are high, exceeding 0·7. The Von-Neumann Ratio shows no evidence of first order serial correlation at a 5% level of significance; with the exception of equation 3.1.2 of *Table Fin. 2* where the Von-Neumann Ratio is relatively large, passing the test at a 1% level of significance only. Most of the

---

* Because of the autoregressive nature of the model the Durbin—Watson statistic (and the Von-Neumann Ratio) are not strictly speaking applicable.

† It should be remembered that there are some ambiguities regarding the parameters of equation (2), as it is a linear approximation of some non-linear mechanism.

coefficients are statistically significant, and they all have the correct *a priori* signs and are of plausible magnitudes. In the equations for ΔFA_3 to ΔFA_9, the relative sizes of the interest rates coefficients are acceptable. In each equation the coefficient of the asset's own rate of interest is larger than the coefficient of the rate of interest of the competing asset.

We now turn to a more detailed analysis of the estimates. The results for Cash and Saving deposits, $\Delta FA_i(i = 1 \ldots 3)$, are considered first, with particular

Table Fin. 1 THE PERSONAL SECTOR'S TRANSACTIONS IN FINANCIAL ASSETS (£m) 1952–66

Index / Variable	Min.	Max.	Mean	Quartile 1	Median	Quartile 3	Standard deviation
ΔFA_1	3·0	77·0	46·47	37·0	48·0	64·0	19·31
ΔFA_2	−130·0	512·0	217·73	149·0	197·0	356·0	162·0
ΔFA_3	93·0	844·0	403·0	195·0	338·0	743·0	258·15
ΔFA_4	−124·0	94·0	17·33	5·0	11·0	56·0	49·99
ΔFA_5	−97·0	197·0	49·8	1·0	41·0	132·0	88·88
ΔFA_6	−246·0	452·0	34·2	−75·0	−40·0	121·0	186·10
ΔFA_7	−8·0	289·0	136·87	92·0	126·0	233·0	89·96
ΔFA_8	−751·0	8·0	−306·2	−396·0	−305·0	−100·0	239·96
ΔFA_9	5·0	105·0	40·5	10·0	32·0	68·5	31·33

Notes

ΔFA_i Transactions in Financial Assets by the personal sector
$\quad i = 1$ Notes and Coins
$\quad i = 2$ Bank Deposits
$\quad i = 3$ Deposits with Financial Institutions other than banks
$\quad i = 4$ National Savings Certificates (excluding interest)
$\quad i = 5$ Other Non-Marketable Government Securities
$\quad i = 6$ Marketable Government Securities
$\quad i = 7$ Local Authority Debt
$\quad i = 8$ Company Securities
$\quad i = 9$ Unit Trust Units

emphasis on three questions: i.e. (1) the empirical selection of the rate, or rates, of interest which represents the opportunity cost of holding money, (2) the definition of money, and (3) the stability of the personal sector's demand for money function. Estimates for Securities, $\Delta FA_i(i = 4 \ldots 9)$, are discussed in sub-section 3.3.2, and in sub-section 3.3.3 we examine the results in the context of a Utility Tree hypothesis.[198]

3.3.1 CASH AND SAVING DEPOSITS

In the bank deposits equation, equation 3.1.2 of *Table Fin. 2*, the rate of interest on deposits with non-bank financial institutions, RSD_t, emerges as the most significant measure of the opportunity cost of holding money by the personal sector. The relative superiority of this rate can easily be observed by comparing equation 3.1.2 with equations 3.1.3 and 3.2.3 of *Table Fin. 3*. The

Table Fin. 2 CASH AND SAVING DEPOSITS (1952–66)

Equation Number	Dependent Variable	A_{it-1} (£m)	Y_t^P (£m)	RSD_t (%)	$RNSC_t$ (%)	E_{Lt} (λ = 0.25) (%)	E_{Lt} (λ = 0.9) (%)	S_{t-1} (£m)	Structural Parameters θ_i	a_i	b_i (× 100)	b_j (× 100)	R^2	VN
3.1.2	ΔFA_{2t}	-0.369 (0.103)	0.184* (0.053)	-270.764 (122.946)		-1422.691 (467.871)		-0.286 (0.139)	-0.369	0.499		-7.34	0.791	2.48
3.2.2	$\Delta FA_{1t} + \Delta FA_{2t}$	-0.395 (0.115)	0.209* (0.059)	-332.136 (137.690)		-1432.107 (523.98)		-0.354 (0.156)	-0.395	0.529		-8.41	0.751	2.57
3.3.2	ΔFA_{3t}	-0.111 (0.051)	0.077 (0.029)	433.008 (225.915)	-427.383 (115.252)		-90.344 (46.845)	-0.1661 (0.120)	-0.111	0.693	39.01	-38.50	0.964	3.01
3.4.2	$\Delta FA_{1,2,3t}$	-0.155 (0.078)	0.164 (0.091)	642.011 (693.000)	-603.9 (344.800)		-252.0 (132.0)	-0.455 (0.330)	-0.155	1.058	41.42	-38.96	0.950	2.98

Y_{t-1}^P instead of Y_t^P

Notes

1. All variables are deflated by the price index of consumer's expenditures, with the exception of RSD, $RNSC$, $E_{Lt}(λ = 0.25)$ and $E_{Lt}(λ = 0.9)$.
2. RSD is the rate of interest on non-bank deposits and is calculated as a weighted average of the rates of interest on: Building Societies' shares, RBS, Building Societies' deposits, RBD, and Trustee Savings Banks deposits, $RTSB$, $RNSC$ is the rate of interest on National Savings Certificates.
3. E_{Lt} refers to exceptional variables, based on the rate of interest on long-dated government securities, R^L.

Table Fin. 3 CASH AND SAVING DEPOSITS: FURTHER RESULTS (1952–66)

Equation Number	Dependent Variable	A_{it-1} (£m)	Y^P_t (£m)	RSD_t (%)	$RNSC_t$ (%)	R^L_t (%)	R^O_t (%)	$E_{Lt}(\lambda=0.25)$ (%)	$E_{Lt}(\lambda=0.9)$ (%)	S_{t-1} (£m)	R^2	VN
3.1.2	ΔFA_{2t}	−0.369 (0.102)	0.184 (0.053)	270.764 (122.945)				−1422.692 (467.871)		−0.286 (0.139)	0.791	2.32
3.1.3	ΔFA_{2t}	−0.21 (0.09)	0.091 (0.04)			−0.516 (0.595)		−1089.0 (557)		−0.11 (0.14)	0.758	1.668
3.2.3	ΔFA_{2t}	−0.14 (0.11)	0.067 (0.031)				−0.310 (0.37)	−1330 (571)		−0.13 (0.14)	0.750	1.763
3.3.3	ΔFA_{3t}	−0.171 (0.096)	0.061 (0.034)							−0.036 (0.144)	0.723	1.802
3.4.3	ΔFA_{4t}	−0.220 (0.113)	0.098 (0.05)	142 (146)						−0.081 (0.16)	0.725	1.928
3.3.2	ΔFA_{3t}	−0.111 (0.051)	0.0775 (0.029)	433.008 (225.915)	−422.382 (115.252)				−90.344 (46.845)	−0.166 (0.120)	0.964	3.015
3.5.3	ΔFA_{3t}	−0.120 (0.06)	0.120 (0.03)	31.00 (166.00)		−259.0 (96.0)			152.0 (75)	−0.208 (0.09)	0.954	1.361
3.6.3	ΔFA_{3t}	−0.450 (0.203)	0.120 (0.09)	188.0 (191.0)			−195.0 (63.0)		−132.0 (62.0)	−0.230 (0.08)	0.955	1.5193

Notes

1. All variables are deflated by the price index of consumers expenditure; with the exception of RSD, $RNSC$, R^L, R^O, and E_{Lt}.
2. RL is the rate of interest on long-dated Government Securities. RO is the F.T. yield on ordinary shares.

explanatory powers of these equations are lower than that of equation 3.1.2. In addition, neither the rate of interest on long-dated government securities, R^L, nor that on equities R^O, is statistically significant. In this respect our results agree with those of Bronfenbrenner and Maver,[16] Teigen,[202] Heller,[86] Laidler[120] and others[79d, 122, 82b] for the United States.

Equation 3.1.2 has another interesting feature. In the more recent monetary discussion, the demand for money is usually conceived as a stable function of its arguments. Moreover, Keynes' 'speculative motive' is regarded, in current debates, as an *ad hoc* explanation of the interest-elasticity of the money-demand function, and as an unsightly crutch which the 'Keynesian' macromodel would do better without. In the words of Professor H. G. Johnson,[98a] 'Keynes' monetary theory has been refined and elaborated by subsequent writers in the Keynesian tradition. Keynes' most extreme departure from previous analysis — his emphasis on the speculative demand for money at the expense of the precautionary — has been gradually abandoned . . . .' Our evidence in this context is in direct contradiction with the voluminous empirical work* on this topic, and may be regarded as typically Keynesian (not Keynesian in the Leijonhufvad[123] sense) in two respects. Firstly, the fact that our expectational variable, E_{Lt}, is statistically significant in equation 3.1.2 provides some evidence in support of Keynes' liquidity preference, in which what matters is the degree of divergence of the absolute level of the rate of interest from its norm.[108b] Comparing equation 3.1.2 with equation 3.5.2 of *Table Fin. 2* shows that the effect of dropping E_{Lt} is to reduce R^2. Indeed, this loss in the explanatory power refutes the allegedly *ad hoc* element of Keynes' theory, and reveals that the speculative behaviour is not something that the Keynesian macromodel would do better without. Secondly, the negative sign of the expectational variable in equation 3.1.2 of *Table Fin. 2* gives support to the 'convergence' hypothesis as first suggested by Keynes.

Connected with the problem of substitutability is the question of the 'proper' definition of money, or which collection of assets corresponds most closely to the theoretical concept of money? More specifically, one is usually asked to choose between narrow money, to include currency plus current deposits, broad money, to include narrow money and time deposits, and broad money plus other forms of liquid assets, notably deposits with non-bank financial institutions. Traditionally, money is defined as 'narrow' money, while Friedman and others[62b, 63,64] argue for the second concept, and Gurley and Shaw[79b] and others favour the third concept.† The Bank of England figures of bank deposits do not separate current and deposit accounts in the sector-financing tables.[9b] The lack of these figures makes it impossible to provide an empirical test of the choice between narrow money and broad money (narrow money plus time

---

* The first attempts to test empirically the Keynesian demand for money were made by Ball[4d] for the U.K. and later by Starleaf and Reimer[192] for the U.S. See also Norton.[160]
† Leijonhufvud[123] (p. 355) argues that Keynes' definition of money is much broader than that used by lated Keynesians. He points out that 'Not only are all kinds of deposits generally included, but Keynes is also willing to draw the line between money and non-money assets more or less wherever analytical convenience dictates in dealing with a specific problem. The flexibility with regard to the definition of money is a natural concomitant of the attempt to compress the essentials of the Liquidity Preference theory within the simplified framework of a two-asset system.'

deposits). However, it is interesting to note that aggregating currency and bank deposits and re-estimating equation 3.1.2 has not led to an improved fit. On the contrary, comparing equations 3.1.2 and 3.2.2 of *Table Fin. 2* shows that the broadening of the concept of money has led to a marked reduction in R^2, from 0·79 to 0·75. Nor is there any evidence in support of the broader definition of money. This can be observed by comparing equation 3.3.2 for deposits with non-bank financial institutions, with equation 3.4.2, in which money is defined to include currency bank and non-bank deposits. The aggregation has led to a reduction in the explanatory power, as measured by R^2 corrected for the degrees of freedom, and none of the estimated coefficients are statistically significant by the standard tests.

The above findings are strikingly similar to those reported by El-Mokadem and Whittaker[52] of the demand for money by the company sector in the United Kingdom. For both the personal and the company sectors: (1) a short-term rate of interest emerges as the most relevant measure of the opportunity cost of holding money; (2) there is evidence of a speculative demand for money, with a Keynesian converging expectational mechanism; though expectations are more heavily weighted by recent experience for the personal sector ($\lambda = 0·25$) than for the company sector ($\lambda = 0·9$); (3) the definition of money as cash plus total bank deposits is superior, in the statistical sense, to the one which also includes non-bank deposits; and (4) the short-term interest elasticity (calculated at the mean values of the variables) is relatively small and of the same order of magnitude, approximately $-0·2$. On the other hand, there is some evidence that the personal sector's demand for money function is less stable than the company sector's demand function. The expectional elasticities are estimated at: $-0·1$ for the former, and $-0·003$ for the latter. This suggests that if, for example, the current long-term bond rate is, say, 9%, and the normal level at the same time is 6% giving a difference of 3% (or 50% of 6%), the demand for money by the personal sector will be reduced by 5%, and that of the company sector by 0·15% only.

3.3.2 SECURITIES

Non-marketable Government Securities

In the evidence submitted to the Radcliffe Committee, various factors were suggested as important determinants of the demand for non-marketable government securities.[32c] It was pointed out that variations in competing interest rates, unmatched by changes in National Savings rates of interest, were responsible for the decline in the demand for these securities in general and Defence Bonds in particular. The threat of inflation and the resultant fall in the value of money was stressed as a 'substantial factor'. Also, changes in non-interest terms and tax concessions were suggested to have influenced the demand for these securities, particularly with respect to the well-to-do saver. Whenever the limit on the holding of National Savings Certificates was raised there was a transfer from one form of saving to another, in favour of National Savings. In addition, there was some evidence that individuals have resorted to the encashment of National Savings when failing to secure loans from their bankers during periods of credit squeeze.

Equation 3.1.4 of *Table Fin. 4* is the Ordinary Least Squares estimate of the demand for National Savings Certificates by the personal sector. In this equation, the estimated parameter of the rate of interest on Building Societies' shares is not well determined; as reflected in the relatively large standard error. However, experiments with other interest rates were less satisfactory. Several measures of price expectations were tried, but gave the wrong signs. Also, dummies were used to capture the effects of changes in non-interest terms, but results obtained were statistically insignificant. This, nevertheless, should not be viewed as evidence that non-interest terms are unimportant. The use of annual data, together with the usual difficulties of formulating appropriate proxies, may be responsible for the failure to obtain significant results. Norton,[160] in what seems to be the only other estimate of the demand for National Savings in the United Kingdom, tested several measures of price expectations and used dummies for non-interest terms on quarterly data. The latter was marginally significant (t ratio was approximately 1·8), while the former was insignificant.

Other non-marketable government securities include Defence Bonds, Premium Bonds, Securities with the Post Office Registrar and Tax Reserve Certificates. Deposits with the National Savings Banks were added to deposits with non-bank financial institutions, a procedure which is adopted by the Bank of England in the Sector-Financing Table.[9b] Equation 3.2.4 of *Table Fin. 4* is the Ordinary Least Squares estimate of the demand for non-marketable government securities (other than National Savings Certificates) by the personal sector. The rate of interest on National Savings Certificates performed satisfactorily as a proxy for the yield on this group of assets. The coefficient of the price expectation variable – defined as the difference between the current price level and the normal level, where the latter is calculated by formula (5) with $\lambda = 0\cdot5$ – has a negative sign and is statistically significant. This confirms the views expressed in the Radcliffe Report that the fear of inflation has an adverse effect on the demand for these assets. None of the expectational variables were significant, and the short-run constraints which were tried did not perform satisfactorily.

Local Authorities' Debt

The lack of a complete series for the rate (or rates) of interest on local authorities' borrowing made it necessary to search for a proxy that can best represent the authorities' interest policy. However, the aggregation of all types of borrowing, anything from as short as three months to as long as 60 years, in one item in the Bank of England figures made the search for a proxy a very difficult task. In equation 3.3.4 of *Table Fin. 4*, the rate of interest on short-dated government securities emerged as the best proxy for the interest on local authorities' borrowing. This is expected in view of the government regulations regarding the local authorities' access to the Public Works Loan Board and the money and capital markets, and is also compatible with the findings of the Radcliffe Committee.[32] For the period 1951–58 it was observed that the

Table Fin. 4 GOVERNMENT SECURITIES, LOCAL AUTHORITIES' DEBT AND PRIVATE SECURITIES (1952–66)

Equation number	Dependent variable	A_{it-1} (£m)	Y^P_t (£m)	$RNSC_t$ ×100 (%)	RBS_t ×100 (%)	R^S_t ×100 (%)	R^O_t ×100 (%)	$EP^{0.5}$ ×100 (%)	P^N_t ×100	$E'^{0.25}_{Lt}$ ×100 (%)
3.1.4	ΔFA_{4t}	−0·122 (0·047)	0·011 (0·006)	1·414 (0·64)	−1·122 (0·97)					
3.2.4	ΔFA_{5t}	−0·132 (0·124)	0·0083 (0·0081)	0·546 (0·185)				−28·84 (8·636)		
3.3.4	ΔFA_{6t}	−0·937 (0·3)	0·388 (0·123)	−2·11 (1·73)		5·22 (1·79)				
3.4.4	ΔFA_{7t}	−0·0676 (0·043)		−0·715 (0·269)		0·855 (0·317)				
3.5.4	ΔFA_{8t}		** −0·091 (0·025)				0·514 (0·261)		8·47 (4·43)	7·76 (4·39)
3.6.4	ΔFA_{8+9t}		** −0·071 (0·027)				0·545 (0·278)		5·41 (4·73)	6·74 (4·69)

Notes

*S_t instead of S_{t-1}.

**Y^P_{t-1}.

R^S Rate of Interest on short-term government securities – percentage.

R^O_t F.T. yield on ordinary shares.

P^N_t a geometric moving average of consumers' price index.

Table Fin. 4 (cont.)

Equation number	Dependent variable	$E^{0.5}_{Lt} \times 100$ (%)	$E^{0.9}_{Lt} \times 100$ (%)	S_{t-1}	$(T^P_t + NIC)$	t	θ_i	a_i	$b_i \times 100$	$b_{iK} \times 100$	R^2	VN
3.1.4	ΔFA_{4t}	-1·084 (0·536)		-0·128 (0·055)			0·122	0·09	11·59	-9·2	0·82	2·47
3.2.4	ΔFA_{5t}						0·132	0·063	4·14		0·73	1·96
3.3.4	ΔFA_{6t}		-3·77 (2·12)		-1·44 (0·489)	-202·2 (50·8)	0·937	0·414	5·571	-2·25	0·74	2·73
3.4.4	ΔFA_{7t}	-2·67 (0·749)		*0·0814 (0·065)			0·0676		12·64	10·58	0·96	2·11
3.5.4	ΔFA_{8t}			0·277 (0·148)					5·65		0·921	2·25
3.6.4	ΔFA_{8+9t}			0·211 (0·158)					7·68		0·910	2·36

E_{Lt} measures of interest rate expectations.
$(T^P_t + NIC)$ Personal Income Taxation plus National Insurance Contributions.
t Time Trend variable.

rate of interest on local authority borrowing kept pace with changes in the rate of interest on short-term government securities, though it was on average slightly higher. Experiments with other interest rates showed a better performance for the rate on National Savings Certificates, and thus suggested that the latter is a close substitute for local authorities' debt. This substitutability was voiced in the evidence to the Radcliffe Committee, particularly in the North-West area. Permanent income gave a very small coefficient and was insignificant, while current saving emerged as the relevant scale variable.

Government Marketable Securities

The demand for government marketable securities by the personal sector is represented in this study by a single equation, which aggregates over all maturities. Ideally, there should be separate equations for securities of different maturities, but this was not possible since the Bank of England figures are given for aggregate transactions and no other information was available regarding the maturity structure of the personal sector's holdings. This, in addition to the inaccuracies of the data mentioned previously, imposed great difficulties in the estimation of the single equation and particularly in the interpretation of the appropriate signs and magnitudes of the parameters, especially those of the interest rates and the expectational variables.

For the purpose of estimation, we have assumed, for simplicity, that there are two categories of government securities held by the personal sector: 'long-term' and 'short-term'. To some extent this may not be a grave misrepresentation of the market realities, in which dealings and formulation of expectation are in terms of 'shorts' and 'longs'. Based on this assumption, while maintaining the theoretical framework adopted in this study and simplifying, the demand equations for short-term and long-term securities may be put in the following form:

$$\Delta GSS_t = a_0 Z_t + a_1 R_t^S - a_2 R_t^L \pm a_3 E_{Lt} - a_4 GSS_{t-1} \qquad (6)$$

$$\Delta GSL_t = \acute{a}_0 \acute{Z}_t - \acute{a}_1 R_t^S + \acute{a}_2 R_t^L \mp \acute{a}_3 E_{Lt} - \acute{a}_4 GSL_{t-1} \qquad (7)$$

where ΔGSS_t and ΔGSL_t are transactions in short-term and long-term Government securities respectively, GSS_{t-1} and GSL_{t-1} are their stocks, and Z_t and $\acute{Z}_t$ are other explanatory variables. By assuming, for simplicity, a Keynesian type expectational variable with $\lambda = 0.9$, and that Z_t does not differ greatly from $\acute{Z}_t$, and aggregating (6) and (7) we obtain:

$$\Delta GS_t = c_0 Z_t + c_1 R_t^S + c_2 R_t^L + c_3 E_{Lt}^{0.9} - a_4 GSS_{t-1} - \acute{a}_4 GSL_{t-1} \qquad (8)$$

where

$$c_0 = (a_0 + \acute{a}_0), c_1 = (a_1 - \acute{a}_1), c_2 = (\acute{a}_2 - a_2) \text{ and } c_3 = (a_3 - \acute{a}_3).$$

Estimation of (8) helps to throw some light on the maturity distribution of the underlying structure. For example, a positive and large coefficient for R_t^S associated with a negative and smaller coefficient for R_t^L and a negative coefficient for $E_{Lt}^{0.9}$ would be an indication that short-term securities have a comparatively strong weight. The negative sign for the expectational variable $E_{Lt}^{0.9}$ in a demand equation for short-term Government securities implies that when capital gains are expected ($E_{Lt}^{0.9}$ is positive as current rate exceeds normal rate but it is expected to fall) investors move out of shorts to longs and vice versa.

Equation 3.4.4 of *Table Fin. 4* is the Ordinary Least Squares estimate for the personal sector's demand for Government securities. Experiments with the rates of interest on short-term and long-term Government securities and the rate on consols showed a better performance for the short-term rate. Official evidence to the Radcliffe Committee[32c] suggested that Building Society shares may be a substitute for Government securities. However, using the rate on these shares instead of the rate on National Savings Certificates proved unsatisfactory. The size of the coefficient for RBS was smaller than the standard error. The relatively better performance of the rate of interest on National Savings Certificates was reported by Norton[160] in his quarterly estimate of the demand for Government securities by the public. He also found that income tax payments represent the relevant short-run constraint. Evidence to the Radcliffe Committee suggested that the threat of inflation reduced the public's desire to invest in Government securities, but experiments with price expectational variables did not give evidence in support of this view. Another argument was put forward by the Bank of England[9a] (Feb. 1959). They noted that sales of Government securities by the banks may lead some other holders to expect the prices of the securities to fall and therefore to shift out of Government securities. This view was difficult to test on annual data. However, Norton found some evidence in support of this hypothesis on the basis of quarterly data. Other factors were also suggested to have some effect on the demand for Government securities. To account for this possibility a time variable was introduced and yielded a significant coefficient. The negative sign of the coefficient for the expectational variable, $E_{Lt}^{0.9}$, may be regarded as evidence of either a strong weight of short-term securities in the personal sector's portfolio, or instability in the gilt-edged market, where the state of expectation about future interest rates is characterized by extrapolative tendencies. However, in this context no firm conclusion can be reached unless more is known about the maturity structure of Government securities' holding by different sectors.

Private Securities

The demand for company and overseas securities, to include quoted and unquoted ordinary shares, preference shares and debentures, was represented in this study by a single equation. Estimates of separate equations for each of these securities were not possible because the Bank of England figures are available only for aggregate transactions. This, in addition to the wide margin of errors in the data, imposed difficulties in the estimation and interpretation of the signs and magnitudes of the parameters. Moreover, there were no reliable figures for the stock of company and overseas securities held by the personal sector. Equation 3.5.4 of *Table Fin. 4* is the Ordinary Least Squares estimate of the personal sector's demand for company and overseas securities. None of the interest rates on competing assets which were tried gave satisfactory results. The positive sign of the coefficient of the expectational variable implies that, when the gilt-edged market is unstable and capital losses are expected, investors move out of Government securities and buy company and overseas securities instead. Thus private securities may be regarded as a substitute for Government securities in the short-run.

Separate figures were available for the personal sector's transactions in Unit Trusts for the post 1957 period only. The limited number of observations imposed some difficulties in estimating a separate equation for this type of asset. Since the underlying assets are generally all equities, the majority of them industrial equities, transactions in unit trusts were aggregated with those of other company and overseas securities and equation 3.5.4 was re-estimated. This is shown in equation 3.6.4 of *Table Fin. 4*. By comparing the two equations it is clear that while the overall fit remained more or less unchanged with no evidence of serial correlation, the aggregation of unit trusts with other private securities resulted in a less satisfactory estimate than that of equation 3.5.4. Since it was not possible to obtain a better estimate for the demand for unit trusts by the personal sector, due to the lack of data, equation 3.6.4 was included in the model.

3.3.3 FURTHER CONSIDERATIONS

In the previous sub-section, estimates have been made for groups of assets, although the theoretical model has been formulated with reference to individual assets. Aggregation over types of assets which are not strictly identical, and over all maturities in the case of securities, is made necessary to us by the lack of detailed information regarding transactions in individual assets. Indeed this represents a serious problem as to the appropriate definitions of variables and parameter estimates. On the other hand, the satisfactory results obtained for the groups of asset equations raise an interesting question with respect to the way funds are allocated among various groups and individual assets. In this sub-section we report the findings of preliminary investigations into the portfolio decision-making process and the implications for the demand for individual assets. It is important to emphasize that our aim is not to present a complete piece of research in this field, but primarily to draw attention to an area where further research is required.

Based on the so-called 'separable utility functions' Strotz[198] has suggested a rational way for the 'individual . . . doing his budgeting by first deciding how to allocate expenditure among the several branches and then making independent decisions as to how best to spend each branch allocation on the commodities within the branch'. He assumed a utility function of the form:

$$U = U[V^D(q_{d1}, \ldots q_{da}), V^B(q_{b1}, \ldots q_{bB}), V^M(q_{m1}, \ldots q_{mu})] \qquad (9)$$

which he called a Utility Tree, whereas the commodities $q_1, \ldots q_N$ are partitioned into M separate subsets, or branches. The commodities in any branch define a branch utility function, while utility U is then made to depend

On these branch utility functions. By maximising (9) subject to the usual budget contraint:

$$\sum_n P_n q_n = Y \tag{10}$$

implicitly determines the maximising values of the Y^M's where the Y^M's are the branch expenditures. For these values of the Y^M's, taken now as given, each branch utility function must be maximal. For fixed branch expenditures, then, the problem of maximizing U splits into the M independent problems of maximising the V's each subject to a constraint involving only the prices of commodities within the branch and the given branch expenditure.

If it is true that individuals follow the Utility Tree approach in budgeting their expenditure, there is no apparent reason why the same assumption can not be extended to include, for example, the allocation of funds among groups and individual assets, or, even more generally, peoples' economic time allocation. It is possible to think of a Utility Tree, which takes the form shown in *Figure 3.1.*

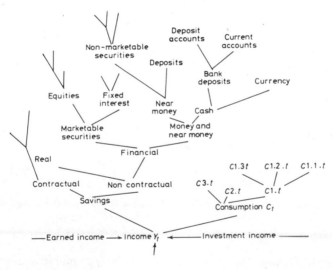

Fig. 3.1

Therefore, it was thought useful to carry out a number of experiments on the basis of the available data. One of these is reported in the following. Firstly, equation 3.3.4 of *Table Fin. 4* was regarded as determining the funds allocated to a sub-branch, say j, of the total deposits with non-bank financial institutions. According to the Utility Tree approach the funds allocated to an asset (i) in the sub-branch j are assumed to be a function of the total funds available for the sub-branch j and the rates of return on all the assets which form the bundle j. Thus we can write:

$$\Delta BSS_t = f_1(\Delta FA_{3t}, RBS_t, RTSB_t, RBD_t) \tag{11}$$

$$\Delta BSD_t = f_2(\Delta FA_{3t}, RBD_t, RBS_t, RTSB_t) \tag{12}$$

$$\Delta TSB_t = f_3(\Delta FA_{3t}, RTSB_t, RBS_t, RBD_t) \tag{13}$$

where ΔBSS, ΔBSD, ΔTSB, ΔFA_3, RBS, RBD and $RTSB$ are net changes in the personal sector's holding of Building Societies' shares, net change in deposits with Building Societies, with Trustee Savings Banks (investment departments), total deposits with non-bank financial institutions, the rate of interest on Building Societies' shares, on Building Societies' deposits and on deposits with Trustee Savings Banks, respectively. Further, equations (11), (12) and (13) were estimated by means of Two Stages Least Squares. The results obtained are shown in *Table Fin. 5*. Judging by the single equation tests, estimates 3.1.5, 3.2.5 and

Table Fin. 5 RESULTS OF TESTING THE UTILITY TREE HYPOTHESIS

Equation number	Dependent variable	ΔFA_{3t}	RBS_t	RBD_t	$RTSB_t$	R^2	VN
3.1.5	ΔBSS_t	0·63 (0·28)	77·66 (184·48)	−129·69 (160·01)	37·34 (159·05)	0·97	0·705
3.2.5	ΔBSD_t	0·075 (0·056)	18·82 (37·36)	3·22 (32·58)	−23·04 (32·39)	0·42	1·48
3.3.5	ΔTSB_t	0·034 (0·063)	−64·83 (42·09)	−36·06 (36·51)	89·03 (36·28)	0·97	1·17
3.4.5	ΔBSS_t	0·69 (0·14)	110·56 (115·29)	−121·36 (149·97)		0·97	0·74
3.5.5	ΔBSD_t	0·06 (0·02)		10·77 (27·79)	−10·71 (20·25)	0·41	1·45
3.6.5	ΔTSB_t	0·12 (0·03)		−62·04 (32·03)	46·56 (24·07)	0·96	1·42

3.3.5 are unsatisfactory. This may be attributed partly to multicollinearity difficulties, particularly between the interest rates. By dropping one interest rate, although the fit remained unsatisfactory, as shown in estimates 3.4.5, 3.5.5 and 3.6.5 of *Table Fin. 5*, it is interesting to note that all the coefficients have the correct *a priori* signs and ΔFA_{3t} is statistically significant. However, on the basis of these results it is not possible to reach a conclusion as to whether the utility tree hypothesis can be used in explaining the personal sector's portfolio decision-making process. Further research is required.

4

Composition of Personal Saving: Real Assets

This chapter is concerned with the personal sector's savings in the form of real assets. These include investments in dwellings, consumer durables, plant and machinery, ships and aircraft, other fixed capital formation, and investment in inventories. In the first section the relationship between the markets for real and financial assets is discussed. This involves a brief review and a critical appraisal of the Keynesian linkage via the rate of interest and the availability of credit doctrines, and then proceeds to outline the hypothesis adopted in this study. The latter is based on the Radcliffe theory which places particular emphasis on the significance of liquidity in influencing investment, while recognising the possible effects of the rate of interest. Thus, the empirical testing of this theory forms part of this chapter's concern. The four following sections describe the models specified for individual items, and demonstrate the estimates obtained. Each of these sections is self-contained in the sense that it deals with all the problems — theoretical, statistical or econometric — that arise in the analysis of each particular asset. This procedure is preferred to the one adopted in the previous chapters in view of the variety of the problems involved, which makes generalisation a very difficult task.

4.1 MARKETS FOR REAL AND FINANCIAL ASSETS

4.1.1 THE KEYNESIAN LINKAGE VIA THE RATE OF INTEREST

Ever since the General Theory the initial integration provided by the Keynesian Interest Theory has remained more or less unchanged in the last thirty years. The rate of interest has remained the primary factor that links the real and the financial markets. On the one hand, the rate of interest is determined by the liquidity preference considerations in a financial market which deals with transactions in financial assets and liabilities. On the other hand, the rate of interest is assumed to enter the investment function explicitly, which reflects the cost—return considerations, i.e. in the Keynesian Model the marginal efficiency of capital *via-a-vis* the rate of interest. This relationship between the rate of interest and investment follows from the assumption that interest charge is part of the cost of holding goods and will, therefore, influence the demand for goods to hold, whether these are commodity stocks, or fixed capital goods. Thus, when the margins of profit are narrow, a rise in interest rate will induce merchants and others to reduce the stocks of commodities they hold, and will also tend to check the demand for the construction of new capital works. Clearly, whether it is short-rates and commodity stocks, or long-rates and constructional works that are in question, the force of the argument depends on how important interest charges are in relation to other elements — including risk.[32a] Accordingly, the longer the useful life of the asset, the stronger the effects of the changes in the rate of interest are likely to be. The demand for house-building and similar constructional works evidently should be among the most interest-sensitive on these theoretical grounds.

A great deal of controversy exists, however, over the interest elasticity of demand for investment goods. Early survey information tends to minimise the role of interest rate. Some implicitly or explicitly imputed a zero elasticity to interest rate effects, on the grounds that short-run variations in investment are never made for purposes other than expansion of productive capacity. This view, which is commonly expressed by those adhering to simple acceleration theories, has been supported by empirical evidence. For example, Tinbergen[206a] in his pioneering study of investment activity in Germany, the United Kingdom, the United States and France, found considerable 'uncertainty . . . concerning the coefficient of interest rates'. Coefficients for France and Germany were close to zero, while those for the United Kingdom were small in the neighbourhood of 0·13 for the pre-war data and 0·1 for the inter-war period. Similar empirical results were obtained in other studies.[111,112]

Various explanations have been given regarding the negative conclusions of the effects of interest rates on investment. For example, Budzeika[20] (p. 271) argued that 'prospective returns from capital projects that might be under consideration are so high, relative to returns on safe financial assets, that the comparison is a little relevance'. Another argument[213] (p. 1) was that 'the high uncertainty about the outcome of an investment, particularly about the results after the first year or so, made the expectation of very high returns a pre-requisite to the undertaking of any project. The minimum acceptable rates of return would be so high and subject to so wide a margin of error that changes of one or two percentage points in the cost of capital could be neglected'. Institutional change in the form of heavy reliance of firms, particularly small firms, on internal funds is also said to weaken the effect of interest rates on investment. In principle, comparisons should be made — on the basis of opportunity cost — between the return on internal funds obtained by capital goods expansion with the return on alternative uses. In practice, as was stated[20], such comparisons are rarely made. Goldfield,[75] (p. 102) on the other hand, takes a different view. He suggested that early regression models suffered from certain technical difficulties, which tended to add to the strength of the negative conclusions regarding the rate of interest effect. In the early post-war period, he pointed out, interest rates showed limited variability and were at low levels, a matter which probably contributed to their lack of success as explanatory variables. In later periods, when interest rates began to rise, the inclusion of highly intercorrelated variables together with the rate of interest — such as profits, sales, etc. — led to serious problems of multicollinearity and consequent difficulty in disentangling the individual effects of the different variables. Another qualification to early studies, he added, was that they ignored the simultaneous nature of the problem, producing both biased and inconsistent estimates.

More recently, there have been a growing number of empirical studies which reported a significant coefficient for the rate of interest. Gehrels and Wiggins,[69a] using quarterly data for the United States manufacturing sector, showed that variations in yields on Industrial Bonds, on Treasury Bills and on Government Bonds (all lagged one year), appeared to have an effect on investment. However, in their interpretation of the results, they pointed out that interest rates were acting as 'indices of credit availability'. Later on, they published a correction to their original article[69b] — brought to their attention by A. Goldberger[69b] — which implied that the structural equation of the model (equation 5) might have been a mis-specification. Glauber and Meyer[71] in their recent study of investment decisions, economic forecasting and public policy, came to the conclusion that an adequate theory of investment behaviour requires the incorporation of the monetary or interest rate effect. They stated that 'specifically, the interest rate was an integral part of any model that provided a good empirical explanation of investment, with high interest rates prevailing late in the upswing of the business cycle. Since good forecasts and structural understanding tend to be even more essential for public policy purposes late in the business cycle than at other times, this interest rate behaviour pattern must be considered relevant if not highly significant'. Similar conclusions were reached by De Leeuw,[40b] Goldfield,[75] Maisel[131] and others[189] for non-business residential construction.

4.1.2 MODIFICATION OF THE KEYNESIAN LINKAGE

From the arguments presented so far in the preceding sub-section, which are only a small sample of the vast amount of literature which exists on this topic, the controversial nature of the debate become obvious. There does not appear to be any consensus of opinion regarding the role that interest rate plays in influencing investment expenditure. Neither is there conclusive empirical evidence.

An alternative or an additional linkage has been suggested by the proponents of 'availability of credit' doctrines.* A common proposition in these theories is the demotion of the rate of interest from a factor of causal significance in determining the level of demand for investable funds to a side effect accompanying — but not directly causing — the change in investment. For example, a rise in the liquidity preference or a decrease in the volume of money will discourage

* Analysis in this sub-section is based, to a great extent on Tussing[208] and Catt.[24]

investment, not because the rate of interest rises, but mainly because holders of funds are now less willing to make more funds available than before, or to maintain the present level. However, there are various explanations of the mechanism by which the availability of credit influences investment. This is due to the ambiguities which exist with respect to what is meant by the availability of credit, particularly as a variable, subject to the influence of monetary policy and to be distinguished from the quantity of money or the rate of interest. According to the 'lock-in effect' version,[178] the impact on investment results from a sequence of reactions to changes in monetary policy. Thus, it is argued, a tightening of monetary policy associated with rising long-term rates of interest would inhibit sales of these securities through the unwillingness of institutional lenders to realise capital losses, by reducing the market values of long-term securities. It would also reduce the liquidity of lenders, portfolios and encourage them to maintain or increase their short-term holdings, while loan rates might remain unchanged, at least at first, since 'administered prices' adjust to new equilibrium levels only with a lag. The theory implied by the lock-in effect proposition is that where banks change the composition of their assets, reducing security holdings and increasing loans, a contribution is made to aggregate effective demand. In addition, the lock-in effect is not just limited to banks, but extends its influence to non-bank lenders also. It is argued that open market purchases or sales — when dealings are with non-bank lenders — increase or reduce, respectively, the funds available to these institutions for lending. Underwriters also respond to tightening credit conditions by discouraging new private security issues during periods of rising rates in order to avoid market losses on their own holdings. Another version of the availability of credit theory is the credit creation doctrine.[176] According to this second approach, Commercial Banks are to be distinguished from other lending institutions by the fact that they can, and always do, 'create credit' with no prior act of voluntary saving on the part of any other economic unit — by virtue of their ability to pay for new assets with newly issued demand deposit liabilities. This means that Commercial Banks are permit an excess of planned investment, over planned saving. In comparison, as pointed out by W. Rifler[176] (p. 203) in his evidence to the Radcliffe Committee, 'other institutions act mainly to gather and lend savings. They are unable to lend more than savers have decided to place with them. Furthermore, they are unlikely to lend appreciably less than they receive; that is, in usual circumstances they do not accumulate idle balances. Hence, these institutions play a neutral role in the saving—investment balance . . . they are not in a position either to disturb the balance or to restore an imbalance between saving and investment'.

Both the 'lock-in effect' and the 'credit creation' versions of the 'availability of credit' theories have been subject to severe criticism. A few examples might help to illustrate the points at issue. In a recent American study Kane and Malkiel[103] showed strong rational economic motives for bankers to shift from securities into loans in periods of high loan demand and tight money, even when the return on the former exceeds that on the latter. A. Tussing[208] observed for the United States that 'during both 1954—57 and 1958—60 tight money periods, Commercial Bank business loans rose at a rate exceeding their post-accord trend value. Life Insurance Companies' holdings show a similar pattern. Mutual Savings

Banks and Mutual Savings and Loan Associations showed less regular behaviour, but were clearly not "locked in" with respect to Government Security Holdings'. Gurley and Shaw[79c] argued that the error in the credit creation version follows from an erroneous definition of saving, which identifies saving with the payment of money for a non-money asset, an act which may signify, but is not the same as, *ex ante* saving. But probably one of the most important criticisms, directed against the credit creation theory, was put forward by A. Tussing.[208] He argued that 'this theory is not a theory of demand. It only says that if there is excess aggregate demand that excess can be financed through the banking system... It does not explain why there must be such an excess'. By contrast, he added, the quantity theory of money, for instance, argues than an increase in the stock of money induces more demand; the interest rate approach argues that increases in the money supply relative to the demand for money reduce interest rate and thereby increase the demand for investment.

Another element of the availability of credit theory which has escaped major criticism is the concept of credit rationing or the 'fringe of unsatisfied borrowers'. Unlike the lock-in effect or the credit creation approaches, the credit rationing theory does not concern itself with implications for the effectiveness of monetary policy, except in a minor way. The fundamental proposition of the latter theory is that there is sufficient imperfection in the loan market so that interest rates do not fulfil the function of a price in clearing the market of all willing borrowers and willing lenders. Under these circumstances lenders will have to use 'credit rationing' in order to cope with the excess demand. It is also argued that the unsatisfied fringe is not merely a frictional imperfection of the money market but is a chronic condition arising out of the rational behaviour of lenders, especially the larger institutions which lead the market. This characteristic of the market was attributed to a number of reasons. A. Catt[24] for example, explained it in terms of the 'difference in viewpoint from which lenders and borrowers approach any investment project', and added that 'for several reasons the typical lender is likely to regard any project submitted to him, particularly at the margin, with rather less enthusiasm than the entrepreneur who wishes to borrow the funds'. In normal market conditions, this relative conservatism on the part of lenders should lead to a rise in the rate of interest offered by borrowers and consequently would eliminate the less-optimistic borrowers until equilibrium is reached. D. Hodgman[92] rules out this possibility of interest rate adjustment by arguing that 'because the chances of default increase as the size of the loan plus interest increase . . . it may become impossible for the borrower to offer a higher rate of interest which does not increase the chance of failure to a degree which is greater than is warranted by the increased rate of interest offered'. The risk of default, Hodgman points out, is set off as a deduction from the stipulated rate of interest, and will be reckoned differently, depending on the liabilities of the lender. This implies, for instance, that the risk discount will be placed at a high level in the case of lending institutions with a high proportion of short-term liabilities. For this reason, lenders and borrowers will differ in their assessment of a particular pay-off distribution, with lenders making much more conservative valuations than borrowers. The resulting inability to discourage the marginal borrowers by a high rate of interest leaves the lender with no option but to choose on the basis of his assessments and reject out of hand those borrowers who are regarded as unsatisfactory. Many additional factors are mentioned in the literature in support of the view that credit rationing is not merely a frictional imperfection. For instance, it is argued that lenders may give preference to their established customers at the expense of others, partly because this enables them to reduce the risk involved and partly out of a sense of obligation. In such a situation new firms might still find themselves in the unsatisfied fringe, even if they have good projects and are willing to pay higher than the market rate of interest.

4.1.3 THE RADCLIFFE REPORT AND THE HYPOTHESIS ADOPTED

An examination of the availability of credit theories — as described in the previous sub-section — reveals three distinctive characteristics of these theories. In the first place, with the possible exception of the credit rationing version, they are primarily concerned with the financial processes of an intended investment, and also with institutions relating ultimate borrowers with ultimate lenders. Neither the lock-in effect nor the credit creation versions deal with motives to invest. To this extent, the availability of credit theories may be defined — as suggested by Tussing[208] — as 'those theories which deal exclusively with the financial mechanism rather than with the variables which influence demand'. Influencing the availability of credit, he added, 'has to do with influencing deficit units' access to financing, as distinct from influencing their desire to borrow or the desire of savers to save'. Secondly, the flow of credit is assumed to be determined mainly by the lending institutions' policies — or by the position of the supply of lending curve — while the demand for credit is regarded as having no influence on the ultimate flow of credit. However, this point has been a cause for confusion, particularly with respect to the credit rationing version. One possible source of confusion in Guttentag's[80] view 'is the emphasis given in the literature to the operations of lenders'. He added that 'it is frequently stated that the older monetary theory emphasised the borrower, whereas the availability doctrine emphasises the lender. Of course, the fact that the lenders administer terms does not mean that the basic forces underlying changes in availability originate on the supply side of the market. It would appear, on the contrary, that for the most part changes in availability originate on the demand side'. The third assumption is that credit rationing does not arise from a frictional imperfection prevailing in the lending market. Resorting to non-price rationing and the resulting unsatisfied fringe of borrowers is seen, by the advocates of this theory, as a chronic condition that is likely to continue.

The conclusions reached by the Radcliffe Committee generally agreed with some aspects of the availability of credit theories. While they failed to find 'convincing evidence' with respect to the interest incentive effect on investment, they stressed the availability of funds as 'obviously crucial for financing con-struction, additions to stocks or other irregular items of expenditure'[32a] (p. 132). In their opinion, an interest charge will be one of the factors to be weighed in the balance when an investment decision is being made. A sharp change in this item may, however, be easily obscured by other factors. But, on the other hand, if the money for financing the project cannot be obtained on any tolerable terms at all, as they put it, 'that is the end of the matter'[32a] (p. 132). Also, similar arguments to those advocated by the lock-in effect school can be found in the Radcliffe Report. In explaining the effects of changes in interest rates on financial institutions' behaviour, they asserted that 'a movement of interest rates — provided that it is not confined to the short end of the market — implies significant changes in the capital values of many assets held by financial institutions. A rise in rates makes some less willing to lend because capital values have fallen, and others because their own interest rate structure is sticky'. Evidence as to the existence of non-price rationing was also mentioned in the Radcliffe Report. Building societies, it was pointed out, reacted to a shrinkage in the inflow of funds by discriminating against old houses, by reducing the loan to value ratio and by warning local builders of their intentions to curtail lending. Such measures have not always been associated with changes in the mortgage rate in view of building societies' tradition of pursuing a policy of stable interest rates. Similar means of non-price discrimination were also reported to have been used by banks in the face, for instance, of official requests to restrict the level of advances.

The Radcliffe recommendations, however, should not be regarded as belonging strictly to the availability of credit theories. In addition to stressing the 'whole liquidity picture', rather than just the 'money at the bank' as the most relevant variable that affects investment, a close examination of the Radcliffe Report reveals at least two more interesting features. These are:

1. While it is true that in both the Radcliffe and the availability theories investment depends on the availability of funds, they are not strictly identical. A necessary assumption in the latter is that the ultimate flow of funds is at the discretion of the lender. With the rate of interest set below the equilibrium level, and given a negatively sloping demand for funds, the volume of lending — and hence the flow of investment — depends on the position of the lending curve. In contrast, the Radcliffe views are not too restrictive in this respect when stating that 'the ease with which money can be raised depends on the one hand on the composition of the spender's assets and on his borrowing power, and on the other hand upon the methods, moods and resources of financial institutions and other firms which are prepared (on terms) to finance other people's spending'.

2. Despite the Radcliffe Committee's failure to find any convincing evidence in support of the direct effects of interest rates on investment, they emphasized the importance of the indirect effects via the influence on the liquidity positions when they described the rate of interest as the 'centre-piece' of monetary action. The argument was that the manipulation of the interest rate structure by the authorities alters the liquidity position of the financial institutions and of firms and people desiring to spend on real resources. A change in liquidity, other things being equal, would affect the flow of investment.

Thus, according to Radcliffe's recommendations it appears that, what came to be known in the literature as a 'circular flow model',[30] is needed. In such models, interest rates and financial flows mutually determine each other. From the solution for financial markets, financial flows then become explanatory variables in expenditure equations. Cohen[30] in a recent contribution has given a clear exposition of the mechanism of a 'circular flow model' and showed its relative superiority by empirical testing. His model bears great similarity to Leontief's closed inter-industry model. However, unlike the Leontief model, the transactions included financial as well as non-financial transactions and the sectoring was along institutional (decision making) instead of commodity or establishment lines.

In this study we argue in support of introducing external finance, in addition to other variables explaining the motives to invest, into investment functions. This permits an empirical analysis of the effects of interest rates on investment, since external finance is endogenously determined in this study. The specified equations for external finance are discussed in the following sub-section. The approach adopted, therefore, is assumed to reflect the ideas expressed in the Radcliffe Report. The liquidity position of the personal sector is brought into the model for real assets determination through the use of external finance. Similar approaches are to be found in recent econometric work. A few examples are: the introduction of bond finance as an explanatory variable in a business fixed investment equation by Dhrymes and Kurz,[41] mortgage borrowing in a housing expenditure equation by Sparks,[189] in addition to Cohen's study cited previously.

4.1.4 THE EXTERNAL FINANCE EQUATIONS

This sub-section is concerned with the personal sector's demand for credit from commercial banks, other financial institutions, and the Public Sector (Government and Local Authorities lending for house purchase). Following the procedure adopted by the Bank of England in the Sector Financing Tables, a distinction is made between bank lending (BL), hire purchase debt (HP), loans for house purchase (HL), and other loans (OL). Since these groups of personal liabilities can be regarded as negative financial assets, the estimated equations are based, in general, on the financial model described in the previous chapter. In addition, the supply side of the market is also considered. Two main expedients are employed. First, supply equations are specified and estimated, or variables which are known to cause significant shifts in the supply of credit are introduced in the demand equation. Second, simultaneous methods of estimation are used instead of Ordinary Least Squares.

Loans for House Purchase

This item covers loans made available to the personal sector by building societies, insurance companies, local authorities, pension funds and banks, in addition to loans to housing associations by the Government and by public corporations. Since building societies are the main suppliers of this type of credit, providing finance for about two-thirds of all private house building, no attempt is made to specify separate supply equations. The aggregate supply equation is considered in conjunction with the lending institutions' portfolios positions and price considerations, with particular reference to building societies' investment and lending policies.

In this study, the supply of mortgage credit is assumed to depend, given the outstanding mortgage debt, on three main factors; namely: the yield from mortgage, the yield from alternative long-term financial assets, and the net changes in funds available to lending institutions. The rate of interest on mortgages advanced by building societies is used as a proxy for mortgage yield. Examination of the lending institutions' investment policies suggests that the rate of interest on long-term Government Securities, lagged one period, can be used as a good approximation for alternative investment. By law, building societies are limited to investment in trustee securities, and although there are no statistics of the acual maturity distribution, it is believed[32a] (p.99) that a substantial proportion of their total non-mortgage investment is in securities with more than five years to run to maturity. Insurance companies normally allocate a significant proportion of their funds to investment in Government Securities. When investing in gilt-edged, and to some extent in deciding how much to put into guilt-edged, they lean heavily on the principle of matching assets to liabilities, and therefore go mainly into the long end of the market[32a] (p. 85). Even when inflation-mindedness encouraged them to go into equities in order to obtain higher yields, evidence to the Radcliffe Committee[32a] (p. 85) suggested that they were still more responsive to changes in the gilt-edged yields. The use of the lagged rate of long-term Government Securities, rather than the current, is chosen in view of the building societies' tradition of maintaining some degree of stability in their interest rates policy; particularly up to 1957 when they appeared to 'drag their feet' when other interest rates were moving. In addition to the rates of interest on mortgage and on long-dated Government Securities, the net increase in deposits at bank and non-bank financial institutions (including insurance companies and pension funds), is considered as an important factor affecting the supply of mortgage credit. When saving deposits and shares and life insurance premiums accumulate in the lending institutions, it is only natural that they seek investment outlets for these funds. The pressure for mortgage acquisition due to an increase in the deposits is probably greatest for building societies. In the evidence to the Radcliffe Committee, three reactions to a shrinkage in the inflow of funds to building societies were mentioned. 'Firstly, the building societies have tended to discriminate against old houses . . . Secondly, the proportion of the valuation which is lent may be dropped from the normal 80%. Thirdly, a society may warn local builders to cut their building programmes because the financing of house purchases looks less certain.'[32a] It is also to be noted that by including the flows of funds to lending institutions as a factor determining the supply of mortgage credit, a link is provided between the money and capital market. This is an important consideration because of the participation of commercial banks and other saving institutions in house lending.

By denoting the outstanding mortgage debt at the beginning of the period by M_{t-1}, the rate of interest on mortgage by RM_t, the rate of interest on long-term Government Securities by R_{t-1}^L, the flows of funds into bank and non-bank financial institutions by ΔFFI_t and assuming that the aggregate supply of mortgage, ΔHL_t^S, function is linear in the variables and the parameters, we have:

$$\Delta HL_t^S = c_0 RM_t + c_1 R_{t-1}^L + c_2 \Delta FFI_t + c_3 M_{t-1} \tag{i}$$

where c_0 and c_2 should be positive and c_1 and c_3 should be negative. For the purpose of providing an indirect estimation of equation (1), the yield on mortgage RM_t is regarded as endogenous and a yield adjustment mechanism is added. Two alternative assumptions are made. The first is to assume the validity of a simple textbook supply and demand analysis. Accordingly, changes in the market yield take place as a result of any disequilibrium in the mortgage market. Thus, the yield adjustment equation takes the form:

$$\Delta RM_t = \psi(\Delta HL_t^S - \Delta HL_t) \qquad (2a)$$

In equation (2a) any changes in the rate of interest on deposits with mortgage lending institutions would influence the mortgage yield only indirectly, by affecting the net inflow of funds to these institutions, given the rates of interest on competing assets. Alternatively, it may be argued that changes in the rate of interest on deposits should lead to corresponding changes in the mortgage rate, independent of the changes in the net inflow of funds. In this case, the yield adjustment equation becomes:

$$\Delta RM_t = \psi(\Delta HL_t^S - \Delta HL_t) + \rho\, \Delta RBS_t \qquad (2b)$$

whereas ΔRBS_t is the change in the rate of interest on building societies' shares – regarded as a proxy for the rate of interest on deposits with mortgage lending institutions. Substituting **for** ΔHL_t^S from equation (1) into equations (2a) and (2b), and re-arranging we obtain:

$$RM_t = d_0 RM_{t-1} + d_1 R_{t-1}^L + d_2 \Delta FFI_t + d_3 M_{t-1} + d_4 \Delta HL_t \qquad (3a)$$

or $$RM_t = d_0 RM_{t-1} + d_1 R_{t-1}^L + d_2 \Delta FFI_t + d_3 M_{t-1} + d_4 \Delta HL_t + d_5 \Delta RBS_t$$
$$(3b)$$

where

$$d_0 = \frac{1}{1 - \psi c_0} \qquad d_1 = \frac{\psi c_1}{1 - \psi c_0} \qquad d_2 = \frac{\psi c_2}{1 - \psi c_0}$$

$$d_3 = \frac{c_3}{1 - \psi c_0} \qquad d_4 = -\frac{\psi}{1 - \psi c_0} \qquad d_5 = \rho \qquad (4)$$

Given the theoretical specification of the demand for mortgage equation ΔHL_t, (3a) and (3b) are estimated by means of the Two Stages Least Squares method. Given (4) and assuming that there are no imperfections or 'credit rationing' in the mortgage market, an indirect estimation of the coefficients of the supply of credit equation (1) is then obtained.

The results are shown in *Table Ra. 1*. M_{t-1} is dropped because the estimated coefficient was statistically insignificant, due partly to the inaccuracy of the data, as will be noted later on. Comparing equations 4.1.1 and 4.2.1 of the yield adjustment mechanism, there is some evidence in support of assumption (2b) with respect to the independent influence of the rate of interest on building societies' shares. This can be observed from the increase in the value of R^2 associated with the reduction in the standard errors of the coefficients, associated with the highly significant coefficient for ΔRBS_t. This is expected in view of the rules applied by building societies. In their evidence to the Radcliffe Committee[32b] (vol. 2) it was stated: 'The broad rule upon which policy in regard to interest rates is based is that it is the duty of a society to hold the balance

Table Ra. 1 LOANS FOR HOUSE PURCHASE (1952–66)

Equation number	Dependent variable	Y_t^P (£m)	S_{t-1} (£m)	RS_{1t} (£m)	RM_t (%)	CF_t (%)	RM_{t-1} (%)	R_{t-1}^L (%)	ΔRBS_t (%)	ΔHL_t (£m)	ΔFFI_t (£m)	R^2	VN
4.1.1	RM_t						0·226 (0·157)	0·919 (0·173)		0·00 251 (0·00 085)	−0·00 072 (0·00 019)	0·973	2·4
4.2.1	RM_t						0·717 (0·081)	0·313 (0·093)	1·253 (0·15)	0·00 033 (0·00 035)	−0·00 014 (0·00 0075)	0·979	2·5
4.3.1	ΔHL_t^S				857·58			−1 000·28			0·4 243		
4.4.1	ΔHL_t	0·0351 (0·007)	−0·119 (0·058)	0·614 (0·252)		−99·49 (16·82)						0·974	1·79

Notes

1. Method of Estimation is the Two Stages Least Squares.
2. RS_{1t}, RM_t, and RBS_t are: investment in dwellings by the personal sector, the average mortgage rate by building societies, and the rate of interest on building societies' shares.
3. ΔFFI is the change in the funds available to lending institutions (bank and non-bank financial institutions including life assurance and superannuation funds).
4. CF is a measure of the cost of borrowing for house purchase, and is equal to $RM(1 - \delta G^{10})$.
5. Parameters of equation 4.3.1 are estimated from (4) given the reduced form parameters of equation 4.2.1.

evenly between its investing members and its borrowing members and to conduct its operations on a narrow margin as prudence will permit'. Usually more than 60% of the rate charged to borrowers is absorbed by the interest rate paid to shareholders. Accepting equation (2b) as a satisfactory approximation of the yield adjustment equation and given the relationship between the reduced form coefficients and the structural parameters — as defined in (4) — the implied values of the coefficients of the supply equation are calculated (equation 4.3.1). Two reservations regarding the estimated supply equation should be noted. Firstly, although the structural parameters c_0, c_1 and c_2 are formed from unbiased estimators of the reduced form parameters, they are not themselves unbiased. They are, however, consistent estimators.[99d] Secondly, equation 4.3.1 can be used for the purpose of predicting the supply of mortgage credit only when there are no imperfections or 'credit rationing' in the mortgage market.

On the demand side, there is the problem of formulating an index which can serve as a proxy for the cost of funds associated with the act of purchasing a house for owner-occupation. In view of the special tax treatment of owner-occupiers, gross rate of interest on mortgage does not provide an appropriate measure of the costs involved, but should be adjusted by a fraction which depends on the magnitude of the tax allowances on borrowed funds and imputed rentals. In this respect, one difficulty arises from the fact that this fraction will vary for different individuals, because although it may not be too unreasonable to regard all individuals as faced with the same pre-tax cost of funds, some will face high and others low marginal tax rates. Any proxy designed to measure the cost of funds should ideally reflect these differences in the tax incidence among individuals. This is not possible with the type of aggregate data available. Denoting the cost of funds by CF, the rate of interest by R and the standard rate of income by G^{10}, for each £1 spent on house purchase, a construction of a variable of the following form:

$$CF_t = R_t(1 - \delta G_t^{10}) \tag{5}$$

may be an acceptable compromise. The letter δ measures the extent of tax discrimination in favour of owner-occupiers. Thus, if imputed rentals are fully taxed, δ would disappear, and if interest on borrowing for house purchase is not allowed δ would be reduced by a proportion depending on the ratio of mortgage debt on owner-occupied housing to the total value of such housing.

Assuming that δ has not changed substantially during the period under review, a direct estimate of δ can be made. To illustrate, let the demand for housing mortgage ΔHL_t be expressed as a linear function of the cost of funds CF_t and a vector of other explanatory variables X_t (including the lagged endogenous variable). Thus we have:

$$\Delta HL_t = h_0 X_t + h_1 CF_t \tag{6}$$

Substituting from (5) into (6) yields:

$$\Delta HL_t = h_0 X_t + h_1 R_t - h_1 \delta R_t G_t^{10} \tag{7}$$

By estimating (7), h_0, h_1 and $h_1\delta$ will be known. Given h_1 and $h_1\delta$, the value of the tax parameter δ can be calculated. However, because of the changes in the tax provisions regarding owner-occupation, this procedure is unrealistic.

For example, the abolition of the Schedule A tax on notional income implies a smaller value of δ for the pre-1964 period. As a rough guess, δ has been given the value of 0·5 for the 1952—64 period and 0·75 for the 1964—66 period.

Equation 4.4.1 of *Table Ra. 1* is the Two Stages Least Squares estimate of the personal sectors' demand for mortgage for house purchases.

It satisfies the economic, statistical, and the econometric criteria. However, there are a few points which warrant some comment. Firstly, equation 4.4.1 represents the demand for mortgage expressed in terms of net rather than gross flows. The reason is that there are no figures available for the latter, except for building societies. Secondly, as mentioned previously, M_{t-1} is dropped because coefficients obtained were either statistically insignificant or showed wrong signs. This may be attributed partly to the inaccuracy of the data for mortgage stock. For example, the *Annual Abstract*'s figures for the stock of mortgages held by building societies for any year relate to 'accounting years ending on any date between 1 February of that year and the 31 January of the following year'. Thirdly, in constructing the cost of funds variable, R_t should ideally be the rate of interest on perpetuities rather than the building societies' recommended rate. Experiments with the rate on consols and the building societies' mortgage rate produced better estimates for the latter, which was, therefore, chosen. Fourthly, although there are no other rates of interest or expectational variables directly entering the demand for mortgage equation, the treatment of the mortgage rate as endogenous has introduced these variables implicitly via ΔFFI_t. Fifthly, the positive sign for the permanent income coefficient may be explained partly by the influence of permanent income on the desired housing stock. Finally, equation 4.4.1 falls short of representing all the forces that determine the demand for housing mortgages. For example, changes in terms of credit (such as the loan to value ratio or the repayment period) do not enter the supply or demand equations.

Other Personal Debt

Under this heading the three remaining items of personal debt are considered: namely bank lending, hire-purchase debt, and other lending.

Equation 4.1.2 of *Table Ra. 2* is the Two Stages Least Squares estimate of the personal sector's demand for credit from commercial banks. Apart from the coefficient of ΔBDT_t which is statistically insignificant, equation 4.1.2 may be regarded as satisfactory as judged by the usual single equation tests. However, several comments regarding this equation seem to be in order.

Firstly, the Bank Rate is used as a proxy for the rates of interest which the banks charge for advances to private borrowers. Overdraft rates are normally arranged on a formula agreed with customers, establishing, generally speaking, a stated margin above Bank Rate subject to a minimum. Although neither the margin nor the minimum is uniform — varying with the type of borrower and the lending risk — the rates change automatically with the change in Bank Rate, unless the minimum rate is applicable. Occasionally borrowing rates may be changed by mutual agreement between bank and customer in appropriate circumstances.

Table Ra. 2 BANK LENDING, HIRE PURCHASE AND OTHER LOANS (1952–66)

Equation number	Dependent variable	A_{it-1} (£m)	Y^P_{t-1} (£m)	BR_t (%)	ΔHPC_t (%)	ΔBDT_t (£m)	ΔFA_{3t} (£m)	Y^d_t (£m)	t	θ_i	a_i	b_i	R^2	VN
4.1.2	ΔBL_t	-0·506 (0·154)	-0·280 (0·136)	-82·14 (29·36)		0·191 (0·193)		0·320 (0·142)	43·02 (18·3)	0·506	-0·553	-162·33	0·67	1·575
4.2.2	ΔHP_t	-0·316 (0·140)	-0·077 (0·034)		-4·631 (0·823)		0·108 (0·092)	0·0914 (0·034)		0·316	-0·244	-14·655	0·778	1·825
4.3.2	$\Delta HP_t + \Delta OL_t$	-0·293 (0·135)	-0·065 (0·032)		-4·237 (0·789)		0·112 (0·088)	0·0787 (0·033)		0·293	-0·222	14·461	0·809	1·632

Notes

1. Method of estimation is the Two Stages Least Squares.
2. The lagged stock in equation 4.3.2 is that of hire purchase only.

ΔBL Change in bank lending to the personal sector.
ΔHP Change in hire purchase debt.
ΔOL Change in other loans.
BR Bank rate.
ΔHPC Change in the percentage downpayment on hire purchase of radio and electrical goods.
ΔBDT Change in total bank deposits.
ΔFA_{3t} Change in deposits with non-bank financial institutions.
t A time trend variable.

Secondly, although the estimated coefficient of the total inflow of funds to the banking sector, ΔBDT_t, is not very satisfactory, its inclusion serves two purposes: (1) On the one hand, it may be regarded as a proxy for the 'availability effect' in the sense of capturing some of the non-price elements of the set of loan terms. Evidence to the Radcliffe Committee[32b] (vol. 2) showed that official requests to restrict the level of advances, which have been in force for most of the period under review, have resulted in a particular type of non-price rationing of advances. (2) On the other hand, this variable provides a direct link between the demand for bank lending and the rest of the personal sector's financial portfolio, since the personal sector's demand for bank deposits is endogenously determined in this study. Norton[160] in his study of the demand for advances by the public in exchange for private securities, used a dummy variable to account for the effect of non-price rationing. Goldfield[75] included a potential demand deposits variable in the demand equation for industrial and commercial loans, for the purpose of capturing the 'availability effect'. This variable bears a great similarity to the one chosen in this study.

Thirdly, the positive and significant coefficient of the time-trend variable, t, may be an indication of omitted variables. Among the possible candidates attempted were inventory investment, investment in consumer durables, investment by unincorporated businesses in plant and machinery, and proxies for the availability of alternative finance. Investment in consumer durables and in plant and machinery did not yield significant coefficients. Inventory investment was marginally significant, but the estimated equation was generally unsatisfactory. This suggests that the traditional bias towards lending for stock accumulation and other self-liquidating transactions still persists.

Fourthly, the coefficient of the lagged stock suggests slow adjustment of actual to desired stocks. This is plausible, as official intervention in the market has often prevented a rapid movement towards an equilibrium level of advances[160].

Fifthly, *a priori* one would expect the demand for bank lending to be negatively correlated with current disposable income. However, this variable shows a significant positive coefficient in equation 4.1.2. One explanation is that income might be acting as a proxy, for example, for sales by unincorporated businesses. Based on the 1952 and 1953 *Surveys of Consumer Finances*, J. Tobin reported positive association between current income and additions to debt, particularly at higher income levels[207c] (p. 65). Another may be found in the sort of argument advocated by Budzeika[20] (p. 68) for a positive association between loan demand and internal funds. Whatever the explanation may be, there is need for care in the interpretation of this coefficient.

Finally, no supply relationship, for bank advances, is specified. Direct estimation is impossible, because no data for the supply of credit are available. Indirect estimation is hindered by the use of a proxy for the rates charged on loans and overdrafts, while Bank rate is defined as exogenous in this study. However, the absence of a supply relationship is not likely to result in a serious identification problem. The view that the 'total of bank advances is a function of the demand by customers' was stressed in the Radcliffe Report as 'a feature of the current banking situation'. During the period covered by this study, banks had a strong desire to expand their advances. The ratio of advances to deposits fell drastically during World War II and it is still relatively low. Even if shifts took place in the supply curve, the effects of these shifts on the estimated demand equation might be reduced by the inclusion of a variable that represents the inflow of funds to the banking sector — since changes in the latter are believed to be one of the main factors that might cause shifts in the supply of credit.

Equation 4.2.2 of *Table Ra. 2* is the Two Stages Least Squares estimate of the personal sector's demand for hire purchase debt. The explanatory power of this equation is satisfactory with no evidence of first order serial correlation, and all coefficients are statistically significant with the exception of the coefficient of ΔFA_3. From equation 4.2.2 it is clear that changes in the terms of trade control, as represented by the changes in the percentage downpayment on the hire purchase of radio and electrical goods, are important determinants of the personal sector's demand for hire purchase debt. This finding confirms the views expressed by the finance houses in their evidence to the Radcliffe Committee[32b] (vol. 2, p. 28) regarding the 'immediate effectiveness of terms of trade control in reducing and stimulating the level of hire purchase activity'. This was attributed to the fact that, as they put it, 'terms of trade control is fair and universal in its application as between one finance house and another . . . It is easily understood (in principle, if not in detail) by finance houses, traders and individuals and seems ideally suited to a fluctuating economy in that it is capable of being tightened or relaxed at any given time with immediate effect'. On the other hand, experiments with the Bank Rate did not yield a significant result, implying that changes in the Bank Rate have no direct effect on the volume of hire purchase. But they may have indirect effects by changing the cost of providing funds to the lending institutions, in view of the nature of their commitments. For example, when a finance house enters into a hire purchase transaction with a customer, it commits itself for a specified period of time and cannot call its funds back any sooner than is stated in the agreement. Thus at any given time a finance house must continue to provide itself with sufficient funds to finance the business on its books until their business runs off and a change in the Bank Rate merely increases or decreases the cost of providing such funds. Under these circumstances, changes in the liquidity position of finance houses and the cost of their borrowing may lead to one form or another of the 'availability effect'. For this reason, deposits with non-bank financial institutions are included, as an explanatory variable, into the demand equation. The positive sign of the coefficient for current disposable income is a cause for alarm, as in the case of bank lending. One possibility, is that income may be acting as a proxy for expenditure on consumer durables (particularly on motor cars). Experiments with these variables gave significant coefficients, but in both cases the coefficients were very high, exceeding unity. Or it may be capturing the effects of the availability of alternative finance, or resulting from multicollinearity difficulties, or suggesting that the linearity assumption is a misspecification. Again there is need for considerable care in the interpretation of this coefficient and hence any conclusion in this study based on this equation should be subject to this important qualification. Finally, equation 4.3.2 of *Table Ra. 2* is the personal sector's demand for both hire purchase debt and other loans (OL_t). No separate equation for OL_t is estimated because of the unspecified composition of this item in the Bank of England Sector Financing Tables. It is to be noted that the lagged stock variable in equation 4.3.2 refers to hire purchase debt only and does not include the stock of other loans because of the lack of data. To this extent, the lagged stock of hire purchase debt should be regarded only as a proxy for the stock of hire purchase debt plus other loans. The general improvement in the estimated coefficients of equation 4.2.2, as shown in equation 4.3.2 of *Table Ra. 2*, gives support to the aggregation of the two items. This is demonstrated by the significant increase in R^2. associated with the reduction in the standard errors of the estimated coefficients. Given equations 4.3.2 and 4.2.2 the personal sector's demand for other lending can be obtained as a residual.

4.2 THE REAL ASSETS EQUATIONS

We now turn to the specification and estimation of the models for the personal sector's investment in dwellings, consumer durables, other fixed capital formation and inventories. *Table Ra. 3* gives a statistical summary of these items.

Table Ra. 3 VARIABLES USED IN THE ESTIMATION OF THE EXTERNAL FINANCE AND REAL ASSETS EQUATIONS (1952–66) (£m)

Variable \ Index	Min.	Max.	Mean	Quartile 1	Median	Quartile 3	Standard deviation
ΔHL	139·0	758·0	384·0	229·0	362·0	572·0	200·77
ΔBL	−103·0	339·0	77·73	−1·0	61·0	193·0	122·60
ΔHP	−102·0	224·0	42·4	18·0	37·0	82·0	74·34
ΔOL	−8·0	73·0	15·93	5·0	13·0	25·0	18·74
RS_1	99·0	688·0	405·53	289·0	382·0	541·0	182·16
RS_2	181·3	426·90	292·43	245·3	300·7	355·8	76·25
RS_3	193·0	293·0	243·53	233·0	238·0	274·0	32·05
$RS_{3.1}$	150·0	333·0	288·73	185·0	230·0	273·0	58·91
RS_4	−5·0	182·0	78·0	62·0	71·0	99·0	42·06

Notes

+ Increase in assets and liabilities.
− Decrease in assets and liabilities.
RS_i Transactions in real assets by the personal sector.
   $i = 1$ Investment in dwellings.
   $i = 2$ Investment in consumer durables.
   $i = 3$ Other fixed capital formation.
   $i = 4$ Investment in inventories.
$RS_{3.1}$ Investment in plant and machinery, ships and aircraft.

4.2.1 INVESTMENT IN DWELLINGS

In this section a stock adjustment model is set up to explain the personal sector's investment in dwellings. A behavioural equation, describing the factors which are assumed to determine the desired stock, is specified first. The invest-ment function is then derived by using a linear Koyck distributed lag. Possible influences of short-run constraints on the planned path of adjustment are also allowed for in the model.

To begin with, let DW_t^*, W_t, Z_t, RR_t and F_t stand for: the desired stock of real assets in dwellings, a measure of the size of the total portfolio in terms of wealth, an index summarising the size of the housing shortage, the ratio of rent to price per unit of housing stock, and external funds available for housing purchases. As a first approximation the desired — or the long-run equilibrium — stock DW_t^* may be expressed as a function of W_t, Z_t, RR_t and F_t — hence we have:

$$DW_t^* = f_1(W_t, Z_t, RR_t, F_t) \tag{8}$$

Since DW_t^* is a theoretical magnitude which is not directly observable the following partial adjustment mechanism is assumed:

$$RS_{1t} = n\,(DW_t^* - DW_{t-1}) + \xi DW_{t-1} \tag{9}$$

where $RS_{1t} = DW_t - DW_{t-1}$ is gross investment in dwellings by the personal sector.

The usual stock adjustment model states that net — rather than gross — investment is a fraction of the gap between the desired level of capital and the level of actual holding. Since gross investment is, by definition, equal to net investment plus replacement for depreciation, gross investment, therefore, can be written as a function of the desired to actual stock gap and the beginning of the period stock holdings. An implicit assumption in (9) is that depreciation at time t may be regarded as a constant proportion, ξ, of the actual stock lagged one period. By assuming that equation (8) is linear in the variables and the parameters, substituting for DW_t^* in (9), and rearranging, the gross investment in dwellings equation takes the following form:

$$RS_{1t} = m_0 W_t + m_1 Z_t + m_2 RR_t + m_3 F_t - (n - \xi)DW_{t-1} \tag{10}$$

The importance of wealth in equation (10) is self-explanatory and was discussed when the financial portfolio model was considered. External finance plays a crucial role in providing the linkage between the real and the financial sub-portfolios. RR may be regarded as a proxy for the gross rate of return on housing. That is, in the long-run equilibrium if there is to be no net addition to the stock of housing over time, rent divided by price per unit of stock must be equal to the sum of depreciation, maintenance and repair expeditures, taxation, and the long-run equilibrium net rate of return on housing. This variable has been used in a number of similar studies, e.g. Muth[151] and Huang.[96] The inclusion of the housing shortage variable Z_t in (10) follows from the fact that the demand for owner-occupied housing cannot be separated from the general circumstances that prevail in the housing market. This variable is of particular significance because the housing market has been in disequilibrium throughout the period under review, as evidenced by the existence of rent controls and local authority waiting lists. Under these circumstances, it is clear that rentals will reflect the pressure of demand for owner-occupied housing only imperfectly.

Before the results obtained from the estimation of equation (10) are analysed, a brief description is given of the variables and the data.

1. The figures used for gross investment in dwellings by the personal sector are the ones prepared by the Central Statistical Office[153] from contractors' output, rather than expenditure figures, with an addition to cover expenditure on architects' and quantity surveyors' fees, expenditure on irremovable equipment not included in the contractors' output series, and expenditure in Northern Ireland. This addition is a constant proportion based on independent estimates of expenditure on private housing derived from statistics of starts, completions and dwellings under construction, together with a house price index. For the period up to 1955, the price index excluded the cost of land, but for the post-1955 period the index used is the one prepared by the Building Societies and includes the cost of land. Conversions and improvements are only included if they are grant aided; otherwise they are included in consumers' expenditure.

2. As in the previous chapter, permanent income (Y_t^P) is used as a proxy for personal wealth, due to the lack of reliable figures for wealth for the period under review.

3. There are no readily available estimates of the size of the housing shortage for the period of the study. A rough estimate* of Z for the census years 1951 and 1961 was made. First the total number of census enumerated households was adjusted in order to estimate the number of households requiring separate dwellings. This involved an estimation of both the number of so-called 'frustrated households' and 'potential households'. Secondly, certain adjustments were made to the census enumerated dwellings so that an estimate of the number of 'reasonably' (defined according to the presence of certain amenities) separate units of accommodation could be obtained. From the adjusted figures of households and dwellings, the size of the housing shortage is derived. The results obtained for the census years 1951 and 1961 are shown in *Table 4.1*, from which the striking similarities† between the housing situation in the two years can be

Table 4.1 ESTIMATES OF THE HOUSING SHORTAGE IN 1951 AND 1961

Year	Dwellings			Households	Housing shortage	Percentage of (5) to		
	(1) Available	(2) Vacancies	(3) Total	(4)	(5)	(1)	(3)	(4)
1951	12 177 271	376 617	12 553 888	13 598 434	1 421 163	11·3	11·7	10·4
1961	14 208 389	515 330	14 723 719	15 611 960	1 403 571	9·5	9·9	9·0

observed. In absolute terms, the size of the housing shortage has remained more or less unchanged, while in relative terms it has shown a slight decline. In view of this stability and the amount of work involved in deriving estimates of the housing shortage for the whole period covered in this study, Z_t is dropped from the final equation.

* Estimates were made only for England and Wales.
† The characteristics of the housing shortage remained unchanged being basically in the small type of dwelling (three rooms or less).

4. The Bank of England figures for house purchase loans were used as a surrogate for external finance, F_t, rather than using the inferred supply of credit which could be derived from equation 4.3.1 of *Table Ra. 1*. The reason is twofold. Firstly, although the coefficients of equation 4.3.1 were formed from unbiased estimators of the reduced form parameters of equation 4.2.1 (*Table Ra. 1*), they are not themselves unbiased. Secondly, estimates obtained from equation 4.3.1 (*Table Ra. 1*) would represent the supply of mortgage credit only under the assumption that there are no imperfections in the loan market, because the supply of mortgage equation 4.3.1 is derived from the rate of interest adjustment equation 4.2.1.

5. The series used for rent and house prices are: the rent component in the Consumer Expenditure Index, and the average value of new houses mortgaged to building societies. It should be noted that while the Central Statistical Office figures of investment in dwellings exclude the cost of land, the building societies' price index includes the cost of land. Also it is not adjusted for changes in the size and quality of a dwelling unit. An alternative house price index — prepared by the Ministry of Public Buildings and Works — was tried. (This index is used by the Central Statistical Office to deflate contractors output and the fixed capital formation series for both public and private housing.) The estimates obtained were quite unsatisfactory. From 1958 to 1966, this index rose only by about 20% which is very low as compared with an increase of 80% in the average tender price for local authority houses over the same period. Equation 4.1.4 of *Table Ra. 4* is the Two Stages Least Squares estimate of the personal sector's investment in dwellings. The value of R^2 is satisfactory and the Von-Neumann ratio shows no evidence of positive or negative serial correlation. Four out of the five coefficients are statistically significant by the usual single equation test, while the size of the fifth coefficient is nearly twice the size of its standard error. The lagged stock variable DW_{t-1} is dropped from the equation because experiments with both the Central Statistical Office and Revell's estimates of the stock of real assets in dwellings — adjusted and extended for the whole period — were not successful. Permanent income lagged one period may be acting as a proxy for the stock of real assets in dwellings lagged one period.

4.2.2 INVESTMENT IN CONSUMER DURABLES

Two behavioural equations are estimated in this section: one describes the personal sector's aggregate net investment in all forms of consumer durables, RS_{2t}, while the other singles out net investment in new and used motor cars and motor cycles, IDM_t. An identity is then used to derive an equation for investment in other consumer durables, IDO_t, in terms of the determinants of RS_{2t} and IDM_t. Investment in motor cars and motor cycles has been accorded separate treatment for obvious reasons. The market (or markets) for motor cars and motor cycles is/are sufficiently different from the markets for other consumer durable goods to merit special attention. Among durable goods, expenditure on motor cars and motor cycles shows more cyclical fluctuations than expenditure on durable household goods. This suggests that precise understanding of the determinants of the demand for motor cars and motor cycles is

Table Ra. 4 INVESTMENT IN DWELLINGS AND CONSUMER DURABLES (1952–66)

Equation number	Dependent variable (£m)	A_{it-1} (£m)	Y_t^P (£m)	Y_{t-1}^P (£m)	Y_t^d (£m)	S_{t-1} (£m)	ΔHL_t (£m)	$(\Delta BL + \Delta HP)_t$ (£m)	Relative prices (1958 = 1)	Structural parameters (4)				R^2	VN
										N_0	N_1	N_2	N_3		
4.1.4	RS_{1t}		0·1709 (0·091)	−0·2204 (0·107)		0·2602 (0·0626)	0·7286 (0·188)		593·26 (205·85) (2)		0·771	2691·74	3·306	0·99	1·36
4.2.4	RS_{2t}	−0·267 (0·051)			0·0824 (0·0148)			0·383 (0·0387) (2)	−351·18 (104·22) (2)	0·267	0·309	−1315·28	1·434	0·99	2·79
4.3.4	IDM_t	−0·406 (0·152)			0·0272 (0·01)			0·143 (0·045) (2)	−218·49 (2)	0·406	0·067	−538·15	0·352	0·91	2·04

Notes

1. Method of estimation is Two Stages Least Squares.
2. Relative prices are: the ratio of rent to the price of an average house, RP, in 4.1.4, the price deflator of consumer durables deflated by the price index of consumer expenditure, PD/PX, in 4.2.4, and the price deflator of motor cars deflated by PX in equation 4.3.4.
3. All variables are deflated by PX.
4. N_0, N_1, N_2 and N_3 are the speed of adjustment coefficient, the structural parameter for current income (disposable and permanent), the structural parameter for relative prices and the structural parameter for external finance respectively.

essential both for forecasting purposes and for devising appropriate stabilisation policies.

The model specified for the personal sector's investment in consumer durables is, in principle, analogous to the capital stock adjustment model for investment in dwellings described in the previous section. However, in the distributed lag equation (12), the term which defines depreciation as a constant proportion, ξ, of the actual stock lagged one period is omitted. This is because figures for net, rather than gross, investment in consumer durables have been used in the estimation.

The desired stock, DU_t^* or DM_t^*, is assumed to depend on income, external finance and relative prices. Current rather than permanent disposable income has been used. It is not obvious *a priori* which form of income might have more influence on the demand for durables. On the one hand, permanent income may be regarded as the appropriate income variable on the grounds that the purchase of consumer durables usually requires large sums and hence more than one year's income has to be taken into account. But, on the other hand, to the extent that consumer durables may be considered as luxuries, expenditure on these commodities may have a high transient income elasticity. Empirical evidence obtained in this study* gave support to this view. As pointed out previously, the inclusion of net investment in consumer durables with the figures of aggregate personal saving led to a small change in the marginal propensity to save out of permanent income, while the marginal propensity to save out of transitory income was greatly increased.

Relating the desired stock to the actual stock by a Koyck-type distributed lag adjustment mechanism and re-arranging yields the following equations:

$$RS_{2t} = u_{01}n_{01}Y_t^d + u_{02}n_{01}F_t + u_{03}n_{01}PD_t - n_{01}DU_{t-1} \tag{11}$$

$$IDM_t = u_{11}n_{11}Y_t^d + u_{12}n_{11}F_t + u_{13}n_{11}PM_t - n_{11}DM_{t-1} \tag{12}$$

where $F_t, PD_t, PM_t, DU_{t-1}$ and DM_{t-1} are: external finance, price of consumer durables, price of motor cars and motor cycles, stock of consumer durables and stock of motor cars and motor cycles respectively. Before the results obtained from the estimation of equations (11) and (12) are analysed, a brief description is given of the variables and data:

1. For the purpose of deriving figures of investments and stocks, a method suggested by Stone and Rowe,[195] and described earlier† has been used. Only one rate of depreciation has been assumed, corresponding to $n = 4$ for total consumer durables, and $n = 2$ for motor cars. These values were found by Stone and Rowe[195] and O'Herlihy[163] to have maximised R^2. The fact that no other values have been tried for n represents a serious weakness of this study, particularly in the case of motor cars where a value of 2 is peculiarly small. In a recent article, Odling-Smee[162b] has suggested that the rate of depreciation 'might be treated as a variable dependent on demand conditions as well as on technical factors' and could be further 'viewed as a psychological concept depending partly on physical deterioration and partly on the desire to own a new and/or technically advanced vehicle'.

* See Chapter 2, page 26.
† See Chapter 2, page 18.

2. The price indices PD_t and PM_t are derived from the 'Blue Book' estimates of expenditure in total durable goods and in new and used motor cars and motor cycles at current and at 1958 prices. No distinction is made between the prices of cars of different vintages. This is obviously an oversimplification, but probably not a very serious one, since it is not too unreasonable to assume that prices of cars of different vintages tend to move together and that gross price elasticities may be regarded as fairly high. Since $RS_{2t}, IDM_t, F_t, DU_{t-1}$ and DM_{t-1} are all measured at constant prices (all deflated by the price index of consumers' goods and services PX_t), PD_t and PM_t have been divided by the same deflator to obtain the relative price indices.

3. The Bank of England figures for hire purchase, ΔHP_t, and bank lending, ΔBI_t, have been chosen as surrogates for external finance, F_t. No figures are available for the inferred supply of credit. Again this may be regarded as a weak feature of this study.

The estimates obtained are shown in equations 4.2.4 and 4.3.4 of *Table Ra. 4*. R^2 is satisfactory and there is no evidence of serial correlation in both equations. All the coefficients have the correct *a priori* signs, and are statistically significant by the usual single equation tests, particularly those of the external finance variables.

4.2.3 OTHER FIXED CAPITAL FORMATION

This item covers investment expenditure by the personal sector in vehicles, plant machinery, ships and aircraft, and buildings other than dwellings (new buildings and works plus purchases — less sales — of land and existing buildings). Fixed capital formation of unincorporated businesses (professional persons, farmers and other sole traders and partnerships) accounts for nearly all capital formation by the personal sector in vehicles and plant and machinery, and most of that in buildings other than dwellings. In the National Income Statistics, the distinction between plant and machinery and vehicles or buildings is not clear-cut. Machinery and equipment form an integral part of buildings and works; for example, lifts and heating and ventilating plants are generally included in buildings; railway-track and gas and water mains are also included in buildings and works, but electricity and telephone lines and cables are classified as plant. Expenditure on repairs* and maintenance is regarded by the Central Statistical Office as expenditure on current operating accounts and not as a part of fixed capital formation.

Two behavioural equations are estimated in this section: one describes the personal sector's gross investment in all fixed assets (other than dwellings and investment in consumer durables) RS_3, while the other singles out what may be termed business investment, $RS_{3.1}$, in vehicles, plant and machinery, and ships and aircraft, made by unincorporated businesses. An identity is then used to derive an equation for investment in buildings (new and existing). Obviously, this procedure is not the ideal one. However, a separate estimate for investment in buildings proved unsuccessful, partly because of the unreliability of the C.S.O. estimates, particularly for transactions in land and existing buildings.

* Expenditure on conversions and improvements of dwellings is included in Investment in Dwellings, if grant-aided.

The model specified for the personal sector's other fixed capital formation is analogous to the capital stock adjustment model for investment in dwellings described in section 4.2.1. Because figures for gross, rather than net, investment have been used in the estimation, the term which defines depreciation as a constant proportion, ξ, of the stock lagged one period is maintained in the formula for the partial adjustment mechanism. For business investment, $RS_{3.1t}$, the desired stock is assumed to depend on wealth, W_t, external finance, F_t, a measure of profitability, Π_t, and an index for initial and investment allowances, ALA_t. Assuming that the desired stock equation is linear in the variables and parameters, relating the desired stock to the actual stock by a partial adjustment mechanism, and rearranging, yields the following equation:

$$RS_{3.1t} = b_0 n_{12} W_t + b_1 n_{12} F_t + b_2 n_{12} \Pi_t + b_3 n_{12} ALA_t - (n_{12} - \xi) BI_{t-1} \quad (13)$$

where n_{12} is the speed of adjustment coefficient, ξ the rate of depreciation, and BI_{t-1} is capital stock lagged one period.

Several comments about equation (13) are in order:

1. It will be noted that although the economic phenomena giving rise to expansion in capital are likely to be more closely related to investment decisions than to investment expenditures, the data used in this study refer to the latter. One way of incorporating the capital stock approach, while distinguishing explicitly between investment decisions and investment expenditures, has been suggested by Goldfield[75] (p. 103–6), which, if adopted, results in an additional term, $RS_{3.1t-1}$, in the business investment equation (13). However, experiments with this formulation proved unsuccessful.

Another distinction which has been suggested,[51] is between the determinants of the desired capital stock at any point in time and the determinants of the speed at which actual stock adjusts towards the desired stock. This implies that the factors which determine the speed of adjustment coefficient, n_{12}, should enter the investment equation explicitly. In this study no attempt is made to account for the explicit determinants of the speed of adjustment coefficient because of a desire to minimise the degree of non-linearity in the structural model.

2. Considerable care is required in the construction of the initial and investment allowances index. These two types of allowances have differing effects on the expected rate of return on capital, although during the current period they cover the same amount of statutory depreciation. This implies that their impact on investment behaviour is not likely to be the same. While investment allowances may be regarded as a 'bonus' increasing the aggregate depreciated value of the asset, initial allowances are a form of accelerated depreciation which leave the aggregate depreciated value (over the whole life) of the asset unaffected.[8] Consequently the relative importance of initial and investment allowances depends on the rate of interest and the average useful life of the asset, a matter which should be taken into account in the formulation of the index, ALA_t. Writing i for the rate of interest, g_1 for the current tax liability, g_n for the expected tax liability, n for the average useful life-time of the asset, Balopoulos[8] used the following formula:

$$w = \frac{(g_1 - g_n(1 + i)^{-n})}{g_1} \quad (14a)$$

in constructing an index of initial and investment allowances. Assuming for simplicity, that $g_1 = g_n$ this gives

$$w = 1 - (1 + i)^{-n} \qquad (14b)$$

Assuming that i and n are known, the relative weights, w, of initial and investment allowances in the index, ALA_t, are obtained by means of (14b). This formula is used in this study, under the assumption that* $i = 7\%$ and $n = 10$ for plant and equipment and $n = 25$ for buildings (other than dwellings). It is important to emphasise that these values are to a great extent arbitrary,† a matter which should be borne in mind in the interpretation of the results.

Another problem is whether or not the initial and investment allowances index should enter the desired stock of capital equation. It may be argued that this factor is likely to affect the 'timing' of investment. Based on the distinction between the investment decision equation and the investment expenditure equation, it follows that ALA_t should enter the latter rather than the former. On the other hand since ALA_t affects the expected rate of return on capital, there is a strong case for including this variable, explicitly or implicitly, in the desired stock equation. Empirically, whether initial and investment allowances should enter one equation or another would have some implications with regard to the structural parameters. If all the relationships are assumed to be linear, the reduced form parameters will remain unchanged.

3. Similarly, it may be argued that the availability of external finance determines the speed of adjustment coefficient, and accordingly does not enter the desired stock equation. Goldfield[75] (p. 106) adopted this view and assumed that the speed of adjustment coefficient depends on the rate of interest. Again, we have not subjected this alternate hypothesis to empirical testing in order to avoid non-linearity.

For present purposes, external finance, F_t, has been defined as the total of bank lending, ΔBL_t, hire purchase, ΔHP_t, and other lending, ΔOL_t. Evidence submitted to the Radcliffe Committee[32a] (p. 325) indicates that 'the joint-stock banks are very important in the finance of small businesses, not only as a major source of capital but because the ordinary business of banking establishes a close contact between businessmen and bank managers'. At the time when the Industrial and Commercial Finance Corporation (I.C.F.C.) was set up, the banks publicly expressed their determination to help the 'small trader', and said that in this connection they would 'have regard to economic justification rather than to the probable duration of an advance when considering applications for credit for small or moderate accounts'. Available evidence[32a] (p. 325) seems to indicate that banks do in fact lend on a large scale to such customers to finance medium-term and long-term requirements. For farmers, the joint-stock banks represent the principal institutional sources of credit[32a] (p. 318); whether for short-term credit ('seed-time to harvest'), medium-term credit for the purchase of live-stock and machinery, or long-term credit for the purchase or improvement of lands and buildings. In addition to borrowing from the banks, hire-purchase credit provides some supplementation, particularly in the medium-term field.

* Balopoulos assumed the same values for i and n.
† Balopoulos reported that several experiments with moderately different assumptions provided very similar results to those obtained when i was assumed equal to 7% and n equal to 10 and 25.[8]

The figures used in the estimation are the Bank of England's figures of actual lending, rather than those for the inferred supply of credit. Again this may be regarded as a weak feature of this study.

4. As a measure of profitability, personal disposable non-wage income, $Y_{2.t}^d$, has been used as a proxy. This index is far from satisfactory. On the one hand, $Y_{2.t}^d$ includes, in addition to self-employment income, rent, interest and dividends. This is because tax figures are only available for the combined item. On the other hand, even self-employment income as such can only represent profits of unincorporated businesses imperfectly. As stated in the National Accounts Statistics, *Sources and Methods*[153] (p. 103), self-employment income should be regarded as 'a combination of labour income and profits, and there is no way of distinguishing between these two elements'. For example, income from farming represents the reward of the manual and managerial labour of farmers and their wives and the return on their capital. Alternate measures of profitability were tried. The percentage ratio of company profits to gross domestic product yielded unsatisfactory results. Experiments with current and lagged personal savings produced a highly significant coefficient for the lagged variable and were associated with a relatively high F value only when the lagged stock variable was dropped from the estimation.

5. Figures for the lagged stock variables have been calculated on the basis of Revell's estimates.[174] *

The estimate obtained for the personal sector's investment in vehicles, plants and machinery and ships and aircraft is shown in equation 4.1.5 of *Table Ra. 5*. Although R^2 is very high with no evidence of serial correlation, and all the coefficients have the correct *a priori* signs, equation 4.1.5 is not very satisfactory. None of the estimated coefficients are statistically significant by the usual single equation test, although the size of each coefficient is greater than the size of its standard error and the F value is highly significant. This is not surprising in view of the multi-collinearity difficulties on the one hand, and the unreliability of the data used — particularly those of non-wage income and the lagged stock — on the other hand. Thus, by dropping BI_{t-1} and substituting $Y_{2.t}^d$ by S_{t-1}, this has led to a marked improvement in the estimate. As shown in equation 4.2.5 of *Table Ra. 5*, a higher F value and well determined parameters are obtained, associated with a slight decline in R^2. However, equation 4.1.5 is preferred because it provides estimates of the structural parameters. Equation 4.3.5 of *Table Ra. 5* is the estimate obtained for the personal sector's investment in all fixed assets (other than dwellings and consumer durables). Total personal disposable income gave a better performance than non-wage income only.

4.2.4 INVENTORY CAPITAL FORMATION

The model specified in this section for the personal sector's inventory investment — held exclusively for business purposes by farmers, professional persons and other sole traders and partnerships — is based on the flexible-acceleration

* See data Appendix.

Table Ra. 5 OTHER FIXED CAPITAL FORMATION AND INVENTORIES

Equation number	Dependent variable (£m)	A_{it-1} (£m)	Income (£m)	Y^P_{t-1} (£m)	S_{t-1} (£m)	F_t (£m)	ALA_t (%)	Structural Parameters (4)						R^2	VN	F Statistic
								C_0	C_1	C_2	C_3	C_4	C_5			
(1) 4.1.5	$RS_{3.1t}$	-0·011	(2) 0·037 (0·026)	0·005 (0·004)		(3) 0·021 (0·017)	0·317 (0·237)	0·011	1·99	3·36	0·454		28·81	0·98	2·41	148·7
(1) 4.2.5	$RS_{3.1t}$			0·012 (0·0005)	-0·031 (0·009)	(3) 0·018 (0·017)	0·410 (0·187)							0·98	2·71	203·6
4.3.5	RS_{3t}	-0·279 (0·128)	(2) 0·072 (0·003)			(3) 0·124 (0·007)		0·279	0·44			0·256		0·97	1·41	153·5
(1) 4.4.5	RS_{4t}	-0·013 (0·011)	(2) 0·059 (0·02) .			(3) 0·049 (0·039)		0·013	3·79					0·83	1·92	25·2

Notes

1. All variables in these equations are deflated by the price index of consumer expenditure PX, with the exception of ALA_t.
2. Non-wage disposable income, $Y^d_{2.t}$, in 4.1.5, Total disposable income, Y^d_t, in 4.3.5, and Income change, ΔY^d_t, in 4.4.5.
3. F_t is external finance as follows: $\Delta BL_t + \Delta HP_t + \Delta OI_t$ in 4.1.5, 4.2.5 and 4.3.5, and ΔBL_t in 4.4.5.
4. C_0 is a speed of adjustment coefficient and C_1, C_2, C_3, C_4 and C_5 are long-run coefficients for F_t, Y^d_t, $Y^d_{2.t}$, Y^P_{t-1}, Y^d_t and ALA_t respectively.

concept.* This approach is commonly used in most recent econometric studies of inventory investment.

Firstly, firms are assumed to have a desired or equilibrium level of inventories which is taken to depend on expected sales and a number of other factors. Thus we have:

$$NV_t^* = f_4 \ (SS_t^E, X_t) \tag{15}$$

where NV_t^*, SS_t^E and X_t are the desired level of inventories, expected sales and a vector of other explanatory variables respectively. An expected rise in sales, which implies a larger scale of operation, will require a larger holding of 'trans-actions' and 'precautionary' stocks,[39] and vice versa. In addition to expected sales, a large number of other factors have been suggested, in the literature, to affect the desired stock of inventories. Three variables are selected for empirical testing: capacity utilisation in manufacturing, ZM_t, as a proxy for the supply conditions faced by unincorporated business, external finance, F_t, representing the cost and the availability of financing inventories, and a measure of price expectations. The methods of constructing capacity utilisation and price expectation indices will be described later on.

Secondly, firms are assumed to plan for a partial adjustment towards the desired stock only. Denoting the planned stock of inventories by NV_t^P we have:

$$NV_t^P = NV_{t-1} + \delta(NV_t^* - NV_{t-1}) \tag{16}$$

Various explanations have been given to this form of adjustment. Among these, Goldfield[75] singles out the following: '(a) time is required to renew stocks of purchased materials; (b) economies of scale in the placement of orders may lead to lumpiness in ordering; (c) an increase in inventories may require new warehouse space, the acquisition of which may introduce lags; and (d) if the variance of expected sales is high, firms may proceed cautiously at first'.

Since both NV_t^P and SS_t^E are theoretical magnitudes not directly observable, two further assumptions are made. A partial adjustment mechanism is used in relating planned to actual inventories, which takes the following form:

$$NV_t = NV_t^P + r(SS_t^E - SS_t) \tag{17}$$

According to (3) the difference between actual and planned inventories depends on the error in anticipating sales. With respect to expected sales SS_t^E, there are two alternatives. On the assumption that errors of prediction are randomly distributed, Darling[39] substituted actual sales for anticipated sales. Alternatively, Lovell[127b] suggested that expected sales may be defined as a linear approximation of lagged and actual sales, that is:

$$SS_t^E = eSS_{t-1} + (1-e)SS_t \tag{18}$$

Assuming that equation (15) is linear in the variables and parameters, substituting (15), (16) and (18) into (17) and rearranging yields:

$$RS_{4t} = \delta v_0 SS_t - (\delta v_0 + r)e\Delta SS_t + \delta v_1 X_t - \delta NV_{t-1} \tag{19}$$

where RS_{4t} is the change in the level of inventories at time t.

* The model specified in this section is very similar to Lovell's[127b].

Before subjecting equation (19) to empirical testing, a brief description is given of the variables and data.

1. The figures used for RS_{4t} and NV_{t-1} are those prepared by the Central Statistical Office of the 'value of physical increase in stocks and work in progress' by the personal sector. Stock appreciation is, therefore, excluded. Estimates of both the value of physical change in stocks and stock appreciation should be regarded as subject to a wide margin of error. The difficulties of making accurate estimates are great, and assumptions and approximations have to be made at a number of stages in the estimation. As pointed out by the Central Statistical Office[153] (p. 407), a major uncertainty arises with regard to the validity of the assumptions made in the adjustment of the accounting data. For example, the inherent assumption in the calculation[153] (p. 407) that stocks change at a uniform rate throughout the period is unlikely to be the case when prices are fluctuating. There is also some doubt surrounding the 'implied equality in movements of the market prices used for the price indices and of actual prices paid during the period'[153] (p. 407).

It will also be noted that aggregate figures of inventories are used in the estimation, and no attention is given to the problem of the composition of inventories. This problem involves the fact that relationships at the level of the single firm will differ widely amongst different firms as well as within a single firm for different commodity groups. In several United States studies inventory investment was disaggregated by stage of fabrication, industry or type of commodities.[38, 177, 127a] Based on the available United Kingdom data, it is possible to disaggregate: by stage of fabrication, into the categories 'materials and fuels', 'work in progress', and 'finished product'; by industry and by ownership. However, estimates of inventories disaggregated by both the stage of fabrication and ownership are not available. In order to account for the effect of aggregation, Duesenberry, Eckstein and Fromm,[46] have argued in favour of introducing inventory investment lagged one period as an additional explanatory variable. Estimates made in this study do not give support to this view.

2. The method used in constructing the capacity utilization index is a simple one. A quadratic trend is fitted to the index of manufacturing output, and the predicted values — calculated from the quadratic equation — are chosen to represent the level of capacity.

For price expectations, three alternative indices have been tried, all based on the price index of consumer goods and services. The first is the one described in the previous chapter and defined as the difference between the current price level and the normal level. The latter was calculated by means of formula (5) with $\lambda = 0.5$. The second is the ratio of the current level of the consumers' expenditure price index to the level of this index lagged one period. Balopoulos[8] (p. 191) reported a highly significant positive coefficient for this ratio price index. The third relates the change in time t in the same price index to its current level. This index was used by Darling[39] in his study of the inventory behaviour of the trade sector in the United States.

Bank lending by the personal sector is used as a proxy for external finance, F_t. Evidence to the Radcliffe Committee[32a] (vol. 2, p. 46) indicated that joint stock banks are a very important source of financing stock-accumulation and other self-liquidating transactions. It should be noted, however, that the figures used in the estimation are those of actual lending, rather than those for the inferred supply of credit. Again this may be regarded as a weak feature of this study.

3. The lack of any readily available figures for sales by unincorporated businesses represented a serious problem in estimating equation (19). Two proxies were tried: the first being personal disposable non-wage income $Y^d_{2.t}$ defined to include rent, interest and dividends in addition to self-employment income, and the second being total personal disposable income Y^d_t. Norton[160] used a similar index to the latter to capture the sales effect in his study of aggregate inventory investment in the United Kingdom. Klein[109p] used income less inventory investment as a measure of sales and this was later chosen by Goldfield[75] (p. 123). However preliminary experimentation with Klein's index proved unsuccessful and it was, therefore, dropped at an earlier stage of testing.

4. Finally, it should be noted that estimation of equation (19) would provide separate estimates of the structural parameters δ, v_0, and v_1, but not r and e.

Estimation of equation (19), with ZM_t, ΔBL_t and an index of price expectation all included, proved unsatisfactory. This was the case whether Y^d_t or $Y^d_{2.t}$ was used as a measure of sales. The estimates were as follows:

$$RS_{4t} = 0.061NV_{t-1} + 0.05\Delta Y^d_t - 0.004Y^d_t - 0.004\Delta BL_t - 1031(\Delta PX/PX)_t$$
$$(0.079) \qquad (0.02) \qquad (0.005) \qquad (0.006) \qquad (455.1)$$
$$- 32.5ZM$$
$$(68.9)$$

$$RS_{4t} = 0.078NV_{t-1} + 0.17\Delta Y^d_{2.t} - 0.022Y^d_{2.t} - 0.0037\Delta BL_t - 675.3(\Delta PX/PX)_t$$
$$(0.059) \qquad (0.057) \qquad (0.022) \qquad (0.054) \qquad (495.5)$$
$$- 48.7ZM_t$$
$$(54.6)$$

Most of the coefficients are statistically insignificant, and the coefficients of the lagged stock, NV_{t-1}, bank lending, ΔBL_t, and the price expectation variable $(\Delta PX/PX)_t$ all have the wrong signs. This is not surprising in view of the unreliability of the figures and the high degree of multicollinearity. By using figures deflated by PX and dropping ZM, the estimate yielded better results, but was still unsatisfactory. Further experiments gave support to the inclusion of one income variable, and showed a better performance for ΔY^d_t. The results obtained are shown in equation 4.4.5 of *Table Ra. 5*, which is chosen to represent the inventory equation in this study.

4.2.5 INTEREST RATES AND INVESTMENT

For the purpose of examining the effects of interest rates on the personal sector's demand for real assets, we calculate the matrix of reduced form coefficients of a model consisting of 11 behavioural equations and 3 identities. The equations are: 3.1.2 and 3.3.2 of *Table Fin. 2*, 4.2.1 and 4.4.1 of *Table Ra. 1*, 4.1.2 and 4.3.2 of *Table Ra. 2*, 4.1.4 and 4.2.4 of *Table Ra. 4* and 5.1.5, 5.3.5 and 5.4.5 of *Table Ra. 5*. The identities are:

Table Ra. 6 INTEREST RATES AND INVESTMENT: MATRIX OF REDUCED FORM COEFFICIENTS

Endogenous ⟍ Exogenous	$\Delta \dot{HL}_t$	ΔBL_t	$(\Delta \dot{HP} + \Delta \dot{OL})_t$	$\dot{RS}_{1t}$	$\overset{\circ}{RS}_{2t}$	$\dot{RS}_{3t}$	$\dot{RS}_{3,1t}$	$\dot{RS}_{4t}$
Y^d_t	0	0·3200	0·0787	0	0·2400	0·1216	0·0083	0·0740
Y^b_t	0·1742	0	0·0088	0·2973	0·0033	0·0011	0·0002	0
Y^P_t	−0·1652	−0·2438	−0·0650	−0·3407	−0·1229	−0·0383	−0·0007	−0·0122
$\dot{S}_{t-1}$	0·0438	−0·0562	−0·0231	0·2921	−0·300	−0·098	−0·0016	−0·0028
$\dot{RL}_{t-1}$	−29·8905	0	0	−21·7782	0	0	0	0
$\dot{RM}_{t-1}$	0	0	0	−49·8881	0	0	0	0
$\dot{RBS}_t$	−68·4712	−26·1345	26·7478	−86·1890	−0·1310	0·0761	0·0127	−1·3077
$\dot{RBS}_{t-1}$	−118·2940	0	0	87·1825	0	0	0	0
$\dot{RBD}_t$	119·6576	−13·0673	13·3739	0·4967	−0·0655	0·0380	0·0064	−0·6538
$RTSB_t$	0·6818	−13·0673	13·3739	0·4967	−0·0655	0·0380	0·0064	−0·6538
$RNSC_t$	0·6818	0	−50·4480	−4·3874	−18·6306	−6·2552	−1·0442	0
$\dot{BR}_t$	−6·0217	−82·140	−4·237	0	−31·4596	−10·1854	−1·7003	−4·1070
$\dot{HPC}_t$	0	0	0	922·1591	−1·7737	−0·5254	−0·877	0
$\dot{RR}_t$	0	−274·4479	0	0	0	0	0	0
$\dot{E}_t(\lambda=0.25)$	451·4124	0	0	−13·9969	−105·1136	−34·0315	−5·6811	−13·7224
$\dot{E}_t(\lambda=0.9)$	−19·2107	0	−11·1171	−0·9669	−4·1058	−1·3785	−0·2301	0
ΔLA_t	−1·3271	0	0	0	0	0	0·3170	0
G^{10}	391·9880	0	0	285·603	0	0	0	0
δ_t	295·165	0	0	215·057	0	0	0	0
$\dot{PX}_t$	−12·4297	43·1469	−129·4272	−9·0563	−906·8363	−10·6987	85·0490	−23·4427
$\dot{PX}_{t-1}$	−1·8406	−224·4192	116·1776	−1·3411	858·1543	−13·4220	−91·6249	14·7790
$\dot{PD}_t$	0	0	0	0	−351·1800	0	0	0
$y^d_{2,t}$	0	0	0	0	0	0	0·368	0
$\dot{y}^d_{t-1}$	0	0	0	0	−0·2740	0	0	−0·0590
DU_{t-1}	−0·0051	−0·0724	0	−0·0037	−0·277	−0·0090	−0·0015	0
$\dot{FA}_{2t-1}$	−0·0016	0	−0·0138	−0·0012	−0·0071	−0·0017	−0·0003	−0·0036
$\dot{FA}_{3t-1}$	0	0·1910	0	0	0·0732	0·0237	0·0039	0
ΔOBD_t	0·0134	0	0	0·0097	0	0	0	0·0096
NIF_t	0·0134	0	0	0·0097	0	0	0	0
BL_{t-1}	0	−0·5060	−0·2930	0	−0·1938	−0·627	−0·1047	−0·0253
HP_{t-1}	0	0	0	0	0·1210	−0·363	−0·0061	0
FCF_{t-1}	0	0	0	0	0	−0·2790	0	0
BI_{t-1}	0	0	0	0	0	0	−0·0110	0
NV_{t-1}	0	0	0	0	0	0	0	−0·0130
t	0	43·0200	0	0	16·477	5·3345	0·8905	2·1510

$$\Delta FFI_t = \Delta FA_{2t} + \Delta FA_{3t} + \Delta OBD_t + NIF_t$$

$$RSD_t = 0 \cdot 5RBS_t + 0 \cdot 25RBD_t + 0 \cdot 25RTSB_t$$

$$\Delta BDT = \Delta FA_{2t} + \Delta OBD_t$$

where: ΔFA_{2t} is the personal sector's bank deposit (changes), ΔFA_{3t} is the personal sector's non-bank deposit (changes), ΔOBD_t is non-personal bank deposits (changes), NIF_t is net increase in life assurance and superannuation funds, and RBS, RBD, $RTSB$ the rates of interest on Building Societies' shares, deposits and deposits with Trustee Savings Banks respectively.

Fourteen variables are treated as endogenous; namely: ΔFA_{2t}, ΔFA_{3t}, ΔHL_t, ΔBL_t, $(\Delta HP + \Delta OL)_t$, RS_{1t}, RS_{2t}, RS_{3t}, RS_{4t}, RM_t, ΔFFI_t, RSD_t and ΔBDT; and 41 variables shown in *Table Ra. 6** as exogenous. To remove the non-linearities, all the equations are linearised around the mean values of the variables. The method used in the linearisation is described by Goldberger.[73a]

Proceeding formally, let the model be written in matrix form as:

$$BY + \Gamma X = 0$$

where B is a 14×14 matrix of coefficients of current endogenous variables, and Γ is a 14×41 matrix of the coefficients of the predetermined variables. If the B matrix is invertible, the reduced form of the model may be written as:

$$Y = \pi X$$

where π is a 14×41 matrix of reduced form coefficients given by $\pi = -B^{-1}\Gamma$. The results are shown in *Table Ra. 6*.

From *Table Ra. 6* it is possible to observe the negative coefficients of the rates of interest in the real assets equations. If we further assume that the absolute changes in the rates of interest are equal: i.e.

$$\dot{RBS}_t = \dot{RBD}_t = \dot{RTSB}_t = \dot{RNSC}_t = \dot{BR}_t = \dot{R}_t^L = \dot{R}$$

therefore, from *Table Ra. 6* it is possible to calculate the effects of $\dot{R}$ on the demand for real assets by the personal sector. The estimated coefficients are as follows:

	$\dot{RS}_{1t}$	$\dot{RS}_{2t}$	$\dot{RS}_{3t}$	$\dot{RS}_{3.1t}$	$\dot{RS}_{4t}$
$\dot{R}$	$-104 \cdot 5431$	$-159 \cdot 5716$	$-51 \cdot 7085$	$-8 \cdot 6303$	$-20 \cdot 4440$

Comparing these coefficients, investment in consumer durables appears to be relatively more sensitive to changes in interest rates than the other forms of real assets, particularly RS_3 and $RS_{3.1}$. This surprising result, which does not conform with *a priori* expectations, may be attributed to the fact that most of the interest rates which appear in the model are of a short-term nature and therefore are likely to have a stronger effect on short-term investment. This question will be examined again within the framework of the complete model.

---

* FCF_{t-1} is the stock of fixed capital formation lagged one period.

5

Composition of Personal Saving: Life Assurance and Superannuation

This chapter is concerned with personal saving in the form of Life Assurance and Superannuation. In section 5.1, a model is specified, describing the factors that determine the personal sector's saving in this form. This is followed in sections 5.2 and 5.3 by the estimation and results.

5.1 SPECIFICATION OF THE MODEL

Personal saving in this form is measured in the United Kingdom National Income Accounts by the net change in the Life Assurance and Superannuation funds. This is made up of individual premiums, employers premiums, investment income, outpayments, and administrative costs. Accordingly, the procedure adopted in this chapter is a disaggregative one. We split the aggregate figure of the net change in funds into its constituents, and specify a model for each component separately.

To begin with, let $NIF_t, PR_{it}, PR_t^R, II_{it}, OUP_{it}$, and ADM_{it} stand for: the net increase in Life Assurance and Superannuation funds, premiums paid by individuals, premiums paid by employers to superannuation funds, investment income, outpayments, and administrative costs (including taxes paid on investment income) respectively. The subscript i takes the value of either 1 or 2, where 1 refers to Life Assurance, and 2 refers to Superannuation schemes. The net change in funds, NIF_t is then defined by the following identity:

$$NIF_t = \sum_i PR_{it} + PR_t^R + \sum_i II_{it} - \sum_i OUP_{it} - \sum_i ADM_{it} \qquad (1)$$

In the following analysis PR_{it}, PR_t^R, II_{it}, and OUP_{1t} are treated as endogenous, while OUP_{2t} and ADM_{it} are treated as exogenous. The reason for defining OUP_{2t} as exogenous is that the formal contractual arrangements which link outpayments to the level of funds are lacking in pension funds organisations.

5.1.1 INDIVIDUAL PREMIUMS

Let PR_{it}^*, the equilibrium level of premiums at time t, depend on the permanent income Y_t^P and a vector of other (current and lagged) explanatory variables X. Thus we have:

$$PR_{it}^* = \Phi(Y_t^P, X) \tag{2}$$

Income is widely recognised as a leading measure of the ability to make an outlay, be it saving or spending. Because of the contractual and continuous nature of this form of saving, permanent income seems to be the appropriate measure. In the vector of other explanatory variables X, a number of factors have been mentioned in the literature. Three of these are considered in the following.*

1. One view which has been put forward is that National Insurance Schemes reduce the need for saving in order to provide for future consumption in certain contingencies such as old age, ill-health, or unemployment. Keynes,† in a lecture presented at the Federal Reserve Seminar in Washington in 1945 expressed the hope that the growth of social security would lead to a substantial decline in private saving, thus helping to avoid secular unemployment without heavy reliance on deficit spending by government. Friedman[62a] stated that 'The availability of assistance from the state would clearly tend to reduce the need for private reserves and so to reduce planned saving'. Thus it may be argued that since Life Insurance, Superannuation and National Insurance schemes all provide similar services to the insured, namely protection, some degree of substitutability between them is very likely.

However, empirical evidence in this respect is insufficient. Based on survey data, Katona[104] (p. 98–9) reported that 'it was possible to contradict the contention that families covered by social security put a smaller proportion of their income into private life insurance than those not covered, other things being equal'. Moreover he reached the conclusion that social security 'may serve as a stimulus to additional saving'. The reason for this, he added, is that 'at the present time and probably for years to come, there is a considerable gap between the standard of living to which an employed family is accustomed and the standard of living provided by social security benefits. . . . It is conceivable, therefore, that the minimal protection afforded by collective insurance plans may even stimulate people to save in order to achieve more adequate protection . . . with these plans people may feel closer to their goal and highly motivated to attain it'. As will be shown later, a wealth index based on entitlement to retirement benefits is formulated. This is then included, and tested, in equations for life insurance and superannuation individual premiums.

2. Another candidate may be the stock of liquid assets held by the personal

---

* I am greatly indebted to Mr. W. Peters, University of Manchester, who contributed significantly to the analysis developed in this section.
† As reported by Musgrave.[148]

sector. Savings in life assurance are sometimes regarded as a form of 'liquid assets' which can be converted into cash quickly. Savings in life assurance derive their liquidity from two distinctive features of the usual life assurance contract; these are the cash surrender value and the option open to the policy-holder to borrow against the cash surrender value without forfeiting his policy. However, there are fundamental differences between life assurance saving and other forms of liquid assets. First of all, life assurance saving is contractual in nature and reflects long-term programmes which, in most cases, have been decided earlier when the policies were first written. In contrast, regular and periodic saving in the form of, say, bank deposits or deposits with building societies, involve a series of decisions which may each require a visit to the saving institutions.[106] Secondly, life assurance saving is motivated basically by the desire for family financial protection in the event of untimely death, while the saving and investment elements in permanent life assurance may be secondary or incidental to the main purpose of providing financial protection.[106] True, some policy-holders are undoubtedly conscious of the cash values of their life assurance, and probably regard these as liquid assets. Even in these cases, however, policy reserves are probably far removed along the spectrum of liquid assets from other liquid assets such as bank deposits, deposits with building societies or with other financial institutions. Conclusions reached, on the basis of survey data conducted by the University of Michigan,[209] revealed that the great majority of life assurance policy-holders were completely unaware of reserves they were building through life assurance. In contrast, saving in other forms of liquid assets is often motivated by a desire to accumulate a certain sum for a planned expenditure such as a down payment on a house, a holiday, or some similar outlay. Also, a typical depositer-saver is more likely to know the exact amount of his deposits, for instance, because he holds a deposit book.

With respect to superannuation's individual premiums, possible effects of liquid assets may arise from two distinctive characteristics of pension saving: namely illiquidity and inflexibility as compared with other forms of saving. Most pension plans do not permit loans or lump-sum payments before retirement and hence are not regarded as a reserve fund for contingencies. Also, the participant is uncertain whether he will benefit from the employer's contribution. This is so, since most plans do not vest the benefits from the employer's contribution in the employees at an early date, for example, should he change jobs before a stipulated age and term of service. Thus, if it can be argued that individuals try to maintain a desired ratio of liquid or illiquid assets, therefore it follows that the stock of liquid assets may exert some influence on the desired level of pensions' premiums.

However, there is great uncertainty regarding the effects of liquid assets. There is the general difficulty of separating the income from the liquid asset effects in saving functions. Also, it is not obvious whether premiums are positively or negatively correlated with liquid assets. An increase in the stock of liquid assets may be associated in the short-run with a fall in the less liquid assets, but followed in the long-run by a rise in liquid assets. Obviously, the answer depends on what is regarded by the individual as desired levels of liquid and illiquid assets, and the relative order of the speed of adjustment coefficients, which, in the final analysis, is a matter of empirical testing.

3. Favourable tax treatment of saving in the form of life insurance and superannuation may be an important determinant of saving in this form. To illustrate, let us recall — briefly — the form the special tax provisions take. Non-favoured saving (a) is made out of fully taxed income, (b) produces investment income which is taxed at the saver's marginal rate, (c) may produce capital gains (untaxed during the period under review), and (d) can be used to purchase an annuity, with payments which are treated in part as investment income, and in part as a non-taxable return of capital. Life insurance saving (a) attracts a rebate, subject to restrictions, at a rate generally of two-fifths of the saver's marginal rate, and (b) produces investment income taxed at 37½%; (c) and (d) remain as before. It is evident that the difference under (a) favours life insurance saving for all those who pay income tax, but the difference under (b) does so only for those liable to pay tax at the standard rate or more. A net sacrifice of consumption at a rate A per year for n years will, if we ignore expenses and the cost of life cover, accumulate after n years to:

$$A\left[\frac{1 + R(1 - tx)}{R(1 - tx)}\right] \left[\left\{1 + R(1 - tx)\right\}^n - 1\right] \tag{3a}$$

if saved directly by a taxpayer subject to a marginal tax rate tx and to:

$$\frac{A}{1 - 0\cdot4tx} \left[\frac{1 + R(0\cdot625)}{R(0\cdot625)}\right] \left[\left\{1 + R(0\cdot625)\right\}^n - 1\right] \tag{3b}$$

if saved through life insurance, capital gains being ignored in both cases. R is the rate of interest. On long insurance contracts, the taxpayer who is subject to a reduced rate at the margin could gain less from the tax relief on premiums (reflected in the $1 - 0\cdot4tx$ divisor) than he loses through the substitution of $0\cdot625$ for $1 - tx$. However, it is probable that the bulk of individually written life business is made with standard rate taxpayers, and in any case, unless tx is very small, n has to be quite large before the value of (3a) exceeds (3b). Therefore, some justification appears to exist in talking in terms of a general tendency to favour life insurance by comparison with other channels of saving in the prevailing tax laws.

With respect to the effects of taxation on life insurance premiums two points are in order. Firstly, the modest concession on investment income enables companies to quote rather better rates than would otherwise be possible, in terms of sum insured per £ of premium. The effect of this on premiums is subject to the familiar uncertainty owing to the opposition of income and sub-stitution effects. One possibility is that premium inflow in stably related to income, so that the effect of the concession is that more insurance is bought. Another is that insurance *targets* are stably related to income so that the effect is to reduce premium income and, via the size of accumulated life funds, investment income before tax as well.* However, these cannot be taken as the

---

* Of course, over the life of any individual insurance contract, with a given value on maturity, if premiums are lower *after-tax* investment income must be higher than in the absence of tax concessions. But, what is true for an individual policy aggregated over the periods need not be true for the industry at an instant of time, with aggregation over the funds associated with all policies.

only or even as limiting possibilities: it is by no means implausible that the tax treatment of life insurance may lead to increased premium inflow (cf. the sales of single-premium insurance bonuses before the 1969 Budget). Secondly, as to the favourable effects of tax rebates on premiums, this seems hardly in doubt. Only if insurance *targets* are reduced in response to an improvement in the terms of trade between current consumption and insurance benefits, which seem hardly likely, will the effect of a tax concession of this form be adverse.†

With respect to the tax treatment of superannuation saving, the rules favour — by comparison with direct saving — virtually all persons who have some tax liability during their contributory life, and in the great majority of cases are more favourable than those relating to life insurance saving. Contributions by employees to approved superannuation funds are fully deductible from income for income tax surtax purposes. Employers' contributions are allowed as expenses for corporation tax purposes (and for income tax purposes in the case of self-employed people). Investment income is untaxed. Capital gains are untaxed and annuity payments are treated as earned income, rather than as — in part — a return of capital.

In addition to the effects of National Insurance, liquid assets and taxation, inflation is probably an important factor influencing the desire to save in the form of life insurance and superannuation. As to the latter, the effect of inflation varies according to the constitution of the scheme[32b] (vol. 2, p. 76). 'In the "salary/ service" type of scheme, where the pension is based on the final salary (or the average annual salary over the last few years before retirement) combined with the number of years of service, the effects of inflation are considerably reduced from the members' point of view in so far as the amount of his pension is concerned. Inflation can, however, cause large deficiencies to arise in this type of scheme, which may have to be met by the employer or the employees (or both), or result in reduced benefits . . . A scheme which provides pensions on the "money-purchase" principle (where the contributions paid each year "purchase" a fixed amount of pension at retirement age according to a pre-arranged actuarial table) is likely to provide little protection against inflation. As a result the pension may prove inadequate in terms of final salary on retirement . . .' As regards saving through life insurance, inflation depreciates the real value of insured benefits, and results in higher premium rates per £ of sum insured by increasing operational costs of insurance companies. However experiments with a number of price expectation indices yielded statistically insignificant results.

Since PR_{it}^* is a theoretical magnitude which is not directly observable, a partial adjustment mechanism is assumed in relating desired to actual premiums. It takes the following form:

$$PR_{it} - PR_{it-1} = p(PR_{it}^* - PR_{it-1}) \qquad (4)$$

where $PR_{it} - PR_{it-1} = \Delta PR_{it}$

† Even if the response to the concessions is to reduce the net-of-tax amount allocated to insurance, the effect of premium income of life insurance companies, which is, of course, measured gross of any individual tax rebates, is favourable as long as the concession brings in some net new business.

Equations (2) and (4) form the basis of the estimates reported in Section 5.3, for individual premiums.

5.1.2 EMPLOYERS' PREMIUMS, INVESTMENT INCOME AND OUTPAYMENTS

We now turn to the problem of specifying equations for employers' contributions, PR_t^R, investment income, II_{it}, and outpayments, OUP_{it}. Firstly, the desired level of employers' contributions, PR_t^{*R}, is assumed to depend, linearly, on the level of employment, N_t. Then by using a partial adjustment mechanism of the type shown in (4), we write:

$$PR_t^R = s_0 N_t + (1 + k)PR_{t-1} \tag{5}$$

Secondly, investment income depends on the stock of assets and a rate of return (multiplicatively). The latter should be chosen in such a way as to reflect the investment considerations adopted by life insurance companies and superannuation funds. Denoting the stock of assets by $SLIF_t$ and $SSUP_t$ for life insurance and superannuation respectively, and R_t for the relevant rate of return, it follows that

$$II_{1t} = s_1 + s_2(SLIF_t \times R_t) \tag{6a}$$

$$II_{2t} = s_3 + s_4(SSUP_t \times R_t) \tag{6b}$$

Finally, outpayments by life insurance companies, OUP_{1t}, are assumed to depend on the stock of life insurance assets and an index reflecting the share of whole life, endowment and other policies, $SWLA_t$ (providing that variations in surrenders and policy loans are small). This gives:

$$OUP_{1t} = s_5 + s_6 SLIF_t + s_7 SWLA_t \tag{7}$$

5.2 SOME STATISTICAL AND ECONOMETRIC CONSIDERATIONS

5.2.1 DATA AND VARIABLES

The Special Tax Treatment

As mentioned earlier, the special tax treatment of life insurance and superannuation may be an important determinant of saving in this form. To summarise the special tax provisions, an index is derived from equations (3a) and (3b). Let σ be defined as the rate of return on long-term investment, G^{10} the standard tax rate, and substitute for R and tx respectively in expression (3b), thus we have:

$$\xi = \frac{A}{1 - 0.4G^{10}} \left\{ \frac{1 + \sigma(0.625)}{\sigma(0.625)} \right\} \left[\left\{ 1 + \sigma(0.625) \right\}^{n-1} \right] \tag{8}$$

By assuming that $n = 20$, the value of R which would equate (3a) and (8) is taken, in this study, to represent what may be called the rate of return on life insurance saving R_t^{LA}. This index is used in the premiums and investment income equations for the purpose of reflecting the special tax provisions. Suppose the rate of return rebates on life insurance premiums has been reduced, associated with an increase in the rate at which investment income is taxed — this would lead to a fall in the rate of return in life insurance saving relative to the rates of return on alternative investment, which is expected to result in the individual reallocating his resources away from life insurance saving — other things being equal. However, it has been argued that this 'rate-of-return' type of reasoning does not, in fact, have much applicability so far as life insurance saving is concerned. The advocates of this view[125] emphasize that the saving and investment elements in life insurance are in most of the cases incidental or secondary to the main purpose of financial protection. It is true, so they argue, that in the calculations of premiums an assumption is made about the rate of return which can be earned on policy reserves. However, the premium is also based upon assumed life expectancy and assumed cost of administering the policy. In a study by the Life Insurance Association of America,[125] it was noted that although the average rate of return earned on assets by life insurance companies showed a continuous rise since 1947, 'the growth rate of life insurance savings has exhibited a broad downward trend during the post-war years'.[125] In the evidence to the Radcliffe Committee[32b] (vol. 2, p. 38) by the British Life Insurance Association, it was pointed out that 'as regards savings through life insurance, the effects of changes in rates of interest are remote and can have but little influence on the volume of new life insurance written. Higher rates of interest enable premium rates to be reduced and/or bonus rates to be increased and these outcomes do help in the development of the business. But they are minor influences compared with the efforts of the life insurance field staff, aided by the unique characteristics of life insurance, viz. the creation of the whole anticipated savings fund immediately on death, and the facilities provided for regular savings over a long future period'[32b] (vol. 2, p. 38). As mentioned previously, in this study R^{LA} is interpreted as a summary index of the special tax provisions, when used in the equation for individual premiums. Also, the same index has been used in the superannuation equations as a proxy, though imperfect, of the favourable tax treatment because of difficulties in formulating a separate index. This may be regarded as a weak feature of this study.

In defining σ, the rate of interest on long-dated government securities, R_t^L, has been used. On the one hand, saving through life insurance and superannuation is a long-run commitment, which implies that a long-run, rather than a short-run, rate is the relevant one. On the other hand, an important principle governing investment policies of life insurance companies is that of matching assets and liabilities. Since these liabilities are predominantly commitments to pay fixed, or substantially fixed sums, at dates many years ahead, therefore life insurance companies tend to invest mainly in long-term securities. Similarly, the long-run nature of the liabilities of pension funds encourage them to invest a significant proportion of their assets in long-dated fixed interest securities. In 1957 investment in Government Securities — mainly long-dated — formed nearly one third of the total assets of life insurance and pension funds, and although inflation and the spread of 'with profits' policies have led to a move towards equities, an appreciable amount has still been going into gilt-edged.

Given R^L, G^{10} for each year and assuming that A is £1, the value of ξ in equation (8) is first calculated. Then an iterative procedure is used in deriving the corresponding value of the return on life insurance saving, R^{LA}. By equating

(3a) and (8) we have:

$$\xi = \left[\left(\frac{f}{f-1}\right) x \, (f^n - 1)\right]$$ (9a)

where $f = (1 + R^{LA}(1 - G^{10}))$. By rearranging we obtain:

$$f_{i+1} = \frac{\sqrt[n]{f_i + \xi(f_i - 1)}}{f_i}$$ (9b)

n was given the value of 20 years.*

The National Insurance Variable

For this variable, a wealth index based on entitlement to retirement benefits is formulated. There are two approaches to the calculations of the present value (the capital value) of the benefit entitlement: one by capitalising and discounting the expected value for the present population, allowing for expected changes in certain demographic and economic states, and the other by capitalising and discounting the expected value for the population in its present state. Obviously, the first approach is more relevant to the government, as it provides an estimate of its liabilities to the public. The second, which avoids some formidable problems, can be advocated and defended on similar grounds to those applied by life insurance companies. The second approach is adopted in this study and a brief description of the method used in the estimation is given in the following:

1. The distribution of the insured population by age and marital conditions for the period 1952–66 is derived first from the 1951 and 1961 Census distributions, assuming a constant rate of increase of population in each age group.

2. An adjustment is then made to the distribution of married population, in order to single out the distribution of married women contracted in and out of National Insurance Schemes. The percentage ratio of the total of married women contracted out to the total number of married women is calculated for each year from the figures published by the Ministry of Social Security. The ratio obtained is assumed to be the same for all age groups.

3. For a single male or female or a married female contracted in, at age i in year j, the present value of retirement benefits is given by:

$$WNI^S(d, i, j) = k(i,j) \times Z_R(i,j) \times b^S(j) \times A_3(j) \times \frac{1}{(1 + P(d))^{m(i)}}$$ (10)

where: k is the number of the population (single or married contracted in), Z_R the probability of survival to retirement age, b^S the retirement benefit (single), P the discount rate ($d = 1, \ldots 13$), m the retirement age, R the present age, and A_3

* The initial value of f was assumed to be 2.

the annuity rate for single people (the capital value of £1 annuity paid at the end of each year) is given by:

$$A_3(i) = \frac{Z_{R+1}}{(1+P)} + \frac{Z_{R+2}}{(1+P)^2} + \dots\dots \frac{Z_{R+X}}{(1+P)^X} \tag{11}$$

4. For a married male, at age i in year j, with a wife contracted out, we have:

$$WNI^M(d,i,j) = [e(i,j) \times \{b^S(j) \times A_1(j) + b^M(j) \times A_2(j)\}] / (1 + P(d))^{m(i)} \tag{12}$$

where: A_2 is the joint annuity rate, A_1 the last survival annuity rate, b^M married couple retirement benefits, $e(i,j) = c(i,j) \times s(i,j)$, c the number of married couples, and s the probability of joint survival to the husband's retirement age (a husband aged i and a wife aged $i - \bar{a}$).

For a married male aged 64·5 surviving to age 64·5 + X, and his wife (contracted out) aged 64·5 − $\bar{a}$ surviving to age 64·5 − $\bar{a}$ + X, A_2 is given by the weighted average of $A_2(\bar{a})$ for each $\bar{a}$.

$$A_2(\bar{a}) = \frac{J_1 K_1}{(1+P)} + \frac{J_2 K_2}{(1+P)^2} + \dots\dots \frac{J_X K_X}{(1+P)^X} \tag{13}$$

$\bar{a}$ is the mean difference between the wife's age and 64·5 when her husband is aged 64·5. The weights are given by the percentage distribution (in 1951) of the difference between the ages of the husband and wife when the husband's age is 64·5. $\bar{a}$ is calculated from the 1951 figures of the distribution of wives 'by their age in relation to their husbands'. This series of $\bar{a}$ is used for the whole period due to the lack of statistical data for the relevant distributions. J is the probability of a husband aged 64·5 surviving to age 64·5 + X, and K is the probability of a wife aged 64·5 − $\bar{a}$ surviving to age 64·5 − $\bar{a}$ + X. A_1 is given by the weighted average of $A_1(\bar{a})$ for each $\bar{a}$

$$A_1(\bar{a}) = \frac{J_1 + K_1 - 2J_1 K_1}{(1+P)} + \dots\dots \frac{J_X + K_X - 2JK_X}{(1+P)^X} \tag{14}$$

In the calculation of the annuity rates, the figures for the probability of survivals after retirement are derived from the 1951 Life Table. In order to account for the bias resulting from the use of the same probability of survival figures for the rest of the period, the discount rate P is reduced by a fraction of 0·25% for each subsequent year in equations (10) and (12). This procedure (using a reduced discount rate to account for the improvement in the probability of survivals) is applied by Life Insurance Companies. Figures for the probability of survivals to retirement age are obtained for each class for each year from the abridged Life Tables published by the Registrar General.

5. For a given $P(d)$ and j the aggregate present value is given by:

$$WNI = \sum_{i=1} WNI^S_{i(1)} + \sum_{i=1} WNI^S_{i(2)} + \sum_{i=1} WNI^S_{i(3)} + \sum_{i=1} WNI^M_i \tag{15}$$

where $WNI^S_{i(1)}$, $WNI^S_{i(2)}$, $WNI^S_{i(3)}$ and WNI^M_i are the present value of retirement benefits for single males, single females, married women contracted in, and married couples respectively. Results obtained are shown in *Table Li. 1*.

Table Li. 1 THE NATIONAL INSURANCE INDEX

Year	2·5	2·75	3	3·25	3·5	3·75	4·0	4·25	4·5	4·75	5·0	5·25	5·5	5·75	6·0
51	6 798	6 513	6 243	5 990	5 753	5 530	5 317	5 119	4 929	4 752	4 584	4 424	4 268	4 115	3 972
52	7 098	7 663	7 341	7 040	6 758	6 495	6 241	6 003	5 781	5 572	5 372	5 183	4 998	4 817	4 649
53	8 797	8 428	8 074	7 743	7 433	7 144	6 866	6 605	6 362	6 133	5 911	5 705	5 500	5 303	5 092
54	9 045	8 664	8 299	7 959	7 641	7 343	7 056	6 788	6 537	6 302	6 076	5 863	5 652	5 449	5 257
55	10 714	10 264	9 833	9 430	9 053	8 700	8 361	8 045	7 748	7 470	7 202	6 950	6 701	6 460	6 234
56	11 697	11 207	10 737	10 296	9 885	9 500	9 129	8 784	8 459	8 154	7 868	7 587	7 314	7 051	6 804
57	11 984	11 481	10 999	10 549	10 127	9 732	9 353	8 997	8 665	8 353	8 052	7 770	7 491	7 223	6 972
58	14 962	14 334	13 732	13 169	12 640	12 147	11 674	11 231	10 816	10 427	10 052	9 700	9 352	9 015	8 700
59	15 542	14 889	14 264	13 677	13 130	12 618	12 126	11 665	11 233	10 829	10 438	10 066	9 703	9 354	9 026
60	16 130	15 452	14 803	14 196	13 628	13 096	12 585	12 108	11 660	11 241	10 838	10 458	10 082	9 720	9 379
61	18 523	17 744	17 000	16 302	15 650	15 039	14 453	13 904	13 390	12 908	12 443	12 007	11 575	11 158	10 767
62	19 676	18 848	18 057	17 316	16 622	15 974	15 351	14 768	14 221	13 710	13 217	12 755	12 293	11 850	11 435
63	22 445	21 502	20 600	19 755	18 964	18 224	17 513	16 847	16 224	15 640	15 078	14 549	14 025	13 520	13 048
64	24 741	23 702	22 706	21 774	20 903	20 088	19 304	18 571	17 884	17 241	16 620	16 038	15 461	14 903	14 352
65	28 944	27 729	26 563	25 474	24 455	23 502	22 586	21 728	20 924	20 170	19 444	18 763	18 087	17 435	16 825

Premiums, Investment Income, Outpayments and Administrative Costs

For these variables, data used in the estimation are derived from published statistics in the 'Blue Book'[25a, 25b] and the *Annual Abstract of Statistics*. One difficulty arises with respect to the definition of the saving element in premiums paid by individuals to Life Insurance Companies. If saving is defined as the postponement of present consumption in favour of future consumption then premiums paid for a 'one-period term' policy should be considered as expenditure for current consumption. But, for insurance contracts with a fixed unchanging premium each year for the rest of the insured life, it may be argued that current saving made by the policy holder amounts to the difference between what he actually paid for a policy and the minimal amount he could have paid for protection in the same period. According to this definition premiums will include an element of saving in the earlier years of the insured's life — the premium is higher than a one year term premium — and an element of dis-saving in the later years. This is because, on the one hand, the premium paid depends directly upon the estimated probability of the death of the insured during the contract period, and because this estimated probability increases with the age of the insured, the premium necessary for protection would increase with age. On the other hand, the premium actually paid by the insured is fixed and unchanging for the rest of his life. In this study, no adjustment is made to the figures of individual premiums to Life Insurance Companies because the data available would make the adjustment possible only under very weak assumptions. In this context, it should be noted that the problem does not arise in the case of annuities and pension funds. Since all premiums can be considered as payments for an income stream which will not begin until after the current period, in this case the entire contribution to a pension fund or an annuity represents a deferred consumption.

5.2.2 THE ESTIMATING FORM OF THE INDIVIDUAL PREMIUMS EQUATION

For the purpose of estimating the equation for premiums paid by individuals to Life Insurance and Superannuation funds, two alternative assumptions are tested regarding the influence of taxation — as summarised by the rate of return index R^{LA}. First, R^{LA} is assumed to influence the desired level of premiums, PR_i^*, directly, while in the second it is assumed to affect the speed at which the actual premiums adjust towards the desired premiums. Assuming that equation (2) is linear in the variables and parameters, and substituting in (3) for PR_{it}^*, two forms of equations — depending on the assumed effect of R_t^{LA} — are estimated. These are:

First Assumption: $PR_{it} = K_0 p Y_t^P + K_1 p R_t^{LA} + pKX + (1-p)PR_{it-1}$ (16a)

Second Assumption: $\Delta PR_{it} = K_0 w(Y_t^P . R_t^{LA}) + wK(X . R_t^{LA}) - w(PR_{it-1} R_t^{LA})$

$$\text{(16b)}$$

where in (16b)*, $p_t = wR_t^{LA}$. The vector X includes the stock of liquid assets L_t and the National Insurance variable WNI_t.

---

* It is to be noted that p, the speed of adjustment parameter in equation (4) assumes a subscript t implying that this parameter varies over time.

5.3 RESULTS

This section begins with *Table Li.2* which gives a statistical summary of the Life Assurance and Superannuation variables.

Table Li. 2 VARIABLES USED IN THE ESTIMATION OF THE LIFE ASSURANCE AND SUPERANNUATION SAVINGS MODEL

Index Variables	Min.	Max.	Mean	Quartile 1	Median	Quartile 3	Standard deviation
PR_{1t}	290·354	1 009·8	579·581	386·965	519·344	837·559	226·450
PR_{1+2t}	345·000	1 046·0	639·750	449·0	596·500	852·00	229·737
PR_t^R	254·00	902·0	547·235	364·0	542·0	760·0	199·832
II_{1t}	91·248	553·540	264·290	149·988	218·368	399·629	147·171
II_{2t}	477·52	316·456	146·883	711·66	124·632	237·371	81·5013
OUP_{1t}	195·648	738·101	377·565	237·38	337·969	520·732	158·144
R_t^{LA}	7·267	10·043	8·457	7·961	8·434	8·814	0·652

Equation 5.1.3 of *Table Li. 3* is the Unrestricted (Ordinary) Least Squares estimate of Life Assurance individual premiums. R^2 is satisfactory and there is no evidence of first order serial correlation. All the coefficients have the correct *a priori* signs, and are greater than the size of their standard errors. However, several comments regarding this equation are in order:

1. Equation 5.1.3 of *Table Li. 3* is based on specification (16b), in which R^{LA} is assumed to affect the speed of adjustment coefficients. Experiments with specification (16a) in which R^{LA} enters the desired premiums equation directly, show a negative coefficient for R^{LA} when tested for Life Assurance premiums. Examples of the estimates obtained are as follows:

$$PR_{1t} = 0·017Y_t^P - 9·03R_t^{LA} + 0·617PR_{1t-1}$$
$$\quad\quad (0·007)\quad (4·07)\quad\quad (0·185)$$

$$PR_{1t} = 0·015Y_t^P - 21·38R_t^{LA} + 0·419PR_{1t-1} + 0·026L_t$$
$$\quad\quad (0·067)\quad\quad (8·83)\quad\quad (0·217)\quad\quad\quad (0·017)$$

The negative sign for R^{LA} may be interpreted as evidence of an adverse income effect, resulting from the tax rebate on premiums and the modest tax concession on investment income of assurance companies which enables them to quote better terms than would otherwise be possible. As mentioned earlier, this can only be the case if assurance targets are reduced in response to an improvement in the terms of trade between current consumption and assurance benefits; which seems hardly likely.

2. All explanatory variables appear in a multiplicative form in equation 5.1.3. By linearizing at the mean value of the variables we obtain:

$$\dot{PR}_{1t} = 0·0129\,\dot{Y}_t^P + 459·41\dot{R}_t^{LA} - 0·0098\dot{L}_t + 0·806\dot{PR}_{1t-1} \qquad (17)$$

It is clear that in (17) R^{LA} has the correct sign and is of a sizeable order. If the coefficient of $\dot{PR}_{1t-1}$ is regarded as measuring the speed of adjustment, the fairly large size of this coefficient in (17) implies a very rapid adjustment to the

Table Li. 3 PREMIUMS, INVESTMENT INCOME AND OUTPAYMENTS (1951–66)

Equation number	Dependent variable (£m)	A_{it-1} (£m)	$Y_t^P \times R_t^{LA}$ (£m)	$L_t \times R_t^{LA}$ (£m)	$SLIF_t \times R_t^L$ (£m)	$SSUP_t \times R_t^L$ (£m)	$SLIF_t$ (£m)	$SWLA_t$ (£m)	t	N_t (mill.)	Intercept	R^2	VN
5.1.3	ΔPR_{1t}	−2·28 (1·73)	0·152 (0·09)	−0·117 (0·110)								0·86	1·85
5.2.3	ΔPR_{1+2t}	−3·94 (2·11)	0·247 (0·123)	−0·169 (0·127)								0·84	1·77
5.3.3	II_{1t}				0·726 (0·119)				5·381 (4·034)		12·177 (11·186)	0·98	1·20
5.4.3	II_{2t}					0·592 (0·106)			3·581 (2·336)		22·506 (6·842)	0·98	1·53
5.5.3	OUP_{1t}						0·103 (0·014)	6·71 (3·36)			−591·8 (293·0)	0·99	1·73
5.6.3	PR_t^R	1·03 (0·014)								0·932 (0·306)		0·87	1·73

desired level of premiums. This is expected in view of the contractual nature of this form of saving.

3. With respect to liquid assets, L_t, further experiments gave some evidence that the short-run effect of this variable may be different from that of equation 5.1.3 of *Table Li. 3*. Thus, instead of regarding L_t as a variable entering the desired premiums' equation, it was treated as a short-term constraint; adding a term to the stock adjustment mechanism in (4). The result obtained is as follows:

$$\Delta PR_{1t} = 335 \cdot 9 + 0 \cdot 213(Y_t^P \times R_t^{LA}) - 11 \cdot 14(PR_{1t-1} R_t^{LA}) + 0 \cdot 057 L_t$$
$$(57 \cdot 8) \quad (0 \cdot 05) \qquad\qquad (2 \cdot 08) \qquad\qquad\qquad (0 \cdot 009)$$

$$R^2 = 0 \cdot 85 \quad VN = 2 \cdot 34$$

The liquid asset coefficient has a positive sign — instead of a negative sign as shown in equation 5.1.3 of *Table Li. 3* — suggesting that in the short-run liquid assets and Life Assurance premiums may be regarded as complements. Moreover, the statistical significance of this equation is superior to that of equation 5.1.3 of *Table Li. 3* (a fairly large R^2 is associated with no evidence of serial correlation) and in addition all the coefficients are highly significant. However, when linearized at the mean value of the variables, the resulting coefficient for R^{LA} has a negative sign, and is therefore rejected.

4. Specifications which included the National Insurance variable yielded unsatisfactory results. This was the case whether *WNI* was treated as a variable entering the desired equation or as a short-run constraint. The estimates obtained are as follows:*

$$\Delta PR_{1t} = 0 \cdot 029(Y_t^P \times R_t^{LA}) - 4 \cdot 46(PR_{1t-1} \times R_t^{LA}) + 0 \cdot 021 \; WNI_{t-1}$$
$$(0 \cdot 040) \qquad\qquad (1 \cdot 67) \qquad\qquad\qquad (0 \cdot 007)$$

$$R^2 = 0 \cdot 645 \quad VN = 2 \cdot 11$$

$$\Delta PR_{1t} = 0 \cdot 073(Y_t^P \times R_t^{LA}) - 2 \cdot 29(PR_{1t-1} \times R_t^{LA}) + 0 \cdot 041(WNI_{t-1} \times R_t^{LA})$$
$$(0 \cdot 055) \qquad\qquad (3 \cdot 00) \qquad\qquad\qquad (0 \cdot 097)$$

$$R^2 = 0 \cdot 63 \quad VN = 1 \cdot 58$$

In both cases, the coefficient of determination, R^2, shows a marked reduction as compared with equation 5.1.3 of *Table Li. 3* and the National Insurance variable has the wrong *a priori* sign.

Equation 5.2.3 of *Table Li. 3* is the Ordinary Least Squares estimate of the total of Life Assurance and Superannuation individual premiums. As compared

---

* It should be noted that the effect of introducing the National Insurance wealth into the equation was to reduce the size of the sample and hence the degree of freedom by 2. This is because estimates of the National Insurance variable were made for the period 1952–65 only. Therefore, equations including this variable are not strictly comparable with equations 5.1.3 and 5.2.3 of *Table Li. 3*.

Experiments with specifications, which included both L_t and WNI_t (or WNI_{t-1}), were quite unsatisfactory.

The figures of *WNI* used in these equations are calculated assuming a 5% discount rate (see *Table Li. 1*). Similar results were obtained when alternative discount rates were assumed.

with equation 5.1.3 for Life Assurance only, although R^2 is slightly reduced, there is a marked improvement in the statistical significance of the estimated coefficients. This may be viewed as evidence of substitutability between Life Assurance and Superannuation. By linearising equation 5.2.3 — *Table Li. 3* — at the mean values of the variables we obtain:

$$(\dot{P}R_{1t} + \dot{P}R_{2t}) = 0{\cdot}021\dot{Y}_t^P + 456{\cdot}42\dot{R}_t^{LA} - 0{\cdot}014\dot{L}_t + 0{\cdot}666(\dot{P}R_{t-1} + \dot{P}R_{2t-1})$$

$$(18)$$

Comparing equations (18) and (17) provides additional evidence as to the possible substitutability between Life Assurance and Superannuation saving. The computed coefficients of both the rate of return on Life Assurance and $\dot{P}R_{1t-1}$ show a negative effect on superannuation individual premiums, $\dot{P}R_{2t}$, of the order $-2{\cdot}99$ and $-0{\cdot}14$ for R_t^{LA} and $\dot{P}R_{1t-1}$ respectively.

Experiments with the National Insurance variable in the total individual premiums, $PR_{1t} + PR_{2t}$, were again unsatisfactory, leading to a reduction in R^2 and a wrong sign for both WNI and R^{LA}. However, a contradictory result was obtained when the net increase in Life Assurance and Superannuation funds, NIF, was used as a dependent variable. The estimate obtained was as follows:

$$NIF_t = -255{\cdot}1 + 0{\cdot}079Y_{t-1}^P - 0{\cdot}024WNI_{t-1} + 0{\cdot}686NIF_{t-1}$$
$$(135{\cdot}8)\quad(0{\cdot}022)\qquad(0{\cdot}009)\qquad\quad(0{\cdot}273)$$

$$R^2 = 0{\cdot}98 \quad VN = 2{\cdot}22$$

Despite the satisfactory fit and the negative sign of the coefficient for WNI there are obvious theoretical objections to an aggregate specification of this form. On the one hand, NIF represents an amalgam of heterogeneous activities: some are carried out by individuals in their capacity as consumers, e.g. PR_i, some are carried out by institutions, e.g. II_i, OUP_i, ADM_i, and PR^R, etc. On the other hand, there is strong reason to believe that WNI_{t-1} in the above estimate is acting as a proxy for something else, as yet unidentified. Otherwise one would have expected WNI to emerge as a significant variable in the premium's equations, which was not the case. Nevertheless, it should be emphasised that the disappointing performance of WNI should not lead to the conclusion that entitlement to National Insurance benefits has no effect on Life Assurance and Superannuation saving. The unreliability of the data and the inadequacy of the proxy used should be borne in mind. Further research in this field seems necessary.

Equations 5.3.3 to 5.6.3 of *Table Li. 3* are the Ordinary Least Squares estimates of Life Assurance investment income, Superannuation investment income, Life Assurance outpayments, and employers' premiums paid to pension funds respectively. According to standard statistical and econometric criteria (goodness of fit, standard error, serial correlation, etc.) the estimated relationships 5.3.3 to 5.6.3 shown in *Table Li. 3* are satisfactory; with the exception of equation 5.3.3 where the Von-Neumann ratio is relatively small. The highly significant coefficients for the time trend variable in equations 5.3.3 and 5.4.3 may be regarded as evidence of omitted variables.

6

An Alternative Model of Aggregate Personal Saving: The Balance Sheet Approach

In Chapter 2, aggregate personal saving was defined as a residual and an aggregate model was specified and estimated. Now we focus attention on the personal sector's balance sheet, and define aggregate personal saving as the rate of change in net worth. On the basis of this definition, we derive an alternative aggregate personal saving model by combining the equations selected in Chapters 3, 4 and 5 for financial assets, real assets and Life Assurance and Superannuation saving. These equations are supplemented by a number of additional equations and identities which help to close the model. A brief summary of the complete model is given in section 6.1, and is followed in section 6.2 by the derivation of the reduced form of the alternative aggregate personal saving model. In section 6.3 we end by comparing the reduced form of the aggregate model of Chapter 2 with the one derived in this chapter.

6.1 THE ALTERNATIVE MODEL

6.1.1 A SUMMARY OF THE MODEL

The final form of the model consists of the following equations. All the stochastic equations are estimated by means of Ordinary Least Squares.

$\boxed{6.1}$ The Aggregate Personal Saving definition: *Money Terms.*

$$S_t = \sum_{i=1}^{9} FA_{it} + \sum_{i=1}^{4} RS_{it} - \Delta HL_t - \Delta BL_t - \Delta HP_t - \Delta OL_t + \sum_{i=1}^{2} PR_{it} + PR_t^R +$$

$$+ \sum_{i=1}^{2} II_{it} - \sum_{i=1}^{2} OUP_{it} - \sum_{i=1}^{2} ADM_{it} + CTX_t - CTR_t + STA_t + UNIP_t$$

6.2 Bank Deposits: *Real Terms*

$$\Delta FA_{2t} = -0.36\,905\ FA_{2t-1} + 0.18\,445\ Y^P_{t-1} - 270.76\,424\ RSD_t -$$
$$[0.10\,285] \qquad\qquad [0.05\,321] \qquad\qquad [122.946]$$

$$- 1\,422.691\ E^{0.25}_{Lt} \quad -0.28\,598\ S_{t-1}$$
$$[467.871] \qquad\qquad [0.1393]$$

$$R^2 = 0.79 \quad VN = 2.48$$

6.3 Bank Deposits Plus Notes and Coins: *Real Terms*

$$[\Delta FA_{1t} + \Delta FA_{2t}] = -0.39\,496\ FA_{2t-1} + 0.20\,904\ Y^P_{t-1} - 332.1365\ RSD_t -$$
$$[0.11\,519] \qquad\qquad [0.0596] \qquad\qquad [137.690]$$

$$- 1432.107\ E^{0.25}_{Lt} - 0.35\,397\ S_{t-1}$$
$$[523.981] \qquad\qquad [0.156]$$

$$R^2 = 0.75 \quad VN = 2.57$$

6.4 Non-Bank Deposits: *Real Terms*

$$\Delta FA_{3t} = -0.11\,115\ FA_{3t-1} + 0.0775\ Y^P_t + 433.0076\ RSD_t -$$
$$[0.05\,087] \qquad\qquad [0.0294] \quad [225.9146]$$

$$-\,427.38\,215\ RNSC_t\ -90.344\ E^{0.9}_{Lt} - 0.16\,609\ S_{t-1}$$
$$[115.2521] \qquad\qquad [46.845] \qquad\quad [0.12\,016]$$

$$R^2 = 0.96 \quad VN = 3.01$$

6.5 National Savings Certificates: *Money Terms*

$$\Delta FA_{4t} = -0.1216\ FA_{3t-1} + 0.01\,105\ Y^P_t + 141.444\ RNSC_t - 112.204\ RBS_t -$$
$$[0.0472] \qquad\qquad [0.0065] \qquad\quad [64.111] \qquad\qquad [97.642]$$

$$- 108.378\ E^{0.5}_{Lt} - 0.128\ S_{t-1}$$
$$[53.641] \qquad\quad [0.055]$$

$$R^2 = 0.82 \quad VN = 2.47$$

6.6 Other Non-Marketable Government Securities: *Money Terms*

$$\Delta FA_{5t} = -0.1325\ FA_{5t-1} + 0.0083\ Y^P_t + 54.603\ RNSC_t - 2884.048\ [PX_t - PN_t]$$
$$[0.1242] \qquad\qquad [0.008] \qquad\quad [18.558] \qquad\qquad [863.634]$$

$$R^2 = 0.73 \quad VN = 1.96$$

6.7 Marketable Government Securities: *Money Terms*

$$\Delta FA_{6t} = -0.9366\ FA_{6t-1} + 0.3885\ Y_t^P - 211.157\ RNSC_t + 522.03\ R_t^S -$$
$$[0.300] \qquad\qquad [0.123] \qquad [173.458] \qquad\qquad [178.896]$$

$$- 376.696\ E_{Lt}^{0.9} - 1.44\ (T_t^P + NIC_t) - 202.44t$$
$$[212.038] \qquad\quad [0.489] \qquad\qquad [50.858]$$

$$R^2 = 0.74 \quad VN = 2.73$$

6.8 Local Authority Debt: *Money Terms*

$$\Delta FA_{7t} = -0.0676\ FA_{7t-1} + 85.527\ R_t^S - 267.463\ E_{Lt}^{0.5} - 71.493\ RNSC_t +$$
$$[0.043] \qquad\qquad [31.748] \qquad [74.99] \qquad\qquad [26.867]$$

$$+ 0.08\ 139\ S_t$$
$$[0.065]$$

$$R^2 = 0.96 \quad VN = 2.11$$

6.9 Private Securities: *Money Terms*

$$[\Delta FA_{8t} + \Delta FA_{9t}] = -0.0712\ Y_{t-1}^P + 54.507\ R_t^O + 674.428\ E_{Lt}^{0.25} + 540.607\ PN_t$$
$$[0.0267] \qquad\quad [27.819] \qquad [468.816] \qquad\quad [473.032]$$

$$+ 0.211\ S_{t-1}$$
$$[0.158]$$

$$R^2 = 0.91 \quad VN = 2.36$$

6.10 Loans For House Purchase: *Money Terms*

$$\Delta HL_t = 0.0357\ Y_t^P + 0.5738\ RS_{1t} - 99.972\ [RM_t(1 - \delta_t G_t^{10})] - 0.1129\ S_t -$$
$$[0.0067] \qquad [0.2169] \qquad\quad [16.35] \qquad\qquad\qquad\qquad [0.055]$$

$$R^2 = 0.97 \quad VN = 1.80$$

6.11 Bank Borrowing: *Money Terms*

$$\Delta BL_t = -0.5021\ BL_{t-1} - 0.274\ Y_{t-1}^P - 82.4397\ BR_t + 0.3177\ Y_t^d +$$
$$[0.1494] \qquad\qquad [0.126] \qquad\quad [29.205] \qquad\quad [0.131]$$

$$+ 0.18\ [\Delta FA_{2t} + \Delta BD_t] + 43.214\ t$$
$$[0.166] \qquad\qquad\qquad\qquad [18.238]$$

$$R^2 = 0.67 \quad VN = 1.58$$

6.12 Total Non-Bank Borrowing: *Money Terms*

$$(\Delta HP + \Delta OL)_t = -0\cdot305\ HP_{t-1} - 0\cdot069\ Y_{t-1}^P - 4\cdot21\ \Delta HPC_t + 0\cdot082\ Y_t^d +$$
$$[0\cdot133] \qquad\quad [0\cdot031] \qquad\quad [0\cdot786] \qquad\quad [0\cdot032]$$
$$+\ 0\cdot130\ \Delta FA_{3t}$$
$$[0\cdot083]$$

$$R^2 = 0\cdot81 \quad VN = 1\cdot61$$

6.13 Investment in Dwellings: *Money Terms*

$$RS_{1t} = 0\cdot16\,176\ Y_t^P - 0\cdot2078\ Y_{t-1}^P + 559\cdot766\ RP_t + 0\cdot687\ \Delta HL_t + 0\cdot2569\ S_{t-1}$$
$$[0\cdot089] \qquad\quad [0\cdot104] \qquad\quad [196\cdot957] \qquad [0\cdot169] \qquad\quad [0\cdot0621]$$

$$R^2 = 0\cdot97 \quad VN = 1\cdot32$$

6.14 Investment in Consumer Durables: *Real Terms*

$$RS_{2t} = 0\cdot082\ Y_t^d - 351\cdot2\ PD_t + 0\cdot385\ [\Delta BL_t + \Delta HP_t] - 0\cdot267\ DU_{t-1}$$
$$[0\cdot015] \qquad [104\cdot2] \qquad\ [0\cdot039] \qquad\qquad\qquad\quad [0\cdot051]$$

$$R^2 = 0\cdot99 \quad VN = 2\cdot79$$

6.15 Hire Purchase: *Money Terms*

$$\Delta HP_t = -0\cdot316\ HP_{t-1} - 0\cdot077\ Y_{t-1}^P - 4\cdot631\ \Delta HPC_t + 0\cdot091\ Y_t^d + 0\cdot108\ \Delta FA_{3t}$$
$$[0\cdot14] \qquad\qquad [0\cdot034] \qquad\qquad [0\cdot823] \qquad\qquad [0\cdot034] \quad\ [0\cdot092]$$

$$R^2 = 0\cdot871 \quad VN = 1\cdot82$$

6.16 Other Fixed Capital Formation: *Money Terms*

$$RS_{3t} = 0\cdot072\ Y_t^d + 0\cdot124\ (\Delta BL_t + \Delta HP_t + \Delta OL_t) - 0\cdot279\ OFCF_{t-1}$$
$$[0\cdot003] \qquad [0\cdot007] \qquad\qquad\qquad\qquad\qquad\quad [0\cdot128]$$

$$R^2 = 0\cdot97 \quad VN = 1\cdot41$$

6.17 Inventory Investment: *Real Terms*

$$RS_{4t} = 0\cdot059\ \Delta Y_t^d + 0\cdot049\ \Delta BL_t - 0\cdot013\ NV_{t-1}$$
$$[0\cdot02] \qquad\quad [0\cdot039] \qquad\ [0\cdot011]$$

$$R^2 = 0\cdot83 \quad VN = 1\cdot92$$

6.18 Individual Premiums: *Money Terms*

$$[\Delta PR_{1t} + \Delta PR_{2t}] = 0\cdot247\ [Y_t^P \cdot R_t^{LA}] - 3\cdot94\ [PR_{1+2t-1} \cdot R_t^{LA}] - 0\cdot169\ [L_t \cdot R_t^{LA}]$$
$$[0\cdot123] \qquad\qquad [2\cdot11] \qquad\qquad\qquad\quad [0\cdot127]$$

$$R^2 = 0\cdot84 \quad VN = 1\cdot77$$

6.19 Employers' Contributions: *Money Terms*

$$PR_t^R = 0.932\ N_t + 1.03\ PR_{t-1}^R$$
$$[0.306] \qquad [0.014]$$

$$R^2 = 0.87 \quad VN = 1.85$$

6.20 Investment Income (Life Assurance): *Money Terms*

$$II_{1t} = 12.177 + 0.726\ [R_t^L\ .\ SLIF_t] + 5.381\ t$$
$$[11.186]\,[0.119] \qquad\qquad [4.034]$$

$$R^2 = 0.98 \quad VN = 1.20$$

6.21 Investment Income (Superannuation): *Money Terms*

$$II_{2t} = 22.506 + 0.592\ [R_t^L\ .\ SSUP_t] + 3.581\ t$$
$$[6.842]\ [0.106] \qquad\qquad [2.336]$$

$$R^2 = 0.98 \quad VN = 1.53$$

6.22 Outpayments (Life Assurance): *Money Terms*

$$OUP_{1t} = -591.8 + 0.103\ SLIF_t + 6.71\ SWLA_t$$
$$[293.3]\ [0.014] \qquad [3.36]$$

$$R^2 = 0.993 \quad VN = 1.73$$

6.23 Stock of Liquid Assets: *Money Terms*

$$L_t = \Delta L_t + L_{t-1}$$

$$= \sum_{i=3}^{5} \Delta FA_{it} + \sum_{i=3}^{5} FA_{it-1} + OLA_t$$

6.24 Personal Disposable Income: *Money Terms*

$$Y_t^d = W_t + OY_t - T_t^P - NIC_t$$

6.25 Income From Employment: *Money Terms* (Index: 1958 = 1)

$$[W_{(o)t}/O_{(o)t}] = 0.8738\ [W_{(o)t-1}/O_{(o)t-1}] - 0.412\ \hat{O}_t + 0.845\ \hat{O}_{t-1} +$$
$$[0.072] \qquad\qquad\qquad [0.187] \qquad [0.216]$$

$$+ 0.173\ PX_t - 0.0102\ U_t$$
$$[0.083] \qquad [0.011]$$

$$R^2 = 0.99 \quad VN = 2.04$$

6.26 The Price Index of Consumers' Expenditure: (Index: 1958 = 1)

$$PX_t = 0.804 \; [W_{(o)x}/O_{(o)t}] + 0.178 \; \hat{O}_t + 0.184 \; G_t^{EX}$$
$$\quad\quad [0.011] \quad\quad\quad\quad\quad\quad [0.104] \quad [0.009]$$

$$R^2 = 0.99 \quad VN = 1.66$$

6.27 Personal Income Taxation: *Money Terms*

$$\dot{T}_t^P = 0.22 \; \dot{W}_t + 0.22 \; O\dot{Y}_t - 16.149 \; \dot{G}_t^P - 41.54 \; \dot{G}_t^6 + 38.9 \; \dot{G}_t^R + 21.04 \; \dot{G}_t^{10} +$$
$$+ 8.4 \; \dot{G}_t^{11} - 16 \; \dot{t}$$

6.28 Employment

$$N_t = 11.9858 + 0.493 \; N_{t-1} + 6.511 \; \hat{O}_t + 0.0918 \; t$$
$$[3.974] \quad [0.169] \quad\quad [1.57] \quad\quad [0.028]$$

$$R^2 = 0.98 \quad VN = 1.74$$

6.29 Rate of Interest on Mortgage: *Percentage*

$$RM_t = 0.717 \; RM_{t-1} + 0.313 \; R_{t-1}^L + 1.253 \; \Delta RBS_t + 0.0003 \; \Delta HL_t$$
$$[0.081] \quad\quad\quad [0.093] \quad\quad\quad [0.15] \quad\quad\quad [0.00035]$$

$$+ 0.00014 \left[\sum_{i=2}^{3} FA_{it} + NIF_t + \Delta OBD_t \right]$$

$$[0.00007]$$

$$R^2 = 0.99 \quad VN = 2.15$$

6.30 Rate of Interest on Building Societies' Shares: *Percentage*

$$RBS_t = [0.61 \; R_t^S + 1.74 \; RR2_t] \; [1 - G_t^{BS}]$$
$$[0.069] \quad\quad [0.38]$$

$$R^2 = 0.99 \quad VN = 1.69$$

6.31 Rate of Interest on Building Societies' Deposits: *Percentage*

$$RBD_t = 0.69 \; RBS_t + 0.042 \; RR9_t$$
$$[0.04] \quad\quad\quad [0.014]$$

$$R^2 = 0.99 \quad VN = 1.46$$

6.32 Rate of Interest on National Savings Certificates: *Percentage*

$$RNSC_t = -3.59 + 0.259\ BR_t + 88.74\ RR1_t$$
$$[2.02]\quad [0.091]\qquad [30.19]$$

$$R^2 = 0.653 \quad VN = 1.79$$

6.33 Rate of Interest on T.S.B. deposits (Investment Accounts): *Percentage*

$$RTSB_t = 0.246\ RNSC_t + 1.13\ RR7_{t-1} + 0.745\ RTSB_{t-1}$$
$$[0.097]\qquad\quad [0.627]\qquad\quad [0.123]$$

$$R^2 = 0.982 \quad VN = 1.81$$

6.34 Rate of Interest on Short-dated Government Securities: *Percentage*

$$R_t^S = 16.35\ RR3_t + 13.0\ RR4_t - 33.9\ RR5_t + 0.274\ RTB_t - 2.76\ RR6_t$$
$$[8.39]\qquad\quad [5.57]\qquad\quad [32.6]\qquad\quad [0.212]\qquad\quad [2.4]$$

$$R^2 = 0.98 \quad VN = 1.29$$

6.35 Rate of Interest on long-dated Government Securities: *Percentage*

$$R_t^L = 7.77\ RR4_t + 2.73\ RR8_t + 0.00\,017 Y_t^d$$
$$[3.21]\qquad\quad [1.16]\qquad\quad [0.00\,002]$$

$$R^2 = 0.95 \quad VN = 1.42$$

6.36 Interest Rate Expectational Variables: *Percentage*

$$E_{Lt}^{0.25} = R_t^L - RN1_t$$
$$E_{Lt}^{0.5} = R_t^L - RN2_t$$
$$E_{Lt}^{0.9} = R_t^L - RN3_t$$

6.37 The Rate of Interest on Saving Deposits: *Percentage*

$$RSD_t = \sqrt[4]{RBS_t^2 \cdot RBD_t \cdot RTSB_t}$$

6.38 The Unidentified Item of the Personal Sector: *Money Terms*

$$UNIP_t = 0.708\ UNIP_{t-1} + 13.84\ t$$
$$[0.201]\qquad\qquad [11.07]$$

$$R^2 = 0.90 \quad VN = 2.28$$

6.39 Permanent Income: *Money Terms*

$$Y_t^P = -384.2345 + 0.20\,646\,Y_t^d + 0.88\,903\,Y_{t-1}^P$$
$$[171.468] \quad [0.1132] \quad\quad [0.1237]$$

$$R^2 = 0.99 \quad VN = 1.26$$

Endogenous Variables

S_t	Personal saving before providing for depreciation and stock appreciation, but adjusted for additions to tax reserves
ΔFA_{2t}	Net change in bank deposits
ΔFA_{1t}	Net change in notes and coins
ΔFA_{3t}	Net change in non-bank deposits
ΔFA_{4t}	Net change in National Savings Certificates (principal)
ΔFA_{5t}	Net change in other non-marketable government debt
ΔFA_{6t}	Net change in marketable government securities
ΔFA_{7t}	Net change in local authority debt
ΔFA_{8t}	Net change in company and overseas securities
ΔFA_{9t}	Net change in unit trust units
ΔHL_t	Net change in borrowing for house purchase
ΔBL_t	Net change in bank borrowing
ΔHP_t	Net change in hire purchase borrowing
ΔOL_t	Net change in other borrowing
ΔRS_{1t}	Investment in dwellings (new)
ΔRS_{2t}	Investment in consumer durables
ΔRS_{3t}	Other fixed capital formation by the personal sector
ΔRS_{4t}	Value of physical increase in stocks and work in progress
PR_{1t}	Individual premiums – Life Insurance
PR_{2t}	Individual premiums – Superannuation
OUP_{1t}	Outpayments by Life Insurance Companies
PR_t^R	Employers' contributions to Superannuation and Pension Funds
II_{1t}	Investment income – Life Insurance
II_{2t}	Investment income – Superannuation
$UNIP_t$	The unidentified item of the personal sector
L_t	Stock of liquid assets
RM_t	Building Societies' recommended mortgage rate
RBS_t	Net rate of interest on Building Societies' shares
R_t^S	Rate of interest on short-dated government securities
R_t^L	Rate of interest on long-dated government securities
$RNSC_t$	Rate of interest on National Savings Certificates
$RTSB_t$	Rate of interest on deposits with Trustee Savings Banks
RBD_t	Net rate of interest on Building Societies' deposits
PX_t	Price index of consumers' expenditure on goods and services (1958 = 1)
Y_t^d	Personal disposable income (net of income tax and National Insurance Contribution)
W_t	Income from employment

N_t	Total civil employment and H.M. Forces
T_t^P	Personal income taxation
E_{Lt}	Interest rate expectational variables – for three values of λ

Predetermined Variables

FA_{2t-1}	Stock of bank deposits – lagged one period
Y_{t-1}^P	Permanent income – lagged one period
S_{t-1}	Personal saving – lagged one period
$RN1_t$	Normal rate of interest ($\lambda = 0.25$)
t	A time trend variable
NIC_t	National Insurance Contributions
FA_{3t-1}	Stock of non-bank deposits – lagged one period
$RN3_t$	Normal rate of interest ($\lambda = 0.9$)
FA_{4t-1}	Stock of National Savings Certificates – lagged one period
$RN2_t$	Normal rate of interest ($\lambda = 0.55$)
FA_{5t-1}	Stock of non-marketable government debt – lagged one period
PN_t	An index of the normal price level ($\lambda = 0.5$)
PX_{t-1}	Price index of consumers' expenditure – lagged one period
FA_{6t-1}	Stock of government securities – lagged one period
FA_{7t-1}	Stock of local authority debt – lagged one period
R^O	F.T. dividend yield on ordinary industrial shares
BL_{t-1}	Stock of bank borrowing – lagged one period
G_t^{10}	Standard tax rate
δ_t	A proxy for tax concessions to owner-occupiers
ΔOBD_t	Non-personal bank deposits
BR_t	Bank rate
ΔHPC_t	Change in the percentage downpayments on the hire purchase of radio and electrical goods
HP_{t-1}	Stock of hire purchase borrowing – lagged one period
DU_{t-1}	Stock of consumer durables – lagged one period
OLA	Other liquid assets
$O_{(o)t-1}$	Index of output – lagged one period
$W_{(o)t-1}$	Income from employment [1958 = 1] – lagged one period
$OFCF_{t-1}$	Total capital stock other than in dwellings and in consumer durables – lagged one period
NV_{t-1}	Stock of inventories – lagged one period
Y_{t-1}^d	Personal disposable income – lagged one period
$SLIF_t$	Stock of Life Insurance funds
$SSUP_t$	Stock of Superannuation funds
R_t^{LA}	Rate of interest on Life Insurance savings
$SWLA_t$	An index of the share of whole life, endowment and other policies
PR_{t-1}^R	Employers' contributions – lagged one period
$\left.\begin{array}{l} PR_{1t-1} \\ PR_{2t-1} \end{array}\right\}$	Individual premiums to Life Insurance and Superannuation funds – lagged one period
G_t^{BS}	Building Societies' composite tax rate

TSB_{t-1}	Stock of deposits with Trustee Savings Banks (investment department) – lagged one period
PD_t	The price deflator of expenditure on consumer durables
$RR1_{t-1}$	Ratio of the stock of National Savings Certificates lagged one period to total national debt
$RR2_{t-1}$	Ratio of the stock of Building Societies' mortgages to the stock of Building Societies' shares and deposits – lagged one period
$\left.\begin{array}{l} RR3_t, \\ RR4_t, \\ RR8_t \end{array}\right\}$	Ratio of outstanding government securities up to 5 years, 3–15 years and over 15 years respectively to total national debt
$RR5_t$	Ratio of changes in gold and foreign reserves to total national debt
$RR7_{t-1}$	Ratio of the stock of Trustee Savings Banks' deposits to the stock of National Savings Certificates – lagged one period
$RR9_{t-1}$	Ratio of the stock of Building Societies' shares to the stock of Building Societies' deposits – lagged one period
$RR6_{t-1}$	Ratio of net total bank deposits to gross domestic product – lagged one period
$RTSB_{t-1}$	Rate of interest on T.S.B. deposits – lagged one period
$\hat{O}_t, \hat{O}_{t-1}$	Capacity utilization indices
U_t	Unemployment percentage
OY_t	Other income
N_{t-1}	Employment – lagged one period
RM_{t-1}	Mortgage rate – lagged one period
RBS_{t-1}	Rate of interest on Building Societies' shares – lagged one period
R^L_{t-1}	Rate of interest on long-dated government securities – lagged one period
OUP_{2t}	Outpayments – superannuation funds
ADM_t	Total administrative costs of Life Insurance and Superannuation Funds
CTX_t	Capital taxes
CTR_t	Capital transfers
STA_t	Stock appreciation
$UNIP_{t-1}$	The unidentified item of the personal sector – lagged one period
RTB_t	Treasury Bill Rate
RP_t	Ratio of rent to the price of an average house mortgage by Building Societies
$\dot{G}^P_t$	Change in aggregate family allowance rate
$\dot{G}^6_t$	Change in aggregate income relief rate
$\dot{G}^{11}_t$	Surtax rate
$\dot{G}^{EX}_t$	A Composite Tax rate index – outlay taxation
G^R_t	Change in aggregate reduced income tax rates
OD_t	Stock of other deposits with non-bank financial institutions

6.1.2 A BRIEF DISCUSSION OF THE MODEL

Most of the above equations have been discussed previously, with the exception of those determining the structure of interest rates, prices and wages, taxation and a number of *de facto* or empirical equations. These are discussed in the following:

Interest Rate Equations

Eleven interest rates entered the model explicitly; namely $R_t^L, R_t^S, RM_t, RBS_t, RBD_t,$ $RNSC_t, RTSB_t, BR_t, R_t^O, RTB_t,$ and R_t^{LA}. Seven were defined as endogenous; $R_t^L, R_t^S, RM_t, RBS_t, RBD_t, RNSC_t$ and $RTSB_t$, while the remaining four were regarded as exogeneous. Four of the seven interest rate equations – i.e. *RBS*, *RTSB*, *RBD* and *RNSC* – are merely technical relationships which are assumed to describe the way financial institutions fix their interest rates. As mentioned previously, R^{LA} serves as a proxy for the special tax treatment of Life Insurance saving. This rate was calculated in relation to the rate of interest on long-dated government securities, by means of equation (8) of Chapter 5. However, this latter equation (8) was not introduced explicitly into the model because of its strong non-linear form. Experiments with various specifications for the dividend yield R_t^O did not give any theoretically satisfactory answer. The exogeneity of the Bank Rate, BR_t, and the Treasury Bill rate in this study does not seem an unreasonable assumption.

This leaves three behavioural interest rate equations, one of them has already been discussed, i.e. RM_t, in Chapter 4. With respect to the rates of interest on government securities, a very simple specification was adopted. Following Okun,[164b] the level of both short and long rates of interest was related to money, income and the existing stocks of government securities of various maturities. The inclusion of the income variable was assumed by Okun to reflect private transactions demand for liquidity. He argued in favour of introducing a potential rather than an actual money variable on the grounds that using the latter does not provide an estimate of the way in which interest rates are affected by monetary policy. In this study no attempt was made to construct a potential money variable, and the ratio of total net deposits to gross domestic products, lagged one period, was tried instead. This variable did not yield a satisfactory estimate in the long-dated rate of interest equation.

The estimates obtained were – in general – statistically satisfactory. However, the exploratory nature of these specifications should be noted. Ideally the determination of these rates should be studied in a more realistic model in which the interactions of both lenders' and borrowers' preferences are appropriately specified. This involves, as a minimum requirement, an explicit presentation of the portfolio-selection decisions of the several economic groups, who are the major holders of both government and private securities. This task falls outside the terms of reference of this study.

Prices, Wages and Employment

1. Three price indices enter the model, either explicitly or as a result of estimating equations in real terms. These are: the price index of consumers' expenditure on goods and services, PX_t, the implicit price deflator of consumer durables, PD_t, and the price of an average house mortgaged by Building Societies, P_t.

The equation for the price index of consumers' expenditure, PX_t, is theoretically based on a specification similar (but not identical) to the one developed by Bain and El-Mokadem.[3d] Thus, it is assumed that post-war inflationary pressure in the United Kingdom was caused mainly by wage increases. The index of income from employment per unit of output is used as a proxy for the latter. In addition, two more variables are assumed to exert some influence on the price level; namely the level of capacity utilisation, $\hat{O}_t$, and a composite outlay taxation rate G_t^{EX}. The former — which is used as a proxy for demand pressure — is calculated as the difference between the level of output (1958 = 1) and its trend value.[3d] The latter, G_t^{EX}, is calculated as follows:

$$G_t^{EX} = [T_t^* / TE_t^*] \tag{1.a}$$

where T_t^* is the budget estimate of the outlay tax revenue expected as a result of changing the tax structure and TE_t^* is the outlay tax revenue, assuming no changes in outlay tax rates and definitions from the base year rates and definitions. TE_t^* is given by:

$$TE_t^* = TE_t \pm d_{t-1} [TE_t/T_{t-1}^*] \pm \ldots \pm d_0 [TE_t/T_0^*] \tag{1.b}$$

where TE_t is the budget estimate of outlay taxation revenue at the existing $(t-1)$ base and d_t is the budget estimate of the effect on the outlay tax revenue of changing the tax structure. G_t^{EX} may be regarded as a proxy summarising the outlay tax structure at time t relative to base year.*

With respect to P_t and PD_t similar specifications were attempted, but the results obtained, though statistically satisfactory, did not conform with *a priori* expectations. Estimated coefficients had the wrong *a priori* signs. Alternative specifications were also tried, but proved unsuccessful. Failing to obtain any satisfactory results, it was decided to define both P_t and PD_t as exogenous.

2. The equations for employment and income from employment are both based on similar (more simplified) considerations to the ones suggested by Bain and El-Mokadem.[3d] Thus, in determining the short-term employment function the labour force may be regarded as a 'quasi-fixed' factor of production, and hence labour inputs will be governed by considerations similar to those which determine changes in capital stock, and will not respond instantaneously to changes in output and demand. This is because the costs of hiring and firing can be sufficiently important to rule out instantaneous adjustment in the short-run. Producers will not generally react to small fluctuations in output by hiring or laying off labour because the short-term costs of maintaining the same labour force are relatively low. But if the situation persists or if producers are faced with large changes in output they will be forced to alter their labour force because the cumulative cost of maintaining too large, or too small, a labour force becomes so substantial that adjustment costs are relatively unimportant. This suggests that both the level of employment lagged one period and the level of

---

* Let T_t^* and TE_t^* be defined, approximately, as follows:

$$T_t^* = R_t^* \text{ (Tax base)}_t \qquad TE_t^* = R_{(o)}^* \text{ (Tax base)}_t$$

where R_t and $R_{(o)}$ are composite rates at time t and base year respectively.

Substituting in (1.a) we have:

$$G_t^{EX} = [R_t^* \text{ (Tax base)}_t]/[R_{(o)}^* \text{ (Tax base)}_t] = R_t/R_{(o)}$$

$$\text{For } R_{(o)} = 1, \ R_t = G_t^{EX}$$

capacity utilisation determine the current level of employment. As suggested by Ball and St. Cyr, a time trend is also included to represent technological change.[7]

The income from employment equation is similar to equation (16) of Bain and El-Mokadem in that they are both reduced forms of a structural model consisting of three equations: determining employment, hours worked and wage rate. However, they differ in two respects. Our equation is linear, while equation (16) of Bain and El-Mokadem is loglinear. Also in the latter, the actual levels of employment, hours and wage rate are determined in relation to their respective full-employment levels. In this study we opted for a simpler specification for the sake of limiting the size of the model.

The Income Tax Equations

In this study, the revenue from personal income taxes at any point in time t is treated as an endogenous variable, while — for simplicity — the revenue from capital taxes and National Insurance contributions, and the *expected* (budget estimate) revenue from outlay taxation, T_t^*, are all defined as exogenous variables. The exogeneity assumption may be acceptable with respect to the *expected* (not the realized) revenue from outlay taxation which may be regarded as under the control of the government, but it is difficult to justify insofar as the revenue from National Insurance contributions is concerned. This is because employement, N_t, and income from employment, W_t, — upon which the revenue from National Insurance contributions depends — are both endogenously determined in this study. The treatment of capital taxes' revenue as exogenous may have some effect on the reduced form parameters of at least two variables; namely the bank rate, BR_t, and the time trend, t. This will be the case if we accept Balopoulos' simple model, according to which the revenue from capital taxes is assumed to depend on the bank rate and a time trend variable. The former was chosen by Balopoulos on the grounds that 'the current money value of both personality and reality is affected by current values of the rate of interest'[8] (p. 121), while the latter (the time trend variable) is acting as a proxy for the 'real value as well as the distribution of real wealth passing on death'[8] (p. 121).

Balopoulos' model of personal income taxation[8] is used in this study. According to this model, the aggregate personal tax liability function depends on three groups of factors:

1. The tax structure: tax definitions, rates and allowances which form the complete set of Government action parameters.
2. The tax bases: the set of variables upon which instruments of tax policy operate.
3. Probability density functions: statistical functions describing the distributions of taxpayers according to several characteristics.

In *this chapter*, we incorporate *Balopoulos' equation* into the model (equation 6.27), because it enables us to show the effects of most of the instruments of income tax policy on aggregate personal saving and its composition by means of genuine rather than composite parameters. However, in *the next chapter* Balopoulos' equation is dropped and a *simpler* specification based on *the same theoretical model* is used instead, on the grounds that the predictive power of the model might be seriously affected by the differences — in the data used, the method of estimation and the degree of non-linearity — between Balopoulos' equation and the present model.

The de facto Equations

To connect the 'loose ends', only two *de facto* equations are included in the present model. One, equation 6.38, was unavoidable for two reasons: firstly because of the definition of aggregate personal saving adopted in equation 6.1 which implicitly accepts the income account estimate of personal saving, and secondly because of the failure to reach any conclusion in a thorough statistical analysis which was carried out of the unidentified item of the personal sector.* The permanent income equation, 6.39, was included so that a study of the incidental effects of income taxation — via the level of disposable income — on aggregate personal saving and its composition can be made.

6.1.3 THE ADEQUACY OF THE MODEL

Each equation of the model has been examined in the previous chapters as such in relation to the economic, statistical and econometric criteria. Before proceeding with the derivation of the reduced form of the alternative model, it is important to see how satisfactory the model is as a whole. Of course, a complete answer depends on the results of examining the reduced form matrix, as well as on the forecasting performance of the model. These are examined later. In this sub-section a summary of the whole model in relation to the first and the second order tests is given. A comparison is also made with the Klein—Ball model and the Klein—Goldberger model.† The results are given in *Tables Ade. 1* and *Ade. 2.*

In the light of the above statistics, it is clear that the model compares well with other models, and to this extent may be regarded as satisfactory. However, one must warn against mechanical and exclusive reliability on these tests. Other subsidiary statistical and economic considerations should be taken into account.

6.2 DERIVATION OF THE REDUCED FORM OF THE ALTERNATIVE MODEL

For the purpose of deriving the reduced form, the structural model has first been linearized at the sample means of the variables using the method suggested by Goldberger.[73a]

* For description of the statistical analysis and the results see the author's Ph.D. thesis 'A Study of Personal Saving in the United Kingdom 1946–1966', University of Manchester, December 1969.

† The relevant statistics for the Klein—Ball and the Klein—Goldberger models are taken from Agarwala[1] (pp. 129–131).

Table Ade. 1 THE ADEQUACY OF THE MODEL: FIRST ORDER TEST

Coefficients	Values of t in the range				
	Below 1	1–1.99	2–2.99	3 –	Total
1. AMEM No.	2	37	44	49	132
%	(1·5)	(28·0)	(33·4)	(37·1)	(100·0)
2. K–B No.	41	30	20	72	163
%	(25·1)	(18·4)	(12·3)	(44·2)	(100·0)
3. K–G No.	2	11	6	17	36
%	(5·6)	(30·6)	(16·7)	(47·1)	(100·0)

Equations	Values of R^2 in the range					
	Below 0·75	0·75–0·79	0·80–0·89	0·90–0·99	0·99–	Total
1. AMEM No.	4	2	6	13	8	33
%	(12·1)	(6·1)	(18·2)	(39·4)	(24·2)	(100·0)
2. K–B No.	3	0	6	18	5	32
%	(9·4)	(0)	(18·8)	(56·2)	(15·6)	(100·0)

Notes

AMEM Present study.
K–B   Klein–Ball.
K–G   Klein–Goldberger.

Table Ade. 2 THE ADEQUACY OF THE MODEL: SECOND ORDER TEST

Equations	The hypothesis of zero auto-correlation is accepted at:		The hypothesis rejected at either level	Total
	5% level	1% level		
1. AMEM				
No.	30	3	0	33
%	(90·9)	(9·1)	(0)	(100)
2. K–B				
No.	10	5	17	32
%	(31·3)	(15·6)	(53·1)	(100·0)
3. K–G				
No.	10	1	3	14
%	(71·5)	(7·1)	(21·4)	(100·0)

Proceeding formally, let the model be written in matrix form as:

$$BY + rX = 0$$

where B is the matrix of coefficients of the endogenous variables, and r is the matrix of coefficients of the predetermined variables, and Y and X are column vectors of endogenous and exogenous variables respectively. The matrix of reduced form coefficients π is given by:

$$\pi = -B^{-1}r$$

The results obtained are shown for aggregate personal saving and its composition in *Table π.1*. Before the detailed analysis of the results is given, several preliminary comments are in order.

1. The reduced form coefficients are impact multipliers measuring the total marginal effect of a unit change in a predetermined variable on each endogenous variable, conditional on other pre-determined variables remaining constant.

It should be noted, however, that because of the existence of many lagged variables in the model, the impact multipliers vary over time and the effect over a longer time span may be considerably different from that reported in the complete model table. Also, some of the predetermined variables are lagged endogenous variables which imply that, in a sense, the calculation has not gone back to ultimate determinants. These multipliers should, therefore, be regarded as initial rather than equilibrium multipliers. In order to derive the latter, the dynamic multipliers may be estimated. These, however, were not estimated in this study.

2. The calculated impact multipliers do not provide a measure of the relative contributions of the predetermined variables in explaining the variations, through time, of the endogenous variables. This depends not only on the magnitude of the multipliers but also on the relative variations of the variables.

3. These impact multipliers should be interpreted with considerable care.

Table π.1 AGGREGATE PERSONAL SAVING AND ITS COMPOSITION: A REDUCED FORM ANALYSIS

End. \ Exog.	$\dot{F}A_{2t-1}$	$\dot{F}A_{3t-1}$	$\dot{F}A_{4t-1}$	$\dot{F}A_{5t-1}$	$\dot{F}A_{6t-1}$	$\dot{F}A_{7t-1}$	$\dot{B}L_{t-1}$	$\dot{H}P_{t-1}$	$\dot{D}U_{t-1}$	$\dot{O}\dot{F}\dot{C}F_{t-1}$
	10^{-4}	10^{-4}	10^{-4}	10^{-4}	10^{-4}	10^{-4}	10^{-4}	10^{-4}	10^{-4}	10^{-4}
$\Delta\dot{F}A_{1\div2t}$	−4 066	0	0	0	0	0	0	0	0	0
$\Delta\dot{F}A_{3t}$	0	−1 145	0	0	0	0	0	0	0	0
$\Delta\dot{F}A_{4t}$	0	0	−1 220	0	0	0	0	0	0	0
$\Delta\dot{F}A_{5t}$	0	0	0	−1 320	0	0	0	0	0	0
$\Delta\dot{F}A_{6t}$	−331	−105	−119	−128	−9 370	0	0	0	0	0
$\Delta\dot{F}A_{7t}$	0	0	0	0	−830	−736	197	131	−244	−247
$\Delta\dot{F}A_{8\div9t}$	−46	−16	−2	−2	0	0	0	0	0	0
$\Delta\dot{H}L_t$	−685	0	0	0	0	0	0	0	0	0
$\Delta\dot{B}L_t$	0	0	0	0	0	0	−5 021	0	0	0
$(\Delta\dot{H}P + \Delta\dot{O}L)_t$	0	−149	0	0	0	0	0	−3 050	0	0
Financial Assets	−3 066	−1 085	−1 337	−1 446	−10 200	−736	5 218	3 181	−244	−247
$\dot{R}S_{1t}$	−32	−11	−1	−1	0	0	0	0	0	0
$\dot{R}S_{2t}$	−262	−47	0	0	0	0	−1 923	−1 187	−2 748	0
$\dot{R}S_{3t}$	−85	−18	0	0	0	0	−623	−378	0	−2 790
$\dot{R}S_{4t}$	−34	0	0	0	0	0	−246	0	0	0
Real Assets	−413	−76	−1	−1	0	0	−2 792	−1 565	−2 748	−2 790
$\dot{P}R_{1\div2t}$	0	0	0	0	0	0	0	0	0	0
$\dot{I}I_{1\div2t}$	0	−124	−123	−122	0	0	0	0	0	0
$N\dot{I}F_t$	0	−124	−123	−122	0	0	0	0	0	0
$UN\dot{I}P_t$	0	0	0	0	0	0	0	0	0	0
$\hat{S}_t$	−4 079	−1 285	−1 461	−1 569	−10 200	−736	2 426	1 616	−2 992	−3 037

Table π.1.1 A REDUCED FORM OF THE AGGREGATE (CONVENTIONAL) MODEL

	$\dot{F}A_{2t-1}$	$\dot{F}A_{3t-1}$	$\dot{F}A_{4t-1}$	$\dot{F}A_{5t-1}$	$\dot{F}A_{6t-1}$	$\dot{F}A_{7t-1}$	$\dot{B}L_{t-1}$	$\dot{H}P_{t-1}$	$\dot{D}U_{t-1}$	$\dot{O}\dot{F}\dot{C}F_{t-1}$
$\hat{S}^C_t$	0	−402	−387	−366	0	0	0	0	0	0

Table π. 1 (cont.)

End. \ Exog.	NV_{t-1}	$SLIF_t$	$SSUP_t$	PR_{1+2t-1}	PR_{t-1}^R	ΔOD_t	Y_{t-1}^P	S_{t-1}	NIC_t	G_t^{BS}	S_t
	10^{-4}	10^{-4}	10^{-4}	10^{-4}	10^{-4}	10^{-4}	10^{-4}	10^{-4}	10^{-4}	10^{-4}	10^{-4}
ΔFA_{1+2t}	0	0	0	0	0	0	2090	-3644	2458	76462	0
ΔFA_{3t}	0	0	0	0	0	0	682	-1709	-8	-99683	0
ΔFA_{4t}	0	0	0	0	0	0	97	-1281	161	38037	0
ΔFA_{5t}	0	0	0	0	0	0	73	0	-17	0	0
ΔFA_{6t}	-12	125	28	589	909	13	3423	0	-14616	0	-1047
ΔFA_{7t}	0	0	0	0	0	0	568	-151	-1527	164	0
ΔFA_{8+9t}	0	17	4	0	125	2	-627	2108	-997	0	3.739
ΔHL_t	0	0	0	0	0	0	-68	492	-508	51485	0
ΔBL_t	0	0	0	80	0	0	-2412	-531	-2731	11239	0
$(\Delta HP + \Delta OL)_t$							-597	-223	-828	-13009	
Financial Assets	-12	108	24	509	784	11	9383	-4413	-10479	-34735	-38786
RS_{1t}	0	12	3	56	86	1	-702	2907	-689	35370	25927
RS_{2t}	0	0	0	0	0	0	-1190	-274	-2216	181	0
RS_{3t}	-133	0	0	0	0	0	-373	-94	-1160	-218	0
RS_{4t}							-118	-26	-724	551	0
Real Assets	-133	12	3	56	86	1	-2383	2513	-4789	35882	25927
PR_{1+2t}	0	388	316	0	0	0	0	0	-9075	0	0
$\grave{I}_{1+2t}$	0	0	0	6668	0	140	-12	42	-2	863	0
NIF_t	0	1418	316	6668	10300	140	-12	42	-9077	863	0
$UNIP_t$	0	0	0	0	0	0	0	0	0	0	0
S_t	-145	1538	343	7231	11170	152	6988	-1860	-24345	2010	-12859

Table π. 1.1 (cont.)

	NV_{t-1}	$SLIF_t$	$SSUP_t$	PR_{1+2t-1}	PR_{t-1}^R	ΔOD_t	Y_{t-1}^P	S_{t-1}	NIC_t	G_t^{BS}	S_t
S_t^C	0	0	0	0	0	2050	-175	615	-3972	14536	0

Table π. 1 (cont.)

End. \ Exog.	G_t^{10}	$\Delta O\dot{B}D_t$	Y_{t-1}^{rd}	$C\dot{T}X_t$	$C\dot{T}R_t$	$O\dot{U}P_{2t}$	$\dot{B}R_t$	$R\dot{T}B_t$	$R\dot{N}1_t$	$R\dot{N}2_t$
	10^{-4}	10^{-4}	10^{-4}	10^{-4}	10^{-4}	10^{-4}	10^{-4}	10^{-4}	10^{-4}	10^{-4}
$\Delta F\dot{A}_{1+2t}$	51 725	0	0	0	0	0	−53 423	−275 199	14 461 400	0
$\Delta F\dot{A}_{3t}$	−161	0	0	0	0	0	−1 048 114	358 778	0	0
$\Delta F\dot{A}_{4t}$	3 388	0	0	0	0	0	366 341	−136 902	0	1 084 000
$\Delta F\dot{A}_{5t}$	−367	0	0	0	0	0	141 421	0	0	0
$\Delta F\dot{A}_{6t}$	−307 525	−74	−52	886	−886	−883	−546 897	1 430 381	575 051	0
$\Delta F\dot{A}_{7t}$	−33 128	0	0	0	0	0	−262 095	381 272	−6 744 280	911 166
$\Delta F\dot{A}_{8+9t}$	−20 977	122	0	0	0	−122	0	0	178 937	0
$\Delta H\dot{L}_t$	39 477	1 803	0	0	0	0	−13 254	−185 304	2 638 871	−185
$\Delta B\dot{L}_t$	−57 468	0	0	0	0	0	−832 252	−40 450	0	0
$(\Delta \dot{H}P + \Delta \dot{O}L)_t$	−17 421	0	0	0	0	0	−136 779	46 821	0	0
Financial Assets	−271 633	−1 999	−52	886	−886	−761	−420 482	1 937 263	5 474 363	1 995 351
$R\dot{S}_{1t}$	19 976	85	0	0	0	−83	−9 106	−127 304	122 929	−128
$R\dot{S}_{2t}$	−46 634	691	0	0	0	0	−362 103	−653	1 010 687	0
$R\dot{S}_{3t}$	−24 435	224	0	0	0	0	−120 160	790	327 221	0
$R\dot{S}_{4t}$	−15 229	88	−590	0	0	0	−40 780	−1 982	129 305	0
Real Assets	−66 322	1 088	−590	0	0	−83	−535 066	−129 149	1 590 142	−128
$P\dot{R}_{1+2t}$	−190 933	0	0	0	0	0	0	0	0	0
$\dot{I}_{1+2t}$	4 378	0	0	0	0	0	7 565	−3 106	0	−15 176
$N\dot{I}F_t$	−186 555	0	0	0	0	0	7 565	−3 106	0	−15 176
$U\dot{N}\dot{I}P_t$	0	0	0	10 000	−10 000	−10 000	0	0	0	0
$\dot{S}_t$	−524 510	−913	642	10 886	−10 886	−10 844	−945 066	1 805 008	7 064 505	1 980 047

Table π.1.1 (cont.)

	G_t^{10}	$\Delta O\dot{B}D_t$	Y_{t-1}^{rd}	$C\dot{T}X_t$	$C\dot{T}R_t$	$O\dot{U}P_{2t}$	$\dot{B}R_t$	$R\dot{T}B_t$	$R\dot{N}1_t$	$R\dot{N}2_t$
$\dot{S}_t^c$	−83 571	0	−2 412	0	0	0	110 772	−45 478	0	222 220

Table π. 1 (cont.)

End. \ Exog.	$RN3_t$	$\dot{R}_t^O$	$\dot{R}P_t$	$\Delta H\dot{P}C_t$	$P\dot{X}_{t-1}$	$P\dot{N}_t$	$P\dot{D}_t$	$\dot{R}_t^{LA}$	$A\dot{D}M_t$	$S\dot{W}LA_t$
	10^{-4}	10^{-4}	10^{-4}	10^{-4}	10^{-4}	10^{-4}	10^{-4}	10^{-4}	10^{-4}	10^{-4}
$\Delta F\dot{A}_{1\div2t}$	0	0	0	0	-7 399 000	0	0	0	0	0
$\Delta F\dot{A}_{3t}$	912 250	0	0	0	9 417 100	0	0	0	0	0
$\Delta F\dot{A}_{4t}$	0	0	0	0	0	0	0	0	0	0
$\Delta F\dot{A}_{5t}$	0	0	0	0	0	28 840 500	0	0	0	0
$\Delta F\dot{A}_{6t}$	3 766 960	48 300	354 822	1 698	876 881	2 999 056	-311 209	407 429	-883	5 923
$\Delta F\dot{A}_{7t}$	407 305	545 070	0	0	0	5 406 100	0	0	0	0
$\Delta F\dot{A}_{8\div9t}$	0	0	5 091 001	0	164 257	-4 934	0	56 428	-122	820
$\Delta H\dot{L}_t$	10 997	0	0	0	748 245	0	0	0	0	0
$\Delta B\dot{L}_t$	0	0	0	0	1 228 932	0	0	0	0	0
$(\Delta H\dot{P}+\Delta \dot{OL})_t$	119 049	0	0	-42 120			0	0	0	0
Financial Assets	4 956 469	593 370	-4 736 179	43 818	753 547	37 240 722	-311 209	351 001	-761	5 103
$R\dot{S}_{1t}$	7 555	0	9 095 177	0	112 844	-3 391	0	38 766	-84	564
$R\dot{S}_{2t}$	37 731	0	0	-17 737	9 688 299	0	-3 512 000	0	0	0
$R\dot{S}_{3t}$	14 762	0	0	-5 223	24 570	0	0	0	0	0
$R\dot{S}_{4t}$	0	0	0	0	304 474	0	0	0	0	0
Real Assets	60 048	0	9 095 177	-22 960	10 130 187	-3 391	-3 512 000	38 766	-84	564
$P\dot{R}_{1\div2t}$	0	0	0	0	0		0	0	0	0
$\dot{\Pi}_{1\div2t}$	-12 771	0	0	0	-131 839	-403 767	0	4 615 500	0	0
$N\dot{F}F_t$	-12 771	0	0	0	-131 839	-403 767	0	4 615 500	-10 000	67 100
$UN\dot{I}P_t$	0	0	0	0	0	0	0	0	0	0
$\dot{S}_t$	5 003 746	593 370	4 358 998	20 858	10 772 495	36 843 434	-3 823 209	5 005 267	-10 845	72 767

Table π. 1.1 (cont.)

	$RN3_t$	$\dot{R}_t^O$	$\dot{R}P_t$	$\Delta H\dot{P}C_t$	$P\dot{X}_{t-1}$	$P\dot{N}_t$	$P\dot{D}_t$	$\dot{R}_t^{LA}$	$A\dot{D}M_t$	$S\dot{W}LA_t$
$\dot{S}_t^C$	187 011	0	0	0	91 605 494	-5 912 323	0	0	0	0

Table π. 1 (cont.)

End. \ Exog.	RM_{t-1} 10^{-4}	$\hat{R}^L_{t-1}$ 10^{-4}	$R\hat{B}S_{t-1}$ 10^{-4}	$R\hat{T}SB_{t-1}$ 10^{-4}	$\hat{\dot{O}}_t$ 10^{-4}	$\hat{W}_{t-1}$ 10^{-4}	$\hat{N}_{t-1}$ 10^{-4}	$\dot{G}^{EX}_t$ 10^{-4}	$\dot{R}R1_t$ 10^{-2}
$\Delta\dot{F}A_{1+2t}$	0	0	0	-624 665	-573 051	-1 021	0	4 219 998	-183 040
$\Delta\dot{F}A_{3t}$	0	0	0	814 374	-4 210 106	-458	0	-2 184 681	-3 591 105
$\Delta\dot{F}A_{4t}$	0	0	0	0	-643 790	-133	0	-36 139	1 255 176
$\Delta\dot{F}A_{5t}$	0	0	0	0	-10 834 581	-1 179	0	-5 617 986	484 546
$\Delta\dot{F}A_{6t}$	0	0	-42 488	0	-15 577 739	-3 225	0	-874 459	-1 873 807
$\Delta\dot{F}A_{7t}$	24 313	10 614	0	14048	-1 268 900	-182	405	-458 222	-1 009 136
$\Delta\dot{F}A_{8+9t}$	-876 589	0	1 531 892	0	3 985 815	825	0	223 744	0
$\Delta\dot{H}L_t$	0	-382 667	0	3 591	2 089 026	427	56	141 786	-45 412
$\Delta\dot{B}L_t$	0	0	0	-91 816	12 434 186	2 426	0	1 393 911	-26 904
$(\Delta\dot{H}P + \Delta\dot{O}L)_t$	0	0	0	106 276	2 756 744	625	0	-99 510	-468 640
Financial Assets	900 902	393 281	-1 574 380	185 706	-46 402 308	-8 851	349	-6 163 932	-4 376 410
$R\dot{S}_{1t}$	-602 217	-262 892	1 052 410	2 467	2 792 686	574	38	173 612	-31 198
$R\dot{S}_{2t}$	0	0	0	-1 483	5 955 704	1 516	0	-1 000 380	-158 832
$R\dot{S}_{3t}$	0	0	0	1 793	4 762 076	974	0	322 085	-61 447
$R\dot{S}_{4t}$	0	0	0	-4 499	2 837 307	594	0	133 344	-1 318
Real Assets	-602 217	-262 892	1 052 410	-1 722	16 347 773	3 658	38	-371 339	-252 795
$P\dot{R}_{1+2t}$	0	0	0	0	36 278 916	7 511	0	2 036 523	0
$\dot{I}_{1+2t}$	0	0	0	-11 401	456 430	73	0	123 036	25 919
$N\dot{F}F_t$	0	0	0	-11 401	36 795 900	7 584	4 586	2 159 559	25 919
$UN\hat{I}P_t$	0	0	0	0	0	0	0	0	0
$\dot{S}_t$	298 685	130 389	-521 970	172 583	6 741 365	2 391	4 973	-4 375 712	-4 603 286

Table π. 1.1 (cont.)

	RM_{t-1} 10^{-4}	$\hat{R}^L_{t-1}$ 10^{-4}	$R\hat{B}S_{t-1}$ 10^{-4}	$R\hat{T}SB_{t-1}$ 10^{-4}	$\hat{\dot{O}}_t$ 10^{-4}	$\hat{W}_{t-1}$ 10^{-4}	$\hat{N}_{t-1}$ 10^{-4}	$\dot{G}^{EX}_t$ 10^{-4}	$\dot{R}R1_t$ 10^{-2}
$\dot{S}^C_t$	0	0	0	-166 947	-13 615 665	-496	0	-16 372 079	379 533

Table π.1 (cont.)

Exog. / End.	$R\dot{R}2_t$ 10^{-4}	$S\dot{T}A_t$ 10^{-4}	$R\dot{R}3_t$ 10^{-2}	$R\dot{R}4_t$ 10^{-2}	$R\dot{R}5_t$ 10^{-2}	$R\dot{R}6_t$ 10^{-2}	$R\dot{R}7_t$ 10^{-2}	$R\dot{R}8_t$ 10^{-2}	$R\dot{R}9_t$ 10^{-4}
$\Delta\dot{FA}_{1+2t}$	−2 873 512	0	−164 215	1 254 220	340 483	27 721	−9 475	−394 796	−53 762
$\Delta\dot{FA}_{3t}$	3 746 213	0	214 088	99 341	−443 890	−36 140	12 352	−24 904	69 959
$\Delta\dot{FA}_{4t}$	−1 429 477	0	−81 692	−149 163	169 379	13 790	0	−29 587	0
$\Delta\dot{FA}_{5t}$	0	0	0	0	0	0	0	0	0
$\Delta\dot{FA}_{6t}$	0	0	853 530	385 954	−1 769 705	−144 082	0	−102 838	0
$\Delta\dot{FA}_{7t}$	−6 148	8 861	227 511	237 109	−471 719	−38 405	214	19 751	1 207
$\Delta\dot{FA}_{8+9t}$	0	0	0	524 031	0	0	0	−184 119	0
$\Delta\dot{HL}_t$	−1 934 865	0	−110 574	−51 953	229 263	18 666	54·47	12 636	308
$\Delta\dot{BL}_t$	−422 362	0	−24 137	−224 236	50 046	4 074	−1 393	−72 043	−7 888
$(\Delta\dot{HP}+\Delta\dot{OL})_t$	488 881	0	27 938	12 964	−57 928	−4 716	1 612	−3 250	9 130
Financial Assets	1 305 422	8 861	1 155 995	2 614 717	−2 396 833	−195 140	2 817·53	−653 836	15 854
$R\dot{S}_{1t}$	−1 329 253	0	−75 964	−35 691	157 504	12 823	37·42	8 681	212
$R\dot{S}_{2t}$	−6 821	0	390	−81 774	808	65·80	−22·49	−28 622	−127
$R\dot{S}_{3t}$	8 248	0	471	−26 198	−977	−79·57	27·20	−9 336	154
$R\dot{S}_{4t}$	−20 696	0	−1 183	−10 988	2 452	199	−68·24	−3 530	−386
Real Assets	−1 348 522	0	−76 286	−154 651	159 787	13 008	−26·11	−32 807	−147
$P\dot{R}_{1+2t}$	0	0	0	4 147 704	0	0	0	1 457 301	0
$\dot{I1}_{1+2t}$	−32 434	0	−1 854	697	3 843	313	−173	763	−979
$N\dot{IF}_t$	−32 434	0	−1 854	4 148 401	3 843	313	−173	1 458 064	−979
$U\dot{NIP}_t$	0	0	0	0	0	0	0	0	0
$\dot{S}_t$	−75 534	10 886	1 077 855	6 608 467	−2 233 203	−181 819	2 618	771 421	14 720

Table π.1.1 (cont.)

	$R\dot{R}2_t$	$S\dot{T}A_t$	$R\dot{R}3_t$	$R\dot{R}4_t$	$R\dot{R}5_t$	$R\dot{R}6_t$	$R\dot{R}7_t$	$R\dot{R}8_t$	$R\dot{R}9_t$
$\dot{S}_t^c$	−474 860	0	−27 137	10 217	56 266	4 581	−2 532	11 171	−14 342

Table π.1 (*cont.*)

Exog. / End.	i 10^{-4}	$\dot{U}_t$ 10^{-4}	$\dot{O}Y_t$ 10^{-4}	G^P_t 10^{-4}	G^6_t 10^{-4}	G^R_t 10^{-4}	G^{11}_t 10^{-4}	$UNIP_{t-1}$ 10^{-4}
ΔFA_{1+2t}	-39 335	25 995	-1 918	-39 701	-102 123	95 633	20 651	0
ΔFA_{3t}	123	146 071	0	124	318	-298	-64	0
ΔFA_{4t}	-2 577	42 525	-126	-2 601	-6 690	6 264	1 353	0
ΔFA_{5t}	279	376 197	14	281	724	-678	-146	0
ΔFA_{6t}	-1 790 540	1 028 987	-3 039	236 037	607 158	-568 571	-122 776	0
ΔFA_{7t}	-176 369	57 974	-84	24 360	62 662	-58 680	-12 671	-627
ΔFA_{8+9t}	15 952	-263 283	778	16 101	41 416	-38 784	-8 375	0
ΔHL_t	9 209	-136 277	397	8 166	21 007	-19 672	-4 248	0
ΔBL_t	473 902	-774 182	2 130	44 109	113 462	-106 251	-22 944	0
$(\Delta HP + \Delta\dot{O}L)_t$	13 248	-199 326	646	13 371	34 395	-32 209	-6 955	0
Financial Assets	-2 488 826	2 824 251	-7 548	168 955	434 601	-406 982	-87 881	-627
$\dot{R}S_{1t}$	11 760	-183 294	538	11 094	28 537	-26 724	-5 771	0
$\dot{R}S_{2t}$	200 230	-483 848	1 729	35 793	92 071	-86 219	-18 618	0
$\dot{R}S_{3t}$	71 927	-310 848	906	18 755	48 243	-45 177	-9 756	0
$\dot{R}S_{4t}$	32 661	-189 175	565	11 689	30 068	-28 157	-6 080	0
Real Assets	316 578	-1 167 165	3 738	77 331	198 919	-186 277	-40 225	0
$P\dot{R}_{1+2t}$	235 816	-2 396 403	7 078	146 549	376 966	-353 009	-76 228	0
$\dot{I}_{1+2t}$	-3 329	-23 548	48	-3 361	-8 644	8 095	1 748	0
$N\dot{I}F_t$	233 324	-2 419 951	7 126	143 188	368 322	-344 914	-74 480	0
$UN\dot{I}P_t$	138 400	0	0	0	0	0	0	7 080
$\dot{S}_t$	-1 938 924	-762 865	3 316	389 474	1 001 842	-938 173	-202 586	-7 707

							OD_{t-1} 10^{-4}
							637

Table π.1.1

	i	$\dot{U}_t$	$\dot{O}Y_t$	G^P_t	G^6_t	G^R_t	G^{11}_t	$UNIP_{t-1}$
$\dot{S}^C_t$	63 552	158 317	3 972	64 144	164 998	-154 512	-33 365	0

First, most of the structural equations have been estimated by means of ordinary least squares. This means that the estimated coefficients are biased and also inconsistent. Owing to the formidable computational burden, plus the usual difficulty of choosing the predetermined variables to be used in the first stage of the estimation, no attempt was made to re-estimate the model using simultaneous methods of estimation. Secondly, there is also the possibility of cross-section bias arising from the incorporation of Balopoulos' personal income tax equation in the present model. Thirdly, the structural model was linearized at the mean values of the variables. This had the effect of limiting the purposes which the model can serve. More specifically, the model is likely to be inefficient if used for forecasting or economic policy purposes. For this reason, a different approach will be used in testing the predictive power of the model. This is discussed in the next chapter.

Due to the complexity of the complete model (there are nearly 3 000 coefficients) it is obvious that a complete analysis of the whole reduced-form matrix becomes impossible in the present circumstances. Therefore for further analysis a submatrix relating instruments of economic policy with the aggregate and composition of saving has been selected. *Table π. 2* records the impact multipliers of 19 predetermined variables on 21 endogenous variables. The predetermined variables may be classified into three categories: the first is composed of the instruments of tax policy which were accounted for in the model. These are changes in: the aggregate family allowance rate, $\dot{G}_t^P$, the aggregate earned income relief rate, $\dot{G}_t^6$, the aggregate reduced tax rate, $\dot{G}_t^R$, the standard income tax rate, $\dot{G}_t^{10}$, the surtax rate, $\dot{G}_t^{11}$, the aggregate expenditure tax rate, $\dot{G}_t^{EX}$, national insurance contributions, $\dot{NIC}_t$, and capital taxes $\dot{CTX}_t$. The second category is composed of variables which act as proxies for discriminatory tax provisions. These are: the rate of return on life insurance saving, $\dot{R}_t^{LA}$, to reflect the special tax treatment of both life insurance saving and, to some extent, superannuation, the proxy, δ_t, which is assumed to measure the special tax treatment of owner-occupiers, and the Building Societies' composite tax rate, $\dot{G}_t^{BS}$. The third category consists of a vector of rates of return, in addition to the Bank rate, BR_t, the Treasury Bill rate, RTB_t, and the change in the percentage downpayment on the hire purchase of radio and electrical goods, ΔHPC_t. The effects of these instruments on personal saving and its composition are analysed with reference to these three categories of predetermined variables. This procedure is adopted for convenience purposes only.

THE FIRST GROUP: $(\dot{G}^P, \dot{G}^6, \dot{G}^R, \dot{G}^{10}, \dot{G}^{11}, \dot{G}^{EX}, \dot{NIC}$ and $\dot{CTX})$

1. With respect to $\dot{G}_t^P$ and $\dot{G}_t^6$, evidence from *Table π. 2* suggests that any increase in personal allowances or earned income relief will result in an increase in aggregate personal saving, associated with an adverse effect on consumption. The impact multipliers of $\dot{G}_t^P$ and $\dot{G}_t^6$ on consumption have negative signs and are equal to $-22.79\,843$ and $-58.64\,429$ respectively. These results contradict those obtained by Balopoulos[8] who reported a strong substitutability in favour of consumption as a result of increasing personal allowances and the earned income relief. This may be explained in terms of differences in the

Table π. 2   INSTRUMENTS OF ECONOMIC POLICY AND PERSONAL SAVING

Exog. End.	G_t^P 10^{-4}	G_t^6 10^{-4}	G_t^R 10^{-4}	G_t^{10} 10^{-4}	G_t^{11} 10^{-4}	G_t^{EX} 10^{-4}	NIC_t 10^{-4}	CTX_t 10^{-4}
$\Delta F\dot{A}_{1+2t}$	$-39\,701$	$-102\,123$	$95\,633$	$51\,725$	$20\,651$	$4\,219\,998$	$2\,458$	0
$\Delta F\dot{A}_{3t}$	124	318	-298	-161	-64	$-2\,184\,681$	-8	0
$\Delta F\dot{A}_{4t}$	$-2\,601$	$-6\,690$	$6\,264$	$3\,388$	$1\,353$	$-36\,139$	161	0
$\Delta F\dot{A}_{5t}$	281	724	-678	-367	-146	$-5\,617\,986$	-17	0
$\Delta F\dot{A}_{6t}$	$236\,037$	$607\,158$	$-568\,571$	$-307\,525$	$-122\,776$	$-874\,459$	$-14\,616$	0
$\Delta F\dot{A}_{7t}$	$24\,360$	$62\,662$	$-58\,680$	$-33\,128$	$-12\,671$	$-458\,222$	$-1\,527$	886
$\Delta F\dot{A}_{8+9t}$	$16\,101$	$41\,416$	$-38\,784$	$-20\,977$	$-8\,375$	$223\,744$	-997	0
$\Delta H\dot{L}_t$	$8\,166$	$21\,007$	$-19\,672$	$39\,477$	$-4\,248$	$141\,786$	-508	0
$\Delta B\dot{L}_t$	$44\,109$	$113\,462$	$-106\,251$	$-57\,468$	$-22\,944$	$1\,393\,911$	$-2\,731$	0
$(\Delta HP+\Delta O\dot{I}.)_t$	$13\,371$	$34\,395$	$-32\,209$	$-17\,421$	$-6\,955$	$-99\,510$	-828	0
Financial Assets	$168\,955$	$434\,601$	$-406\,982$	$-271\,633$	$-87\,881$	$-6\,163\,932$	$-10\,479$	886
$R\dot{S}_{1t}$	$11\,094$	$28\,537$	$-26\,724$	$19\,976$	$-5\,771$	$173\,612$	-689	0
$R\dot{S}_{2t}$	$35\,793$	$92\,071$	$-86\,219$	$-46\,634$	$-18\,618$	$-1\,000\,380$	$-2\,216$	0
$R\dot{S}_{3t}$	$18\,755$	$48\,243$	$-45\,177$	$-24\,435$	$-9\,756$	$322\,085$	$-1\,160$	0
$R\dot{S}_{4t}$	$11\,689$	$30\,068$	$-28\,157$	$-15\,229$	$-6\,080$	$133\,344$	-724	0
Real Assets	$77\,331$	$198\,919$	$-186\,277$	$-66\,322$	$-40\,225$	$-371\,339$	$-4\,789$	0
$P\dot{R}_{1+2t}$	$146\,549$	$376\,966$	$-353\,009$	$-190\,933$	$-76\,228$	$2\,036\,523$	$-9\,075$	0
$\dot{H}_{1+2t}$	$-3\,361$	$-8\,644$	$8\,095$	$4\,378$	$1\,748$	$123\,036$	-2	0
$N\dot{I}F_t$	$143\,188$	$368\,322$	$-344\,914$	$-186\,555$	$-74\,480$	$2\,159\,558$	$-9\,077$	0
$UN\dot{I}P_t$	0	0	0	0	0	0	0	0
$\dot{S}_t$	$389\,474$	$1\,001\,842$	$-938\,173$	$-524\,510$	$-202\,586$	$-4\,375\,712$	$-24\,345$	$10\,886$

Table π. 2   (cont.)

Exog. End.	$\dot\delta_t$ 10^{-4}	$\dot R_t^{LA}$ 10^{-4}	$\dot G_t^{BS}$ 10^{-4}	$\dot{RN1}_t$ 10^{-4}	$\dot{RN2}_t$ 10^{-4}	$\dot{RN3}_t$ 10^{-4}	$\dot R_t^{O}$ 10^{-4}	$\dot{RP}_t$ 10^{-4}
$\Delta\dot{FA}_{1+2t}$	0	0	76 462	14 461 400	0	0	0	0
$\Delta\dot{FA}_{3t}$	0	0	−99 683	0	0	912 250	0	0
$\Delta\dot{FA}_{4t}$	0	0	38 037	0	1 084 000	0	0	0
$\Delta\dot{FA}_{5t}$	0	0	0	0	0	0	0	0
$\Delta\dot{FA}_{6t}$	0	0	0	0	0	3 766 960	0	0
$\Delta\dot{FA}_{7t}$	−1 047	407 429	164	575 051	911 166	407 305	48 300	354 822
$\Delta\dot{FA}_{8+9t}$	0	0	0	−6 744 280	0	0	545 070	0
$\Delta\dot{HL}_t$	37 739	56 428	51 485	178 937	−185	10 997	0	5 091 001
$\Delta\dot{BL}_t$	0	0	11 239	2 638 871	0	0	0	0
$(\Delta HP{+}\Delta\dot{OL})_t$	0	0	−13 009	0	0	119 049	0	0
Financial Assets	−38 786	351 001	−34 735	5 474 363	1 995 351	4 956 469	593 370	−4 736 179
$\dot{RS}_{1t}$	25 927	38 766	35 370	122 929	−128	7 555	0	9 095 177
$\dot{RS}_{2t}$	0	0	181	1 010 687	0	37 731	0	0
$\dot{RS}_{3t}$	0	0	−218	327 221	0	14 762	0	0
$\dot{RS}_{4t}$	0	0	551	129 305	0	0	0	0
Real Assets	25 927	38 766	35 882	1 590 142	−128	60 048	0	9 095 177
$P\dot{R}_{1+2t}$	0	0	0	0	0	0	0	0
$\dot{II}_{1+2t}$	0	4 615 500	863	0	−15 176	−12 771	0	0
$\dot{NIF}_t$	0	4 615 500	863	0	−15 176	−12 771	0	0
$\dot{UNIP}_t$	0	0	0	0	0	0	0	0
$\dot{S}_t$	−12 859	5 005 267	2 010	7 064 505	1 980 047	5 003 746	593 370	4 358 998

Table π. 2 (*cont.*)

Exog. End.	$\Delta H\dot{P}C_t$ 10^{-4}	$R\dot{T}B_t$ 10^{-4}	$\dot{B}R_t$ 10^{-4}	$[\dot{R}_t^{LA} - RN3_t]$ 10^{-4}	$[\hat{\dot{G}}_t^{10} - \hat{\dot{G}}_t^{BS}]$ 10^{-4}
$\Delta F\dot{A}_{1+2t}$	0	$-275\,199$	$-53\,423$	0	$-24\,737$
$\Delta F\dot{A}_{3t}$	0	$358\,778$	$-1\,048\,114$	$-912\,250$	$99\,522$
$\Delta F\dot{A}_{4t}$	0	$-136\,902$	$366\,341$	0	$-34\,649$
$\Delta F\dot{A}_{5t}$	0	0	$141\,421$	0	-367
$\Delta F\dot{A}_{6t}$	0	$1\,430\,381$	$-546\,897$	$-3\,766\,960$	$-307\,525$
$\Delta F\dot{A}_{7t}$	$1\,698$	$381\,272$	$-262\,095$	124	$-33\,292$
$\Delta F\dot{A}_{8+9t}$	0	0	0	0	$-20\,977$
$\Delta H\dot{L}_t$	0	$-185\,304$	$-13\,254$	$45\,431$	$-12\,008$
$\Delta B\dot{L}_t$	0	$-40\,450$	$-832\,252$	0	$-68\,707$
$(\Delta H\dot{P} + \Delta O\dot{L})_t$	$-42\,120$	$46\,821$	$-136\,779$	$-119\,049$	$-4\,412$
Financial Assets	$43\,818$	$1\,937\,263$	$-420\,482$	$-4\,605\,468$	$-236\,898$
$R\dot{S}_{1t}$	0	$-127\,304$	$-9\,108$	$31\,211$	$-15\,394$
$R\dot{S}_{2t}$	$-17\,737$	-653	$-362\,103$	$-37\,731$	$-46\,815$
$R\dot{S}_{3t}$	$-5\,223$	790	$-120\,160$	$-14\,762$	$-24\,217$
$R\dot{S}_{4t}$	0	$-1\,982$	$-40\,780$	0	$-15\,780$
Real Assets	$-22\,960$	$-129\,149$	$-535\,066$	$-21\,282$	$-102\,204$
$\dot{P}R_{1+2t}$	0	0	0	0	$-19\,093$
$I\dot{I}_{1+2t}$	0	$-3\,106$	$7\,565$	$4\,628\,271$	$3\,513$
$N\dot{I}F_t$	0	$-3\,106$	$7\,565$	$4\,628\,271$	$-187\,418$
$U\dot{N}IP_t$	0	0	0	0	0
$\dot{S}_t$	$20\,858$	$1\,805\,008$	$-945\,066$	$1\,521$	$-526\,520$

structure of the two models, the data used, as well as the method of estimation. More important is the fact that in this study the discriminatory effects of taxation on consumption and saving were not taken into account.

2. Apart from $\overset{\cdot}{G}^{iP}$ and $\overset{\cdot}{G}^6$ all the remaining instruments of income taxation and National Insurance show an adverse effect on aggregate personal saving, as indicated by the negative signs of the impact multipliers of $\overset{\cdot}{G}^R_t, \overset{\cdot}{G}^{10}_t$ and $\overset{\cdot}{G}^{11}_t$. Another interesting result is the relatively small impact multiplier of the surtax rate, with the possible implications regarding the seriousness of the disincentive effects of progressive taxation on saving. Considering the composition of personal saving, it is interesting to note that: (1) although an increase in $\overset{\cdot}{G}^R$ or $\overset{\cdot}{G}^{10}$ or $\overset{\cdot}{G}^{11}$ results in a net fall in aggregate personal saving, this will be associated with an increase in the holding of both cash and National Savings Certificates. The increase in the former is possibly to meet short-term consumption plans while the increase in the latter may be explained in terms of the tax concessions associated with the holding of certificates which become more attractive as tax rates increase. (2) Any change in the standard income tax rate results in a change in the same direction in investment in dwellings. This may be explained in terms of the tax concessions associated with owner-occupier housing.

3. The negative sign for the impact multiplier of the rate on outlay taxation, G^{EX}, on aggregate saving may be regarded as an indication of a strong adverse income effect outweighing the substitution effect. On the other hand, it is interesting to note the positive signs of the impact multipliers of $\overset{\cdot}{G}^{EX}$ on the long-term forms of saving: i.e. real assets, with the exception of investment in consumer durables; and Life Assurance and Superannuation saving.

4. The positive sign of the impact multiplier of capital taxation on aggregate personal saving may be explained with reference to a fixed-sum saver who aims at fulfilling a specific target. However, this result should be viewed with some reservation, since capital taxes were defined as exogenous in this study.

THE SECOND GROUP: $(\overset{\cdot}{\delta}_t, \overset{\cdot}{G}^{BS}_t,$ and $\overset{\cdot}{R}^{LA}_t)$

1. The proxy, $\overset{\cdot}{\delta}_t$, which reflects the tax concessions associated with owner-occupied housing shows a negative impact multiplier with respect to aggregate personal saving. It is made up of two elements: a positive component consisting mainly of the investment in dwellings multiplier equal to +2·5927, and a negative, but larger, multiplier for loans for house purchase equal to −3·7739. Thus, the negative sign of the net multiplier is mainly due to the increase in mortgage (a dis-saving element) associated with the act of purchasing a house for owner-occupation. However, this should not be taken as conclusive evidence that the favourable tax treatment of owner-occupiers has adverse effects on aggregate personal saving. It is important to emphasise that the proxy used in the empirical testing, $\overset{\cdot}{\delta}_t$, was assigned arbitrary values (0·55 before the abolition of Schedule A and 0·75 after). Also, this variable may be an inadequate proxy for owner-occupiers purchasing their houses outright.

2. To examine the effects of the tax concessions on life assurance and super-annuation saving we calculate the contribution which may be attributed to these

concessions as such. This is given by:

$$C\dot{T}C_{1t} = \pi_1 \dot{R}_t^{LA} - \pi_2 \dot{R}N3_t$$

where CTC is the contribution of the tax concessions, and π_1 and π_2 are relevant impact multipliers. This formula assumes that, if the tax concessions are abolished, life assurance and superannuation saving will yield a rate of return equivalent to $RN3$. If we further assume that:

$$\dot{R}_t^{LA} = \dot{R}N3_t = 1$$

it is possible to calculate $C\dot{T}C_{1t}$. The results are shown in *Table π. 2.* They reveal that tax concessions on life assurance and superannuation have a net favourable effect on aggregate personal saving – the relevant CTC_{1t} has a positive sign and is equal to 0·1521. This, however, results from a combination of differing effects on the various forms of saving, a positive effect on life assurance and superannuation saving associated with a negative, but smaller in size, effect on the other forms of saving, particularly financial saving.

Similarly, the contribution of the special tax treatment of deposits with Building Societies* is given by:

$$C\dot{T}C_{2t} = \pi_3 \dot{G}_t^{BS} - \pi_4 \dot{G}_t^{10}$$

This formula assumes that, if the special tax concessions are abolished, the rate of return on Building Societies' deposits will be taxed at the standard income tax rate. If we further assume that:

$$\dot{G}_t^{BS} = \dot{G}_t^{10} = 1$$

$C\dot{T}C_{2t}$ is calculated. As shown in *Table π. 2,* the result indicates a net negative effect on aggregate personal saving and all forms of personal saving; with the exception of deposits with non-bank financial institutions.

THE THIRD GROUP: ($\dot{R}N$, $\dot{R}N2$, $\dot{R}N3$, $\dot{R}^O$, $\dot{R}P$, $\Delta H\dot{P}C$, $R\dot{T}B$, $B\dot{R}$)

Table π. 2 shows that (1) with the exception of BR, all interest rates have positive impact multipliers with respect to aggregate personal saving, and (2) the signs of the interest rates' impact multipliers for the various forms of saving suggest that the composition of aggregate personal saving is affected by the relative interest rates. This may be taken as an evidence that changes in interest rates not only influence the composition of personal saving, but also lead to a net favourable effect on the aggregate level of personal saving, a conclusion which neither the Radcliffe Committee[32a] nor the Commission on Money and Credit was able to reach. As to the negative multiplier for $B\dot{R}_t$ on aggregate personal saving, this may be attributed to the adverse effect which a rise in the Bank rate has on holdings of financial and real assets, and vice versa.

---

* Income tax on interest on Building Societies' deposits is deducted at source at a somewhat reduced rate. It should be noted that this form of tax discrimination is only beneficial to those who pay tax at the standard rate, but works to the disadvantage of savers in the lower income group who cannot reclaim any of the tax paid on their behalf by the Society.

6.3 THE TWO AGGREGATE MODELS COMPARED

In Chapter 2 aggregate personal saving was defined from the personal sectors' income account as a residual, and an aggregate model, based on the permanent income hypothesis, was derived and estimated by means of the Iterative Maximum Likelihood Method. The estimated reduced form for the broad definition of saving (to include investment in consumer durables) was as follows:

Aggregate Personal Saving: Income Approach* — *Real Terms*

$$S_t = 0.723 \ Y_t^d - 0.2412 \ \Delta Y_t^d - 0.205 \ L_t + 0.1373 \ L_{t-1} - 0.67 \ C_{t-1} \quad 6.1(b)$$

First (1) we define Y_t^d and L_t as endogenous, (2) include the equations for $L_t, \Delta FA_{3t}, \Delta FA_{4t}, \Delta FA_{5t}, Y_t^d, W_t, PX_t, \dot{T}^P, RNSC_t, RBS_t, RS_t, RBD_t, RTSB_t,$ R_t^L and Y_t, (3) linearise the equations around the sample means of the variables, and (4) then derive the reduced form of the model. The results are shown in *Table π. 1.1.*

Now we are in a position to compare the reduced forms of the Income Account Aggregate Saving function — referred to as the conventional model. S_t^C — and the Balance Sheet Aggregate Saving function — referred to as the Alternative model S_t^A.

Before we look at the numerical results, let us examine the difference between the two approaches with respect to the derivation of the aggregate model. Consider *one individual* and *F forms of saving;* we may, accordingly, distinguish between two ways of deriving the aggregate saving function:

The Conventional Method

$$\text{Step One} \quad \sum_{i=1}^{F} \sum_{j=1}^{P} S_{ij} = S \quad i = 1, \dots F, j = P = 1$$

Step Two $\quad S = \phi(X)$

The Alternative Method

Step One $S_{ij} = \phi_{ij}(X)$

$$\text{Step Two} \quad S = \sum_{i=1}^{F} \sum_{j=1}^{P} S_{ij} \quad i = 1, \dots F, j = P = 1$$

Comparing the two methods, it is obvious that the alternative method has the advantage of being more flexible than the conventional method. At least it allows variability in the functional form between the various forms of saving. It also simplifies the specification since the model builder will be concerned with the theoretical specification of a model dealing with a relatively homogenous form of saving. Moreover, if we further distinguish between the single-equation conventional model, i.e. X is exogenous, and the simultaneous-equation con-

* See Equation 2.2.9 of *Table Agg. 9* (Chapter 2).

ventional model, i.e. X consists of G^Δ endogenous and $G^{\Delta\Delta}$ exogenous, it becomes clear that the single-equation conventional model — which is commonly adopted — is less satisfactory. Firstly, there is the limitation that for the purpose of estimation it is necessary that

$$X < N$$

where N is the size of the sample. In this case one is forced to choose among the explanatory variables the ones to be included, with the probability of the omitted variables' mis-specification increasing, the smaller the size of the sample. Secondly, suppose that the X (exogenous) vector includes: an ability to save variable, say income; a shift variable, say a wealth variable; and a vector R of rates of return to account for incentives to save,

$$X = [Y^d \; | W | \; R]$$

With respect to the choice of rates of return to be included, we have the following alternatives, each of which is faced with certain difficulties:

Alternatives		*Difficulties*
1. $R = R_i$	$i = 1, \ldots F$	Sample size limitations mainly
2. $R = \sum_{i=1}^{F} k_i R_i$	$i = 1, \ldots F$ k_i weight	Problem of choosing weights
3. $R = R_i$	$i = Z \quad Z = 1$ *and/or* 2 and/or $\ldots F$	Which rate (or rates) of return to select, and hence to include in the single equation
4. $R = \sum_{i=1}^{Z} k_i R_i$	$i = Z$ *and/or* 2 $\ldots$ and/or $\ldots F$	Problems associated with 2 and 3

Faced with these difficulties, the common practice has been to omit R, and then derive the conventional model with income and shift variables only. In this case, the aggregate saving function becomes, in my view, simply a *technical*, rather than a behavioural, relationship in just the same way as the production function. It says something regarding the *ability to save* out of a given income, and very little, if nothing at all, regarding the *incentive to save*. It should be emphasized that this criticism is valid only in so far as the conventional single-equation model is concerned, but its validity with respect to the conventional simultaneous model depends on the number and the type of variables included in G^Δ.

Turning to the empirical results, there appears to be more evidence in favour of the alternative model. Comparing the reduced forms of the two models — as shown in *Tables $\pi.1$* and *$\pi. 1.1$* — the superiority of the alternative model for policy-making purposes can be observed. It is evident that some policy questions which are allowed for in the alternative model cannot be examined if the conventional model is used. One example is the question of the effects on aggregate personal saving of the tax discrimination in favour of Life Assurance and super-annuation saving. Moreover, a close analysis of the results shows that from the policy-making point of view the two models do not always lead to the same, or even similar, conclusions. For example, suppose that the policy-maker aims to increase aggregate personal saving. Given the conventional model, this may be achieved by *increasing* the Bank rate, while the *opposite* action is required if we base our policy on the alternative model. In this case, the course of action which one adopts is the one which takes into account more factors than the other; i.e. the alternative model.

It should be emphasised, however, that both aggregate models, as presented in this study, are derived under inappropriate aggregation assumptions. The assumption of linearity, which was adopted for mathematical simplicity, is obviously unrealistic as it implies that the aggregate saving function is independent of the pattern of income distribution. As shown by Balopoulos,[8] this leads to serious policy implications, for it implies that fiscal policy has no discriminatory effects on saving and consumption. The failure to allow for the distributional effects is a weak feature of this study.

7

Application of Models

Econometric models may be solved or applied in at least two ways:

In a direct way; that is, given an econometric model and a set of exogenous or predetermined variables, our aim is to predict the corresponding endogenous variables. This is sometimes called solving the model in the 'economic theory' way.[8,61]

In an indirect way; in this case attention is focussed on the exogenous variables. That is, assuming a fixed target model for example, we take the endogenous, or target variables, as given and derive the values of the instrumental (exogenous) variables, which achieve the given targets. This exercise is sometimes called solving the model in the 'economic policy' way.[61]

In this chapter we are primarily concerned with testing the predictive power of the models which have been discussed previously. We begin, in section 7.1, with a technical introduction in which we deal with the problems of generating forecasts and verifying their accuracy. This is followed, in section 7.2, by the results of testing the predictive power of the model. Some concluding remarks and suggestions for further research are put forward in the final section.

7.1 SOME TECHNICAL CONSIDERATIONS

Following Theil,[203c] there are three essential aspects of forecasting: generation, verification and purpose of predictions. The first deals with the particular predictive technique used, while the second and the third are concerned with the degree to which the forecasts could be imperfect and with the evaluation of alternative forecasting techniques and the decision on an 'optimal' or best forecasting technique respectively.[61]

7.1.1 GENERATION OF PREDICTIONS

For the purpose of this study, we distinguish between two methods of generating predictions of the endogenous variables. In the first, we deal with one equation at a time, and given the *actual or realised* values of the *explanatory variables* in each equation, predictions of individual dependent variables are derived. The vector of explanatory variables may include variables which are defined as endogenous in the complete model. In the second, a distinction is made between endogenous and predetermined variables, and simultaneous predictions of the endogenous variables are generated, given the values of the predetermined variables and the complete model. These two methods are referred to later as the 'unconditional' forecast for the former* and the 'conditional' forecast for the latter.

To obtain conditional forecasts of the values taken by the endogenous variables, given the values taken by the predetermined variables, it is conventional to estimate the reduced form of the model first, i.e. to solve the system by expressing the endogenous variables as explicit functions of the predetermined variables. Given the matrix of reduced form coefficients and by substituting the numerical values of the predetermined variables, one then obtains conditional forecasts of the values taken by the current endogenous variables. The derivation of the matrix of reduced form coefficients presents no problems when the model is linear in the variables. With respect to non-linear models, until recently an attempt was often made to linearize the model around certain values of the variables, the sample means of the variables if the model is used for analytical purposes, or the most recent values of the variables if the model is used for predictions. At the present time non-linear models are simulated in the computer. This, of course, was made possible by the development of large computers. The models presented in this study — as shown in Chapter 6 — contain non-linearities. To derive the conditional forecasts, these models were simulated in the computer. For this purpose, two simplifying assumptions were made:

1. The stochastic term was ignored. This might have affected the results of the simulation, for, as pointed out by Klein and Goldberger[111] (p. 75), even if the disturbances were zero on the average in each equation separately, 'the forecast equations will depend on non-linear functions of the separate disturbances, and, in general, the estimated covariances of these disturbances will have to be taken into account'.

2. Equation 6.27 of personal income taxation was dropped, since this equation is a linearised form of a highly non-linear model which was developed and estimated by Balopoulos.[8] Instead, a simpler version was estimated, in which wage and non-wage incomes were used as proxies for tax bases, and the standard income tax rate as a proxy for the tax structure. The estimate obtained was as follows:

$$T_t^P = -1944 \cdot 8 + 0 \cdot 23\,114\,(W_t + TI_t) + 0 \cdot 21\,846\,OY_t - 1727 \cdot 212\,G_t^{10} -$$
$$ (479 \cdot 8)\ (0 \cdot 044) \qquad\qquad (0 \cdot 1107) \qquad\qquad (1075 \cdot 22)$$

$$-\,123 \cdot 77\,t \hfill (6.27a)$$
$$(26 \cdot 39)$$

where TI_t is transfer income. $R^2 = 0 \cdot 996$ VN = 1·8

* It is unconditional in the sense that predictions are not conditional on the solution of the complete system, but, of course, it is conditional on the values of the explanatory variables and the mathematical and statistical form of the single equations.

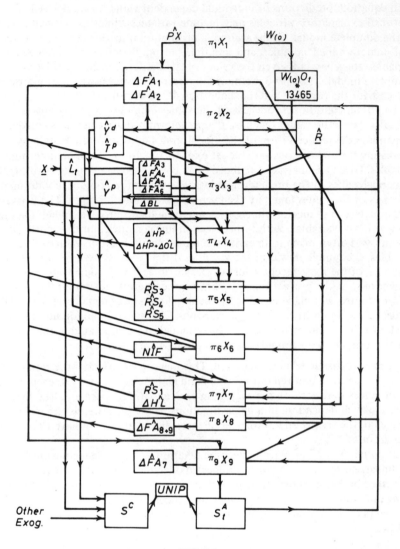

FIG. 7.1

With these assumptions, we proceed by solving five blocks of simultaneous equations (6.25, 6.26; 6.24, 6.27a, 6.30, 6.31, 6.32, 6.33, 6.34, 6.35, 6.2, 6.3; 6.10, 6.13, 6.29; 6.28, 6.19; and 6.1, 6.8) and the rest of the model is solved one by one. A flow diagram of the system is presented in *Figure 7.1*.

7.1.2 VERIFICATION OF PREDICTIONS

In measuring the quality of forecasts, Theil's Inequality Coefficient, U, and its decompositions are used.

Let P_i and A_i stand for predicted and realised *changes* respectively ($i = 1 \ldots n$), U is defined as:

$$U = \sqrt{\Sigma(P_i - A_i)^2 / \Sigma A_i^2} \qquad U \geqslant 0$$

U assumes the value of zero for perfect predictions; i.e. $A_i = P_i$, and is equal to unity if $P_i = 0$ (no-change extrapolation) but it has no upper bound, i.e. the predictive power of a particular forecasting technique may be worse than no-change extrapolation. The first set of Theil's Inequality Coefficient is given by:

$$\text{The bias proportion } U^M = (\bar{P} - \bar{A})^2 / \frac{1}{n} \Sigma (P_i - A_i)^2$$

$$\text{The variance proportion } U^V = (S_P - S_A)^2 / \frac{1}{n} \Sigma (P_i - A_i)^2$$

$$\text{The covariance proportion } U^C = 2(1 - R)S_P S_A / \frac{1}{n} \Sigma (P_i - A_i)^2$$

and the second set by:

$$\text{The regression proportion } U^R = (S_P - RS_A)^2 / \frac{1}{n} \Sigma (P_i - A_i)^2$$

$$\text{The disturbance proportion } U^D = (1 - R^2)S_A^2 / \frac{1}{n} \Sigma (P_i - A_i)^2$$

where

$$U^M + U^V + U^C = 1$$

$$U^M + U^R + U^D = 1$$

A and P are the actual and predicted *levels* of the variables and S_A, S_P, R are the standard deviations of A and P and the simple correlation coefficient between A and P respectively. We shall also use P' to denote a linearly corrected prediction.

7.2 RESULTS

The tests which are reported in this section are confined to the 'within the period' predictive power of the models. For both conditional and unconditional forecasts, the analysis begins by a bird's eye view, and is followed by a variable by variable and a year-to-year investigation.

VARIABLE ΔFA_{2t} EQUATION NUMBER: 6.2

TYPE OF PREDICTION: UNCONDITIONAL

Index	1952 1966	1952 1956	1957 1961	1962 1966
U	0·4 623 (0·522)	0·3 665 (0·972)	0·2 846 (0·999)	0·6 503 (0·956)
U^M	0·0 005	0·1 101	0·0 060	0·0 002
U^V	0·0 670	0·2 098	0·0 001	0·0 178
U^C	0·9 325	0·6 801	0·9 939	0·9 820
U^R	0·0 002	0·0 947	0·0 180	0·0 485
U^D	0·9 993	0·7 952	0·9 759	0·9 513
R	0·8 864	0·9 447	0·9 596	0·7 676
α	−1·667	−23·24	−3·09	−1·87
β	1·0 071	1·1 360	0·962	0·841

Year	ξ	A	P	P'
1952		83·63	56·99	
1953	−0·5 147	140·52	84·59	82·93
1954	−0·1 387	171·26	156·19	154·63
1955	1·0 069	−144·28	−34·87	−38·00
1956	0·4 626	26·54	76·81	76·71
1957	−1·0 934	203·49	84·68	83·43
1958	0·6 349	188·00	256·99	255·70
1959	−0·2 416	381·71	355·46	354·98
1960	−0·1 362	194·09	179·29	176·18
1961	−0·1 472	181·03	165·03	163·16
1962	0·4 146	278·19	323·24	322·58
1963	0·7 167	324·82	402·70	401·92
1964	−0·2 728	402·84	373·20	371·88
1965	−1·1 063	435·00	314·78	312·48
1966	0·6 204	206·87	274·29	271·48

Prediction – Realisation Diagram

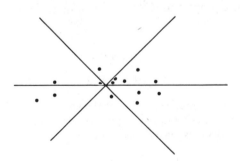

VARIABLE $\Delta FA_{1t} + \Delta FA_{2t}$

TYPE OF PREDICTION: UNCONDITIONAL

EQUATION NUMBER: 6.3

Index	1952 1966	1952 1956	1957 1961	1962 1966
U	0·4 809 (0·521)	0·3 864 (0·968)	0·3 005 (0·997)	0·6 192 (0·970)
U^M	0·0 000	0·0 524	0·0 021	0·0 001
U^V	0·0 616	0·2 423	0·0 089	0·0 069
U^C	0·9 384	0·7 053	0·9 890	0·9 930
U^R	0·0 001	0·1 045	0·0 035	0·0 586
U^D	0·9 999	0·8 431	0·9 944	0·9 413
R	0·8 765	0·9 345	0·9 540	0·7 982
α	0·2 547	−17·1	2·0 961	−2·626
β	0·9 954	1·1 549	0·9 818	0·8 416

Year	ξ	A	P	P'
1952		126·64	123·06	
1953	−0·5 634	204·92	135·72	135·93
1954	−0·2 581	244·83	213·13	213·35
1955	0·9 235	−91·01	22·42	23·70
1956	0·4 464	65·82	120·65	119·93
1957	−1·0 200	231·24	105·95	106·02
1958	0·6 301	213·00	290·39	290·37
1959	−0·3 112	448·31	410·09	409·43
1960	−0·1 090	244·33	230·94	232·20
1961	−0·2 799	227·97	193·59	194·08
1962	0·4 822	280·96	340·19	339·93
1963	0·7 128	366·79	454·34	453·79
1964	−0·2 388	469·39	440·06	439·98
1965	−1·1 084	500·42	364·28	365·02
1966	0·6 688	237·12	319·27	320·36

Prediction − Realisation Diagram

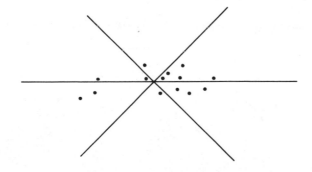

VARIABLE ΔFA_{3t}

EQUATION NUMBER: 6.4

TYPE OF PREDICTION: UNCONDITIONAL

Index	1952 1966	1952 1956	1957 1961	1962 1966
U	0·4 122 (0·529)	0·6 124 (0·964)	0·4 338 (0·974)	0·1 894 (0·993)
U^M	0·0 001	0·0 203	0·1 577	0·2 761
U^V	0·0 016	0·0 348	0·2 983	0·4 763
U^C	0·9 982	0·9 449	0·5 440	0·2 476
U^R	0·0 351	0·0 232	0·1 453	0·5 075
U^D	0·9 648	0·9 565	0·6 970	0·2 164
R	0·8 979	0·7 855	0·9 248	0·9 954
α	2·8 556	−3·986	−29·62	12·390
β	0·9 145	0·8 907	1·2 312	0·8 718

Year	ξ	A	P	P'
1952		111·11	112·16	
1953	0·9 998	154·74	226·23	219·24
1954	−0·9 220	290·80	225·80	222·67
1955	0·2 075	245·28	259·91	265·41
1956	0·1 077	191·08	198·67	205·51
1957	−0·9 052	200·41	136·59	144·10
1958	0·8 401	186·00	245·23	244·25
1959	−0·6 078	387·67	344·82	334·10
1960	0·0 260	333·00	334·83	342·20
1961	0·7 654	328·54	382·50	381·12
1962	0·0 984	511·09	518·03	504·68
1963	0·0 647	677·92	682·48	670·68
1964	−0·2 631	688·55	670·00	673·53
1965	0·0 830	717·08	722·93	722·85
1966	−0·3 977	651·68	623·64	634·48

Prediction – Realisation Diagram

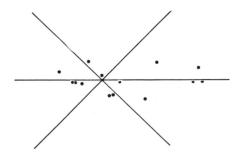

VARIABLE ΔFA_{4t}

TYPE OF PREDICTION: UNCONDITIONAL

Index	1952 1966	1952 1956	1957 1961	1962 1966
U	0·3 854 (0·525)	1·5 582 (0·897)	0·1 877 (0·999)	0·2 732 (0·987)
U^M	0·0 034	0·1 546	0·0 016	0·0 064
U^V	0·1 074	0·3 611	0·5 144	0·2 357
U^C	0·8 891	0·4 843	0·4 840	0·7 579
U^R	0·0 173	0·6 907	0·4 416	0·1 341
U^D	0·9 792	0·1 547	0·5 568	0·8 596
R	0·9 244	0·489	0·9 901	0·9 674
α	1·3 283	10·923	1·1 233	−2·183
β	1·0 581	0·2 101	1·1 447	1·1 154

EQUATION NUMBER: 6.5

Year	ξ	A	P	P'
1952		11·00	29·73	
1953	0·3 562	29·00	41·32	44·41
1954	0·3 935	35·00	48·61	51·08
1955	−0·9 454	31·00	−1·70	−2·50
1956	−0·9 251	56·00	24·00	24·92
1957	0·9 723	11·00	44·63	45·30
1958	−0·4 845	94·00	77·24	82·42
1959	0·3 284	85·00	96·36	97·83
1960	0·0 402	57·00	58·39	58·17
1961	0·0 682	−7·00	−4·64	−6·89
1962	−0·5 215	5·00	−13·04	−12·06
1963	−0·3 969	−7·00	−20·73	−20·90
1964	−0·3 839	26·00	−39·28	−39·83
1965	1·1 868	−124·00	−82·95	−84·93
1966	−0·1 946	10·00	3·27	11·99

Prediction − Realisation Diagram

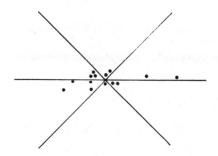

VARIABLE ΔFA_{st}

TYPE OF PREDICTION: UNCONDITIONAL

Index	1952 1966	1952 1956	1957 1961	1962 1966
U	0·6 883 (0·503)	0·9 094 (0·835)	0·4 828 (0·876)	0·7 804 (0·887)
U^M	0·0 075	0·8 673	0·2 833	0·0 048
U^V	0·0 246	0·0 035	0·7 047	0·0 685
U^C	0·9 680	0·1 292	0·0 120	0·9 267
U^R	0·0 469	0·0 005	0·6 962	0·0 610
U^D	0·9 456	0·1 322	0·0 205	0·9 342
R	0·7 430	0·9 048	0·9 975	0·5 662
α	−3·275	−26·196	18·87	−5·9 758
β	0·8 328	0·9 720	1·7 093	0·7 289

EQUATION NUMBER: 6.6

Year	ξ	A	P	P'
1952		−68·00	−122·58	
1953	0·4 632	−50·00	−24·34	−34·91
1954	0·5 789	5·00	37·07	19·24
1955	0·7 399	−11·00	29·99	22·54
1956	0·2 065	14·00	25·44	16·07
1957	0·5 211	47·00	75·87	62·25
1958	−0·9 491	149·00	96·42	84·88
1959	−0·6 725	206·00	168·74	162·17
1960	0·1 236	173·00	179·85	180·95
1961	0·2 291	110·00	122·69	127·83
1962	0·0 440	58·00	60·44	65·45
1963	0·1 780	82·00	91·86	82·92
1964	−1·3 935	140·00	62·80	62·73
1965	−0·8 731	54·00	5·63	24·82
1966	1·7 541	−80·00	17·18	20·06

Prediction − Realisation Diagram

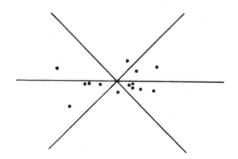

VARIABLE ΔFA_{6t} EQUATION NUMBER: 6.7

TYPE OF PREDICTION: UNCONDITIONAL

Index	1952 1966	1952 1956	1957 1961	1962 1966
U	0·3 497 (0·524)	0·3 529 (0·976)	0·1 911 (0·974)	0·2 677 (0·965)
U^M	0·0 014	0·0 016	0·2 673	0·3 253
U^V	0·1 760	0·2 414	0·3 852	0·2 655
U^C	0·8 226	0·7 570	0·3 476	0·4 093
U^R	0·0 627	0·1 075	0·3 397	0·3 175
U^D	0·9 359	0·8 910	0·3 930	0·3 573
R	0·9 407	0·9 417	0·9 928	0·9 871
α	−1·9 075	12·488	32·772	−17·480
β	1·1 029	1·1 416	1·1 267	0·8 672

Year	ξ	A	P	P'
1952		286·00	219·30	
1953	1·2 733	110·00	295·71	294·80
1954	−0·1 702	−87·00	−111·82	−136·56
1955	−1·0 943	452·00	292·40	329·55
1956	−0·1 439	92·00	71·02	29·89
1957	1·3 642	−181·00	17·96	8·43
1958	−0·7 612	121·00	9·98	27·73
1959	−0·1 559	−56·00	−78·74	−101·21
1960	−0·1 912	302·00	274·12	306·20
1961	0·2 435	−94·00	−58·49	−97·51
1962	−0·6 034	−40·00	−128·00	−133·41
1963	0·1 044	−246·00	−230·77	−252·32
1964	0·4 355	−67·00	−3·48	19·58
1965	−0·1 567	−75·00	−97·85	−102·93
1966	0·2 073	−4·00	26·24	34·75

Prediction − Realisation Diagram

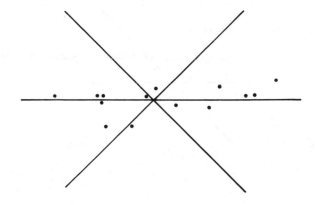

VARIABLE ΔFA_{7t}

TYPE OF PREDICTION: UNCONDITIONAL

EQUATION NUMBER: 6.8

Index	1952 1966	1952 1956	1957 1961	1962 1966
U	0·4 577 (0·534)	0·6 965 (0·947)	0·3 256 (0·975)	0·3 576 (0·999)
U^M	0·0 100	0·1 641	0·5 671	0·0 043
U^V	0·0 193	0·0 020	0·0 568	0·0 277
U^C	0·9 707	0·8 339	0·3 761	0·9 680
U^R	0·1 266	0·2 416	0·0 256	0·1 100
U^D	0·8 634	0·5 943	0·4 072	0·8 858
R	0·8 969	0·4 976	0·9 704	0·9 402
α	0·3 241	11·6 660	−16·65	−3·469
β	0·8 412	0·4 736	1·0 666	0·8 868

Year	ξ	A	P	P'
1952		−8·00	−37·54	
1953	1·4 792	21·00	75·02	62·16
1954	0·2 402	34·00	42·77	39·64
1955	0·0 937	47·00	50·42	48·14
1956	−0·5 244	123·00	103·85	95·14
1957	−0·8 075	126·00	96·51	101·04
1958	0·1 950	108·00	115·12	117·17
1959	0·7 122	92·00	118·01	116·74
1960	0·6 772	144·00	168·73	156·87
1961	−0·0 715	241·00	238·39	223·72
1962	−1·1 285	289·00	247·79	247·04
1963	−1·0 189	205·00	167·79	187·37
1964	1·4 357	130·00	182·43	186·34
1965	0·0 553	268·00	270·02	248·11
1966	−0·2 393	233·00	224·26	231·53

Prediction − Realisation Diagram

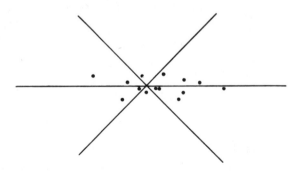

VARIABLE $\Delta FA_{8t} + \Delta FA_{9t}$

TYPE OF PREDICTION: UNCONDITIONAL

Index	1952 1966	1952 1956	1957 1961	1962 1966
U	0·5 887 (0·502)	0·5 657 (0·861)	0·2 857 (0·987)	0·7 331 (0·819)
U^M	0·0 003	0·0 105	0·0 850	0·0 126
U^V	0·1 114	0·6 254	0·1 057	0·2 478
U^C	0·8 883	0·3 642	0·8 092	0·7 397
U^R	0·0 001	0·3 574	0·2 002	0·0 026
U^D	0·9 995	0·6 321	0·7 148	0·9 849
R	0·7 867	0·8 888	0·9 590	0·6 629
α	0·8 243	2·3 514	0·1 633	−10·231
β	0·9 909	1·6 335	0·8 648	1·0 615

EQUATION NUMBER: 6.9

Year	ξ	A	P	P'
1952		−37·00	−14·20	
1953	0·6 505	−104·00	−40·24	−39·39
1954	−0·0 995	−100·00	−109·75	−108·87
1955	−0·6 487	8·00	−55·58	−55·16
1956	0·2 961	−102·00	−72·98	−71·42
1957	−0·3 075	−62·00	−92·14	−91·41
1958	−0·5 534	−150·00	−204·24	−202·12
1959	−0·0 540	−347·00	−352·29	−349·62
1960	0·3 349	−363·00	−330·18	−329·51
1961	−0·1 116	−298·00	−308·94	−308·61
1962	−0·1 407	−362·00	−375·79	−374·25
1963	−0·0 923	−512·00	−521·05	−518·77
1964	0·3 594	−572·00	− 536·77	−535·72
1965	1·5 651	−692·00	−538·60	−538·08
1966	−1·3 602	−495·00	−628·32	−628·08

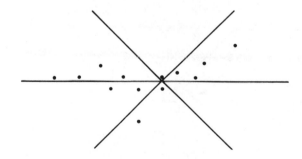

Prediction – Realisation Diagram

VARIABLE ΔHL_t EQUATION NUMBER: 6.10

TYPE OF PREDICTION: UNCONDITIONAL

Index	1952 1966	1952 1956	1957 1961	1962 1966
U	0·4 107 (0·499)	0·4 633 (0·892)	0·4 931 (0·984)	0·3 707 (0·922)
U^M	0·0 007	0·0 105	0·3 568	0·0 774
U^V	0·5 757	0·9 610	0·5 126	0·7 271
U^C	0·4 235	0·0 285	0·1 305	0·1 956
U^R	0·3 618	0·9 340	0·4 256	0·6 039
U^D	0·6 374	0·0 554	0·2 176	0·3 187
R	0·9 253	0·9 931	0·9 635	0·9 648
α	−17·245	−13·061	−55·18	−25·195
β	1·4 467	1·9 395	1·6 359	1·6 008

Year	ξ	A	P	P'
1952		139·00	145·37	
1953	−0·0 594	168·00	165·29	159·79
1954	−0·5 968	236·00	208·76	209·72
1955	−0·3 523	276·00	259·92	253·36
1956	0·7 920	215·00	251·15	222·80
1957	−0·3 878	229·00	211·30	192·40
1958	0·4 664	227·00	248·29	239·66
1959	−0·5 229	362·00	338·13	370·52
1960	0·7 843	380·00	415·80	422·59
1961	1·0 358	369·00	416·28	415·24
1962	−0·2 953	414·00	400·52	397·35
1963	−1·3 732	572·00	509·32	534·65
1964	−1·1 708	758·00	704·56	746·53
1965	0·6 987	695·00	726·89	695·75
1966	0·7 004	721·00	752·97	761·62

Prediction – Realisation Diagram

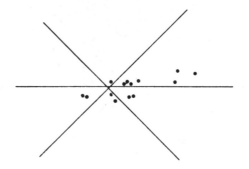

VARIABLE ΔBL_t

EQUATION NUMBER: 6.11

TYPE OF PREDICTION: UNCONDITIONAL

Index	1952 1966	1952 1956	1957 1961	1962 1966
U	0·6 038 (0·526)	0·7 645 (0·866)	0·4 588 (0·940)	0·6 979 (0·790)
U^M	0·0 014	0·8 085	0·4 722	0·3 812
U^V	0·0 002	0·0 032	0·1 343	0·1 755
U^C	0·9 984	0·1 883	0·3 935	0·4 432
U^R	0·0 976	0·0 006	0·1 971	0·0 070
U^D	0·9 010	0·1 909	0·3 307	0·6 118
R	0·8 193	0·9 329	0·9 643	0·6 893
α	−1·627	−47·94	44·189	−42·97
β	0·8 128	0·9 783	0·8 250	1·1 264

Year	ξ	A	P	P'
1952		−103·00	−168·38	
1953	0·2 408	−7·00	14·50	−9·12
1954	0·5 367	72·00	119·93	94·54
1955	0·4 600	−1·00	40·08	44·43
1956	0·9 841	5·00	92·88	73·68
1957	−0·2 503	3·00	−19·35	−16·42
1958	0·3 877	193·00	227·62	183·94
1959	−1·0 369	339·00	246·40	234·78
1960	−1·1 081	257·00	158·04	190·29
1961	−0·5 040	61·00	15·99	59·48
1962	−1·3 472	221·00	100·69	91·63
1963	0·2 877	90·00	115·69	133·78
1964	−0·1 658	129·00	114·19	108·03
1965	1·6 008	−33·00	109·96	111·90
1966	0·3 393	−60·00	−29·70	−31·94

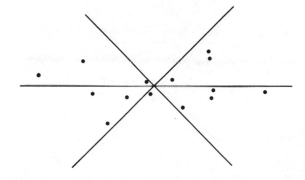

Prediction − Realisation Diagram

VARIABLE $(\Delta HP + \Delta OL)_t$

EQUATION NUMBER: 6.12

TYPE OF PREDICTION: UNCONDITIONAL

Index	1952 1966	1952 1956	1957 1961	1962 1966
U	0·2828 (0·534)	0·2 043 (0·8 417)	0·2 722 (0·9 795)	0·1 784 (0·996)
U^M	0·0 236	0·8 270	0·2761	0·1 254
U^V	0·0 436	0·0 341	0·0 822	0·0 139
U^C	0·9 328	0·1 388	0·6 416	0·8 608
U^R	0·1 113	0·0 287	0·1 354	0·0 015
U^D	0·8 652	0·1 443	0·5 884	0·8 731
R	0·9 647	0·9 967	0·9 778	0·9 860
α	−3·9 617	−14·915	13·7 599	5·2 882
β	0·9 108	1·0 374	0·9 068	1·0 072

Year	ξ	A	P	P'
1952		31·00	−31·95	
1953	0·6 883	41·00	62·46	55·69
1954	0·3 352	115·00	125·45	113·96
1955	0·2 037	84·00	90·35	88·59
1956	0·7 204	−58·00	−35·54	−28·84
1957	0·9 132	41·00	69·47	54·14
1958	−0·4 029	97·00	84·44	76·60
1959	−0·8 907	220·00	192·23	179·78
1960	−1·5 319	44·00	−3·76	12·23
1961	0·7 566	4·00	27·59	25·09
1962	1·6 419	−9·00	42·19	34·82
1963	0·0 940	67·00	69·93	58·93
1964	−0·3 368	136·00	125·50	116·32
1965	−0·7 961	93·00	68·18	70·27
1966	0·3 698	−29·00	−17·47	−11·58

Prediction – Realisation Diagram

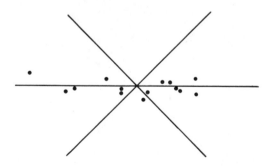

VARIABLE RS_{1t}

TYPE OF PREDICTION: UNCONDITIONAL

Index	1952 1966	1952 1956	1957 1961	1962 1966
U	0·5 414 (0·498)	0·7 855 (0·7 282)	0·6 026 (0·812)	0·1 579 (0·9 953)
U^M	0·0 006	0·3 338	0·7 561	0·0 997
U^V	0·0 120	0·5 066	0·0 916	0·2 231
U^C	0·9 874	0·1 596	0·1 522	0·6 772
U^R	0·2 092	0·6 161	0·0 083	0·1 651
U^D	0·7 902	0·0 501	0·2 356	0·7 352
R	0·7 346	0·8 069	0·6 802	0·9 882
α	12·1 629	27·856	25·9 308	−6·1 852
β	0·6 779	0·2 803	1·2 531	1·0 792

EQUATION NUMBER: 6.13

Year	ξ	A	P	P'
1952		99·00	115·77	
1953	1·0 864	167·00	204·70	182·82
1954	0·9 930	221·00	255·46	239·13
1955	1·4 385	260·00	309·92	293·44
1956	−0·9 152	289·00	257·24	270·29
1957	0·2 239	296·00	303·77	311·18
1958	−0·4 057	314·00	299·92	310·82
1959	−0·8 123	382·00	353·81	353·15
1960	−1·7 933	466·00	403·77	408·92
1961	−0·6 778	520·00	496·48	498·83
1962	0·7 625	522·00	548·46	551·46
1963	0·1 481	541·00	546·14	550·53
1964	−0·0 329	669·00	667·86	639·16
1965	−0·2 642	688·00	678·83	687·83
1966	0·5 412	649·00	667·78	686·46

Prediction – Realisation Diagram

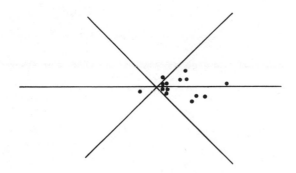

VARIABLE RS_{2t} EQUATION NUMBER: 6.14

TYPE OF PREDICTION: UNCONDITIONAL

Index	1952 1966	1952 1956	1957 1961	1962 1966
U	0·3 738 (0·5 297)	0·2 320 (0·923)	0·4 676 (0·9 454)	0·3 666 (0·934)
U^M	0·0 368	0·2 644	0·4 525	0·1 014
U^V	0·0 349	0·3 347	0·0 545	0·8 395
U^C	0·9 284	0·4 009	0·4 930	0·0 591
U^R	0·0 000	0·2 754	0·1 140	0·8 092
U^D	0·9 632	0·4 602	0·4 335	0·0 894
R	0·9 301	0·9 875	0·9 512	0·9 938
α	6·1 643	12·3 170	24·3 092	−8·563
β	1·0 000	1·1 408	0·8 574	1·5 075

Year	ξ	A	P	P'
1952		216·6	301·7	
1953	−0·8 374	302·7	264·4	270·56
1954	0·0 153	345·6	346·3	352·46
1955	−0·2 164	343·9	334·0	340·16
1956	0·1 377	200·5	206·8	212·96
1957	0·2 952	253·6	267·1	273·26
1958	−1·1 172	332·9	281·8	287·96
1959	0·2 011	424·4	433·6	439·76
1960	−1·5 304	350·5	280·5	286·66
1961	−0·1 224	229·0	223·4	229·56
1962	0·3 192	226·7	241·3	247·46
1963	−0·8 549	336·8	297·7	303·86
1964	0·0 634	374·4	377·3	383·46
1965	1·0 013	263·7	309·5	315·66
1966	0·7 587	162·6	197·3	203·46

Prediction − Realisation Diagram

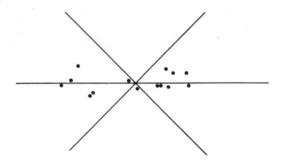

VARIABLE RS_{3t}

TYPE OF PREDICTION: UNCONDITIONAL

Index	1952 1966	1952 1956	1957 1961	1962 1966
U	1·1 986 (0·4 496)	0·8 777 (0·857)	1·1 735 (0·4 856)	1·5 409 (0·427)
U^M	0·0 127	0·6 028	0·3 569	0·3 401
U^V	0·0 213	0·0 108	0·0 478	0·0 131
U^C	0·9 660	0·3 865	0·5 954	0·6 468
U^R	0·4 140	0·0 070	0·4 146	0·2 429
U^D	0·5 733	0·3 903	0·2 285	0·4 170
R	0·3 971	0·8 350	0·1 162	0·0 613
α	4·8 458	22·966	22·9 703	0·2 167
β	0·3 374	0·9 190	0·0 799	0·0 745

EQUATION NUMBER: 6.16

Year	ξ	A	P	P'
1952		197·0	180·6	
1953	0·0 271	193·0	194·3	200·93
1954	−0·5 295	233·0	207·6	202·77
1955	−1·1 446	262·0	207·1	229·11
1956	−0·4 149	209·0	189·1	242·25
1957	−0·0 646	200·0	196·9	209·76
1958	−0·4 003	238·0	218·8	211·19
1959	0·4 024	237·0	256·3	249·02
1960	−0·4 941	274·0	250·3	246·33
1961	−1·1 550	293·0	237·6	266·56
1962	−0·4 170	255·0	235·0	278·28
1963	−0·8 423	288·0	247·6	257·35
1964	1·9 368	233·0	325·9	305·63
1965	0·8 402	274·0	314·3	265·28
1966	0·9 298	267·0	311·6	291·53

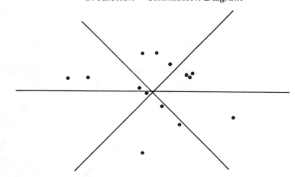

Prediction − Realisation Diagram

VARIABLE RS_{4t}

EQUATION NUMBER: 6.17

TYPE OF PREDICTION: UNCONDITIONAL

Index	1952 1966	1952 1956	1957 1961	1962 1966
U	0·4 633 (0·5 302)	0·4 786 (0·961)	0·3 883 (0·9 826)	0·4 489 (0·994)
U^M	0·0 356	0·3 980	0·3 026	0·1 569
U^V	0·0 010	0·0 071	0·0 001	0·0 194
U^C	0·9 634	0·5 949	0·6 974	0·8 236
U^R	0·0 383	0·0 067	0·0 173	0·0 982
U^D	0·9 261	0·5 953	0·6 801	0·7 449
R	0·8 943	0·9 116	0·9 451	0·9 219
α	2·5 283	9·1 094	−4·3 125	5·5 676
β	0·9 077	0·9 545	0·9 477	0·8 676

Year	ξ	A	P	P'
1952		−17·9	23·3	
1953	−0·4 439	38·6	29·8	27·92
1954	−1·3 519	50·6	23·8	27·69
1955	−0·0 807	45·5	43·9	47·04
1956	0·0 757	34·0	35·5	38·95
1957	−0·5 145	30·8	20·6	24·37
1958	0·5 448	14·0	24·8	27·88
1959	0·6 406	38·8	51·5	50·57
1960	−0·2 573	67·0	61·9	62·30
1961	0·0 404	48·9	49·7	53·83
1962	0·8 474	15·7	32·5	36·54
1963	−0·4 972	53·8	44·3	44·19
1964	−0·2 320	87·8	83·2	83·01
1965	−1·3 468	51·8	25·1	33·42
1966	0·7 617	15·5	30·6	35·09

Prediction − Realisation Diagram

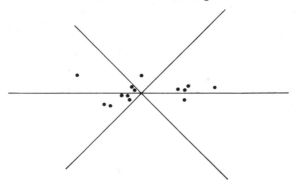

VARIABLE $\Delta PR_{1t} + \Delta PR_{2t}$

TYPE OF PREDICTION: UNCONDITIONAL

Index	1951 1966	1951 1955	1956 1960	1961 1966
U	0·6 695 (0·4 958)	0·3 155 (0·964)	0·7 011 (0·9 929)	0·6 637 (0·857)
U^M	0·0 002	0·0 129	0·4 466	0·0 623
U^V	0·0 072	0·7 378	0·0 275	0·0 100
U^C	0·9 926	0·2 493	0·5 260	0·9 277
U^R	0·0 726	0·6 416	0·0 074	0·0 534
U^D	0·9 272	0·3 455	0·5 460	0·8 844
R	0·7 617	0·9 807	0·7 916	0·7 796
α	0·9 089	−1·5 879	−4·0 008	8·7 320
β	0·8 077	1·3 726	0·9 173	0·8 352

EQUATION NUMBER: 6.18

Year	ξ	A	P	P'
1952	0·1 647	19·00	23·99	25·29
1953	−0·0914	32·00	29·23	28·17
1954	0·0 284	27·00	27·86	29·56
1955	−0·0564	38·00	36·29	35·41
1956	0·4 251	36·00	48·88	47·70
1957	0·2 700	49·00	57·18	54·02
1958	0·3 195	49·00	58·68	57·73
1959	0·1 901	43·00	48·76	49·72
1960	−0·1 383	58·00	53·81	52·64
1961	0·3 010	53·00	66·12	62·24
1962	−0·4 202	77·00	64·27	63·01
1963	−1·5 922	101·00	52·76	58·33
1964	−1·5 714	93·00	45·39	56·99
1965	1·5 982	−2·00	46·42	56·28
1966	0·4 165	77·00	89·62	72·91

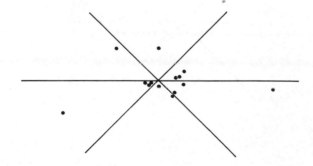

Prediction − Realisation Diagram

VARIABLE PR_t^R

EQUATION NUMBER: 6.19

TYPE OF PREDICTION: UNCONDITIONAL

Index	1951 1966	1951 1955	1956 1960	1961 1966
U	0·2106 (0·389)	0·2503 (0·9514)	0·2216 (0·835)	0·2144 (0·6711
U^M	0·0008	0·6047	0·2168	0·0142
U^V	0·2978	0·2485	0·3673	0·7126
U^C	0·7014	0·1469	0·4159	0·2732
U^R	0·0037	0·0071	0·3728	0·0409
U^D	0·9955	0·3882	0·4104	0·9448
R	0·6181	0·3875	−0·5658	0·3927
α	−3·7259	−21·319	147·785	−47·689
β	1·0843	1·4767	−2·5719	1·9 506

Year	ξ	A	P	P'
1952	0·2165	317·00	319·54	318·47
1953	0·7400	341·00	349·68	348·71
1954	0·9215	364·00	374·81	373·94
1955	−0·0094	399·00	398·89	398·11
1956	−0·5763	442·00	435·24	434·57
1957	−1·4731	497·00	479·72	479·18
1958	−0·4825	542·00	536·34	535·93
1959	0·6683	575·00	582·84	582·56
1960	−0·3112	621·00	617·35	617·20
1961	0·0963	664·00	665·13	665·13
1962	0·3163	706·00	709·71	709·84
1963	−0·5891	760·00	753·09	753·34
1964	1·2020	795·00	809·10	809·51
1965	0·8064	836·00	845·46	845·99
1966	−1·2029	902·00	887·89	888·54

Prediction − Realisation Diagram

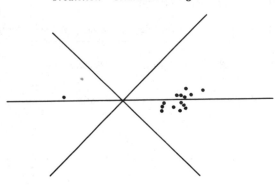

VARIABLE II_{1t}

TYPE OF PREDICTION: UNCONDITIONAL

EQUATION NUMBER: 6.20

Index	1950 1966	1950 1954	1955 1959	1960 1966
U	0·5 718 (0·4 304)	0·8 215 (0·634)	0·8 415 (0·8 472)	0·4 901 (0·652)
U^M	0·0 031	0·2 760	0·6 857	0·0 573
U^V	0·0 055	0·0 243	0·0 069	0·1 071
U^C	0·9 914	0·6 997	0·3 074	0·8 356
U^R	0·2 242	0·5 469	0·1 290	0·1 877
U^D	0·7 727	0·1 772	0·1 853	0·7 551
R	0·4 405	−0·6 380	−0·0 270	0·1 326
α	14·590	21·4 825	25·0 571	36·633
β	0·4 767	−0·8 924	−0·0 334	0·2 116

Year	ξ	A	P	P'
1952	0·2 744	110·6	116·7	123·91
1953	−0·0 315	122·8	122·1	130·67
1954	−1·1 109	150·0	125·3	138·58
1955	−0·1 979	160·2	155·8	167·35
1956	1·0 165	171·5	194·1	190·95
1957	1·2 998	191·7	220·6	209·50
1958	0·9 805	218·4	240·2	229·41
1959	−0·1 124	254·9	252·4	249·20
1960	0·6 656	284·1	298·9	290·46
1961	0·7 466	331·6	348·2	329·25
1962	0·6 342	348·2	362·3	360·82
1963	−1·3 853	399·6	368·8	372·61
1964	−1·3 718	465·6	435·1	431·11
1965	−1·2 009	536·4	509·7	501·21
1966	1·0 030	553·5	575·8	569·77

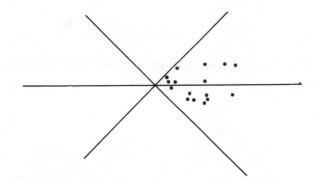

Prediction − Realisation Diagram

VARIABLE II_{2t}

EQUATION NUMBER: 6.21

TYPE OF PREDICTION: UNCONDITIONAL

Index	1950 1966	1950 1954	1955 1959	1960 1966
U	0·4 691 (0·453)	0·5 057 (0·8 847)	0·5 309 (0·9 039)	0·4 932 (0·720)
U^M	0·0 028	0·0 656	0·8 148	0·0 536
U^V	0·0 162	0·4 721	0·0 916	0·0 566
U^C	0·9 810	0·4 623	0·0 936	0·8 898
U^R	0·2 114	0·1 808	0·0 056	0·3 184
U^D	0·7 858	0·7 535	0·1 796	0·6 279
R	0·7 535	0·8 333	0·1 156	0·7 099
α	4·8 625	−0·7 589	5·7 214	12·4 850
β	0·6 884	1·4 816	0·3 978	0·5 860

Year	ξ	A	P	P'
1952	−0·1 019	62·4	61·1	63·25
1953	−0·3 448	71·2	66·8	70·29
1954	0·3 997	66·0	71·1	75·99
1955	0·1 489	83·8	85·7	84·42
1956	0·2 664	102·5	105·9	103·88
1957	0·7 210	114·3	123·5	121·82
1958	0·8 699	124·6	135·7	133·89
1959	0·3 135	140·1	144·1	142·89
1960	0·2 900	164·9	168·6	164·58
1961	0·9 169	183·4	195·1	190·55
1962	−1·4 498	224·8	206·3	204·03
1963	−1·8 494	234·4	210·8	220·02
1964	−0·2 743	246·3	242·8	245·05
1965	1·3 166	261·6	278·4	273·26
1966	−0·2 900	316·4	312·7	301·64

Prediction − Realisation Diagram

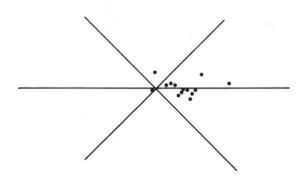

VARIABLE OUP_{1t}

TYPE OF PREDICTION: UNCONDITIONAL

EQUATION NUMBER: 6.22

Index	1951 1966	1951 1955	1956 1960	1961 1966
U	0·3 079 (0·4 587)	0·5 512 (0·8 233)	0·8 037 (0·7 991)	0·2 517 (0·722)
U^M	0·0 000	0·0 161	0·2 144	0·0 244
U^V	0·0 063	0·5 096	0·2 962	0·0 067
U^C	0·9 937	0·4 742	0·4 894	0·9 689
U^R	0·0 354	0·7 624	0·7 053	0·0 645
U^D	0·9 646	0·2 214	0·0 803	0·9 111
R	0·8 621	0·7 944	−0·0 423	0·7 796
α	3·5 905	7·5 264	20·5 688	12·4 486
β	0·8 988	0·4 135	−0·0 125	0·8 239

Year	ξ	A	P	P'
1952	−0·6 434	220·16	208·39	212·19
1953	−0·1 957	230·96	227·38	230·24
1954	0·2 668	237·38	242·26	244·71
1955	0·3 662	259·10	265·80	266·51
1956	−0·3 553	292·81	286·31	287·15
1957	−0·4 865	314·19	305·29	307·62
1958	−0·2 575	337·97	333·26	334·92
1959	1·0 441	350·11	369·21	369·64
1960	1·3 852	373·47	398·81	397·47
1961	−0·4 663	443·35	434·82	432·20
1962	−0·8 107	488·03	473·20	473·77
1963	−0·0 978	520·73	518·94	519·40
1964	0·3 143	572·18	577·93	575·73
1965	1·1 966	633·98	655·87	650·99
1966	−1·2 879	738·10	714·54	709·98

Prediction – Realisation Diagram

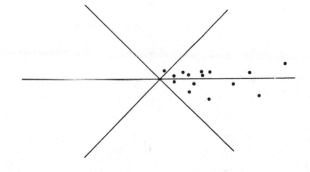

VARIABLE S_t^C (BROAD DEFINITION)

TYPE OF PREDICTION: UNCONDITIONAL

EQUATION NUMBER: 6.1(b)

Index	1950 1966	1950 1954	1955 1959	1960 1966
U	0·3 734 (0·4 782)	0·4 913 (0·960)	0·7 022 (0·9 862)	0·2 715 (0·743)
U^M	0·0 041	0·0 401	0·3 064	0·1 324
U^V	0·0 557	0·0 421	0·0 096	0·2 322
U^C	0·9 402	0·9 178	0·6 840	0·6 354
U^R	0·0 007	0·2 163	0·0 317	0·1 431
U^D	0·9 952	0·7 436	0·6 619	0·7 245
R	0·9 159	0·8 335	0·7 934	0·9 708
α	−5·4 016	29·656	−33·896	19·212
β	1·0 120	0·7 366	0·8 562	1·1 233

Year	ξ	A	P	P'
1952	−0·9 790	653·9	565·8	561·52
1953	0·6 845	817·9	879·5	876·80
1954	1·1 179	822·6	923·2	919·06
1955	1·2 868	926·6	1 042·4	1 039·63
1956	0·3 867	1 037·6	1 072·4	1 068·74
1957	−0·6 989	1 141·1	1 078·2	1 073·28
1958	1·0 934	987·9	1 086·3	1 080·24
1959	0·0 967	1 236·5	1 245·2	1 242·88
1960	−0·8 834	1 621·4	1 541·9	1 540·15
1961	−1·5 168	1 827·6	1 691·1	1 686·53
1962	0·0 411	1 588·1	1 591·8	1 583·58
1963	0·7 301	1 633·3	1 699·0	1 694·92
1964	−0·4 634	1 994·6	1 952·9	1 951·32
1965	−0·0 111	1 873·7	1 872·7	1 865·84
1966	0·2 089	1 699·0	1 717·8	1 710·53

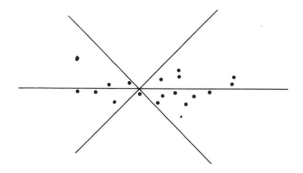

Prediction – Realisation Diagram

VARIABLE S_t^C (NARROW DEFINITION)

EQUATION NUMBER: 2.6.6

TYPE OF PREDICTION: UNCONDITIONAL

Index	1949 1966	1949 1953	1954 1958	1959 1966
U	0·6 009 (0·455)	0·6 615 (0·919)	0·8 663 (0·8 926)	0·4 651 (0·705)
U^M	0·0 073	0·0 026	0·4 896	0·3 245
U^V	0·1 188	0·0 551	0·2 689	0·1 829
U^C	0·8 739	0·9 423	0·2 414	0·4 925
U^R	0·0 012	0·0 580	0·0 980	0·0 673
U^D	0·9 915	0·9 395	0·4 124	0·6 081
R	0·7 462	0·6 120	0·8 141	0·9 111
α	−6·9 502	15·0 101	−167·83	56·405
β	0·9 696	0·7 570	1·5 331	1·1 773

Year	ξ	A	P	P'
1952	−0·8 773	437·3	317·6	306.92
1953	0·8 656	515·2	633·3	620·40
1954	1·0 862	477·0	625·2	614·91
1955	0·9 301	582·7	709·6	695·58
1956	−0·4 112	837·6	781·5	768·51
1957	0·7 051	787·3	883·5	875·16
1958	1·5 319	655·0	864·0	854·72
1959	0·6 913	812·1	896·6	882·31
1960	−1·1 339	1 270·9	1 116·2	1 100·01
1961	−1·7 899	1 598·6	1 354·4	1 344·91
1962	0·1 510	1 361·4	1 382·0	1 381·63
1963	0·1 847	1 387·8	1 413·0	1 404·48
1964	0·1 371	1 620·2	1 638·9	1 624·32
1965	−0·3 973	1 610·0	1 555·8	1 550·81
1966	−0·5 197	1 636·4	1 565·5	1 559·90

Prediction – Realisation Diagram

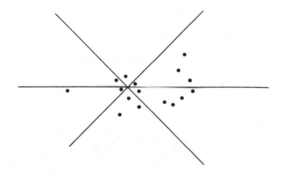

VARIABLE ΔFA_{st} EQUATION NUMBER: 3.5.4

TYPE OF PREDICTION: UNCONDITIONAL

Index	1952 1966	1952 1956	1957 1961	1962 1966
U	0·5 476 (0·5 134)	0·5 420 (0·880)	0·2 708 (0·9 958)	0·7 249 0·853)
U^M	0·0 001	0·0 405	0·2 600	0·0 224
U^V	0·0 579	0·5 404	0·0 418	0·1 424
U^C	0·9 420	0·4 191	0·6 982	0·8 352
U^R	0·0 068	0·2 918	0·0 939	0·0 079
U^D	0·9 931	0·6 677	0·6 462	0·9 697
R	0·8 098	0·8 923	0·9 684	0·6 338
α	−1·7 025	−5·6 197	10·0 319	−17·99
β	0·9 434	1·5 025	0·9 106	0·9 008

Year	ξ	A	P	P'
1952		−37·00	−21·02	
1953	0·7 654	−104·00	−35·72	−37·49
1954	−0·0 610	−100·00	−105·44	−107·06
1955	−0·5 999	8·00	−45·52	−50·30
1956	0·3 069	−102·00	−74·62	−71·65
1957	−0·2 668	−67·00	−90·80	−93·14
1958	−0·6 462	−165·00	−222·65	−215·55
1959	−0·0 739	−377·00	−385·59	−372·93
1960	0·2 327	−376·00	−355·24	−358·17
1961	−0·2 683	−305·00	−328·94	−333·30
1962	−0·1 276	−396·00	−407·38	−403·29
1963	−0·0 336	−572·00	−575·00	−566·58
1964	0·5 280	−649·00	−601·90	−601·91
1965	1·5 473	−751·00	−612·96	−616·70
1966	−1·3 981	−600·00	−724·73	−727·92

Prediction − Realisation Diagram

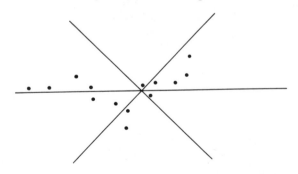

VARIABLE $\Delta RS_{3.1t}$

TYPE OF PREDICTION: UNCONDITIONAL

Index	1952 1966	1952 1956	1957 1961	1962 1966
U	0·4 520 (0·5 115)	0·3 855 (0·947)	0·5 091 (0·8 654)	0·2 792 (0·944)
U^M	0·0 035	0·2 326	0·5 037	0·0 431
U^V	0·2 485	0·3 807	0·1 199	0·5 293
U^C	0·7 481	0·3 867	0·3 764	0·4 276
U^R	0·0 680	0·2 693	0·0 008	0·6 287
U^D	0·9 285	0·4 981	0·4 955	0·3 283
R	0·8 853	0·9 621	0·5 592	0·9 743
α	1·6 706	−4·6 474	6·3 913	3·7 021
β	1·1 657	1·2 632	0·9 443	0·7 577

EQUATION NUMBER: 4.1.5

Year	ξ	A	P	P'
1952		180·4	173·4	
1953	0·5 485	175·6	182·7	181·41
1954	0·3 245	193·1	197·3	199·23
1955	−0·5 794	209·8	202·3	202·15
1956	0·9 271	175·2	187·2	181·78
1957	−0·0 309	190·1	189·7	190·43
1958	−1·0 971	217·0	202·8	203·23
1959	0·0 077	228·6	228·7	228·97
1960	−0·0 695	238·4	237·5	237·30
1961	−0·6 644	249·0	240·4	239·06
1962	1·4 834	223·7	242·9	240·22
1963	0·4 790	249·1	255·3	258·87
1964	−0·1 545	272·4	270·4	272·26
1965	−0·0 927	271·0	269·8	267·70
1966	−0·5 408	272·3	265·3	262·68

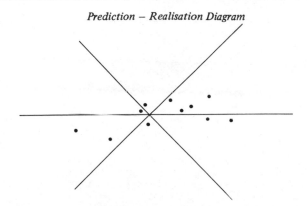

Prediction − Realisation Diagram

VARIABLE ΔPR_{1t} EQUATION NUMBER: 5.1.3

TYPE OF PREDICTION: UNCONDITIONAL

Index	1951 1966	1951 1955	1956 1960	1961 1966
U	0·7042 (0·4814)	0·4862 (0·920)	1·4252 (0·7406)	0·7115 (0·829)
U^M	0·0001	0·0001	0·5623	0·0720
U^V	0·0305	0·4582	0·0337	0·0339
U^C	0·9695	0·5417	0·4039	0·8940
U^R	0·0474	0·2308	0·3304	0·0337
U^D	0·9525	0·7691	0·1072	0·8942
R	0·7218	0·9044	−0·1761	0·7372
α	0·4494	−0·4352	7·6944	7·8779
β	0·8238	1·3485	−0·1134	0·8489

Year	ξ	A	P	P'
1952	0·0683	20·65	22·54	23·63
1953	−0·6301	42·37	24·93	24·63
1954	0·5268	7·44	22·02	26·06
1955	0·0502	29·52	30·91	27·22
1956	0·4762	28·37	41·55	39·88
1957	0·4596	36·17	48·89	45·72
1958	0·5224	38·32	52·78	50·30
1959	0·1680	42·30	46·95	45·88
1960	−0·0712	52·97	51·00	49·92
1961	0·0715	56·46	58·44	57·93
1962	−0·2251	64·56	58·33	58·45
1963	−1·7827	101·94	52·60	55·16
1964	−1·0958	80·03	49·70	59·36
1965	1·4777	15·00	55·90	60·60
1966	0·0817	77·02	79·28	68·40

Prediction − Realisation Diagram

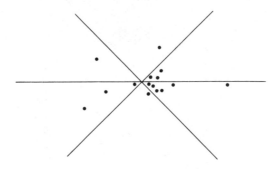

7.2.1 UNCONDITIONAL FORECASTS

A Bird's-Eye View

Table P. 1 gives a survey of overestimation, underestimation, and turning point errors for twenty-five variables, from which it is possible to conclude that there are on average turning point errors in nearly one out of six cases. In the remaining five cases, underestimation is greater than overestimation. As noted by Theil[203c] underestimation is a very common type of prediction error. This result can also be observed from the prediction—realisation diagrams as shown beneath the variables' unconditional forecasts tables.

Individual Variables

The variables' unconditional forecasts tables give estimates of: Theil's Inequality Coefficient and its sampling variance (in parentheses), the first and second-set decompositions, the correlation coefficient and the parameters of the linear corrections. If the first column in the twenty-five tables is considered the following may be observed:

1. The average value of Theil's Inequality Coefficient is approximately 0·5. This implies that the *RMS* prediction error is 50% of the *RMS* error which would have resulted had the method of no-change extrapolation been adopted. Moreover, it is to be noted that only in one case, RS_{3b} did U exceed unity; i.e. the predictive power of this equation is worse than no-change extrapolation.

2. With respect to the first-set decomposition, it is clear that the mean square prediction error is mainly due to incomplete covariation. While the bias and the variance proportions are of the order 4% and 8% on average respectively, the covariance proportion is on average greater that 87%. As to the second set proportions, their values are more or less of the same order as the corresponding values of the first set. The average values of the regression and stochastic proportions are of the order 5% and 90% respectively. The former is smaller than the variance proportion, while the latter is slightly greater than the covariance proportion.

3. In the unconditional forecasts tables, estimates of the coefficients α and β of the Least Squares regressions:

$$A_t = \alpha + \beta P_t$$

are given. It can easily be observed that the intercept is positive and the coefficient β is less than unity with seven and eight exceptions respectively. The latter result seems, in the first instance, surprising, since in view of our previous conclusions regarding the underestimation of change, one would have expected $\beta > 1$. This may be explained by the slope effects as discussed by Theil.

Individual Year's Analysis

So far we have discussed the accuracy of the forecasts of the individual variables, with no reference given to the years for which these forecasts were made. We now

Table P. 1 UNCONDITIONAL FORECASTS

	ΔFA_2	ΔFA_{1+2}	ΔFA_3	ΔFA_4	ΔFA_5	ΔFA_6	ΔFA_7	ΔFA_8	ΔFA_{8+9}	ΔHL	ΔBL	$(\Delta HP+\Delta OL)_t$
Overestimation	5	5	5	5	6	6	7	5	4	2	7	6
Underestimation	7	7	5	6	6	6	5	6	7	9	6	7
Turning point	2	2	4	3	2	2	2	3	3	3	1	1
Total	14	14	14	14	14	14	14	14	14	14	14	14

	RS_1	RS_2	RS_3	$RS_{3.1}$	RS_4	II_1	II_2	ΔPR_1	ΔPR_{1+2}	PR^R	OUP_1	$S^C_{(N)}$	$S^C_{(B)}$	Total	%
Overestimation	6	7	4	4	4	8	8	7	4	8	6	6	8	143	39
Underestimation	7	6	4	8	9	8	7	6	8	7	8	7	8	170	47
Turning point	1	1	6	2	1	0	1	2	3	0	1	4	1	51	14
Total	14	14	14	14	14	16	16	15	15	15	15	17	17	364	100

(N) narrow definition – Equation 2.6.6.
(B) broad definition – Equation 6.1(b).

Table P. 2 ANALYSIS OF INDIVIDUAL YEARS

Type of prediction	1953	1954	1955	1956	1957	1958	1959	1960	1961	1962	1963	1964	1965	1966
1. Unconditional	0·7141	0·5916	0·6481	0·5831	0·7000	0·6164	0·7348	0·7616	0·5385	0·7874	0·8660	0·8718	1·0800	0·8246
2. Conditional	0·4359	0·5568	0·6083	0·6000	0·7211	1·102	0·7681	1·020	0·8718	0·8246	0·7141	1·214	1·24	0·9163

consider the extent to which the prediction quality remained unchanged over time. Firstly, estimates of Theil's Inequality coefficient and its decomposition are given in the unconditional forecasts tables, from which one may conclude that there has been an improvement in the quality forecast for the more recent years. Theil's Inequality Coefficients for the period 1961–66 were *below* the whole periods coefficients in 15 out of 25 cases, while for the period 1951–56 they were *above* the whole period coefficients in 16 out of 25 cases. Secondly, in carrying out the year to year analysis we calculate the standardised prediction error by means of the formula

$$\xi_{it} = (P_{it} - A_{it})/\sqrt{\frac{1}{n} \sum_{s} (P_{is} - A_{is})^2} \qquad \begin{aligned} i &= 1 \ldots K \quad (K \text{ variables}) \\ t &= 1 \ldots n \quad (n = 14) \end{aligned}$$

which has been suggested by Theil.[203c] The results are shown in the conditional forecast tables. Consider for each t the *RMS* of the twenty-five values of ξ_{it}; that is the square root of

$$\frac{14}{25} \Sigma \frac{(P_{it} - A_{it})^2}{\Sigma(P_{is} - A_{is})^2}$$

which are shown in *Table P. 2*.

In two years the standardised prediction errors are close to 1, in 1965 it is 8% larger, and for the rest of the period the average is approximately 0·68. The high values for the more recent years should not be taken as evidence that the prediction performance has been subject to a decreasing trend, since high values might result from extreme realised changes.

7.2.2 CONDITIONAL FORECASTS

To obtain the conditional forecasts, two models, namely the conventional-simultaneous equation model and the alternative model,* were simulated in the computer. Preliminary experiments showed that the results obtained were sensitive, particularly those for financial assets, to errors of predicting R^L, the rate of interest on long-dated government securities. For this reason, the equation for this rate was dropped from the complete model, and the realised, instead of the predicted, values were used in the simulation. The results obtained of the continous simulation for 15 years for aggregate personal saving and its composition are analysed in the tables of conditional forecasts.

Table P. 3 UNCONDITIONAL AND CONDITIONAL FORECASTS

Type of prediction	Overestimation	Underestimation	Turning points	Total
1. Conditional	39	47	15	100
2. Unconditional	46	33	21	100

* See Chapter 6, section 6.3.

A Bird's-Eye View

Table P. 3 gives a survey of the percentage of overestimation, underestimation and turning point errors. By comparing the conditional and unconditional forecasts it is clear that while in the latter underestimation is greater than overestimation, in the former the opposite is the case, i.e. overestimation is greater than underestimation and there are also more turning point errors.

Individual Variables

Turning now to the estimates of Theil's Inequality Coefficient, as shown in the conditional forecasts table, one observes the following:

1. The average value of Theil's Inequality coefficient is equal to 0·8752; i.e. the *RMS* prediction error is 88% of the *RMS* error which would have resulted if the method of no-change extrapolation had been adopted. However, in five equations $[\Delta FA_3, \Delta FA_6, \Delta FA_{8+9}, RS_3$ and $S_t^A]$ U has exceeded unity, and this implies that prediction errors are worse than no-change extrapolation in these cases. By comparing these statistics with the corresponding ones for the unconditional forecasts, it is possible to conclude that the predictive power of the unconditional forecasts was superior to that of the conditional forecasts. This is not surprising, owing to the accumulation of errors in the conditional forecasts, since errors of predictions in one year or one variable influence predictions of other variables and subsequent years.

2. With respect to the decomposition, incomplete covariation as well as errors in the unsystematic element represent the major source of prediction errors. This conclusion agrees with the one reached for the unconditional forecasts except that the relevant statistics differ. For the latter, the covariance and the stochastic proportions are larger than the corresponding ones for the conditional forecasts, and vice versa with respect to the bias, variance and regression proportions. The average values for the decompositions are as follows:

	U^M	U^V	U^C	U^R	U^D
Conditional	0·0 887	0·1 008	0·8 105	0·2 694	0·6 419
Unconditional	0·0 437	0·0 84	0·8 723	0·0 503	0·9 060

From these statistics, it is evident that the accumulation of errors in the conditional forecasts has led to a substantial increase in both the regression proportion by more than 5 times and the bias proportion which has nearly doubled.

3. The average of the slope coefficient β is less than unity. This confirms the conclusion reached previously (The Bird's-Eye View) that overestimation errors are larger than underestimation errors.

Individual Year's Analysis

As shown in *Table P. 2,* the standardised prediction errors are close to unity in two years, greater than unity in 4 years, and for the rest of the period the average

TYPE OF PREDICTION: CONDITIONAL   VARIABLES: AGGREGATE SAVING AND ITS COMPOSITION

Variables \ Index	U	U^M	U^V	U^C	U^R	U^D	R	α	β
$\Delta FA_2 t$	0·6294 (0·5181)	0·0029	0·0055	0·9916	0·0647	0·9324	0·7923	6·3343	0·8313
$\Delta FA_{1+2} t$	0·6662 (0·5130)	0·0073	0·0074	0·9853	0·0693	0·9234	0·7664	9·8947	0·8133
$\Delta FA_3 t$	1·0191 (0·5249)	0·0376	0·2197	0·7427	0·5601	0·4023	0·6744	19·3754	0·4363
$\Delta FA_4 t$	0·8301 (0·4610)	0·0033	0·0463	0·9505	0·0703	0·9264	0·6013	−1·9488	0·7320
$\Delta FA_5 t$	0·7059 (0·5107)	0·0009	0·0045	0·9946	0·0909	0·9083	0·7398	0·8367	0·7766
$\Delta FA_6 t$	1·1900 (0·5063)	0·0202	0·0774	0·9024	0·4656	0·5142	0·5179	−29·7578	0·3888
$\Delta FA_7 t$	1·4330 (0·3592)	0·0323	0·0148	0·9529	0·5224	3·4453	0·1041	14·2757	0·0881
$\Delta FA_{8+9} t$	1·0725 (0·4902)	0·6396	0·0238	0·3366	0·0056	0·3548	0·7422	80·0402	0·8980
ΔHL_t	0·7119 (0·5289)	0·1072	0·0002	0·8926	0·1415	0·7513	0·7006	−0·6316	0·6934
ΔBL_t	0·9648 (0·5228)	0·1557	0·2366	0·6077	0·4706	0·3737	0·8074	26·0457	0·5494
$(\Delta HP + \Delta OL)_t$	0·4732 (0·5303)	0·0138	0·1982	0·7880	0·3592	0·6270	0·9270	2·8497	0·7655

TYPE OF PREDICTION: CONDITIONAL VARIABLES: AGGREGATE SAVING AND ITS COMPOSITION (*Cont.*)

Index / Variables	U	U^M	U^V	U^C	U^R	U^D	R	α	β
RS_{1t}	0·9868 (0·5262)	0·2158	0·1617	0·6225	0·3869	0·3973	0·7830	22·6757	0·5605
RS_{2t}	0·8896 (0·5160)	0·1596	0·0661	0·7743	0·3899	0·4506	0·5395	15·1756	0·4079
RS_{3t}	1·3864 (0·4812)	0·2781	0·0636	0·6584	0·3518	0·3702	0·5219	12·5456	0·3856
RS_{4t}	0·9492 (0·4836)	0·2182	0·0001	0·7817	0·1334	0·6484	0·6418	9·3612	0·6485
$PR_{1+t\,t}$	0·5626 (0·4377)	0·0020	0·0393	0·9587	0·4568	0·5412	0·4069	35·6409	0·3266
PR_t^R	0·2169 (0·4075)	0·0240	0·3521	0·6239	0·0064	0·9696	0·5725	−3·8538	1·1317
II_{1t}	0·5758 (0·4300)	0·0031	0·0055	0·9914	0·2242	0·7727	0·4405	14·5898	0·4767
II_{2t}	0·4691 (0·4525)	0·0028	0·0162	0·9810	0·2114	0·7858	0·7535	4·8625	0·6884
OUP_{1t}	0·3079 (0·4587)	0·000	0·0063	0·9937	0·0354	0·9646	0·8621	3·5905	0·8988
S_t^A	2·6601 (0·4800)	0·000	0·4610	0·5390	0·9024	0·0976	0·1416	104·3710	0·0450
S_t^C	0·5552 (0·5024)	0·0262	0·2120	0·7617	0·0097	0·9641	0·7606	−30·0152	1·0936

TYPE OF PREDICTION: CONDITIONAL; ESTIMATES OF THE RESIDUAL

Year	ΔFA_{2t}	ΔFA_{1+2t}	ΔFA_{3t}	ΔFA_{4t}	ΔFA_{5t}	ΔFA_{6t}	ΔFA_{8+9t}	ΔFA_{7t}	ΔHL_t	ΔBL_t
1952	47·1193	33·8313	43·5841	-45·7058	22·0215	306·7912	21·0585	86·8528	4·2802	123·0935
1953	81·3145	100·2082	-9·2497	-39·5543	-37·9405	50·0128	-12·3179	-29·0305	-25·5665	-6·3201
1954	62·1113	87·6002	-19·509	2·0919	-24·0308	-251·0507	65·6264	-77·3015	-6·3825	-47·2926
1955	-41·764	-32·5203	-43·4308	17·939	-56·2218	25·2061	127·0785	-12·6335	24·5528	44·9107
1956	-0·5673	5·5506	-12·4946	42·4871	1·5100	-13·0853	40·9547	28·7225	5·7107	-47·3259
1957	143·9598	153·5236	-117·9353	26·6266	41·6618	-527·3091	98·6159	-79·5707	-19·958	7·8332
1958	-52·9281	-57·6599	-165·982	37·6511	67·1697	-594·6377	133·2311	-158·9163	-96·7765	-118·4902
1959	8·0346	15·5645	-216·7114	41·5505	36·0334	-343·4614	86·0911	-158·7306	-50·2170	119·3824
1960	-17·6844	-26·4176	57·0014	-77·657	-47·0065	447·6949	55·7765	-8·5903	-104·625	192·4824
1961	39·0543	63·2763	15·6082	-22·5645	-19·3822	42·6718	109·2984	91·3856	-69·9915	139·1914
1962	-156·9771	-175·0758	116·7956	6·7370	54·5451	96·6889	158·5857	-12·4942	-72·8645	63·7878
1963	-87·5199	-98·7253	-73·6631	22·6286	-8·7699	-379·1701	114·6650	-45·1950	6·3150	47·5628
1964	52·9235	56·7520	76·0369	-14·9074	34·1225	68·9517	81·1309	-10·8762	115·4975	286·090
1965	173·1181	-199·1829	180·2649	-116·2132	52·1513	508·2352	-25·2536	182·2174	18·4163	-38·1841
1966	-135·5345	-163·1721	-74·4387	36·2816	-75·3070	222·2014	266·3642	65·0839	5·5141	-15·1840

TYPE OF PREDICTION: CONDITIONAL; ESTIMATES OF THE RESIDUAL (*cont.*)

Year	$(\Delta HP + \Delta OL)_t$	RS_{1t}	RS_{2t}	RS_{3t}	RS_{4t}	PR_{1+2t}	PR_t^R	S^A	S^C
1952	81·5 587	85·1 812	5·8 010	55·3 057	−19·2 015	−3·6 073	−1·9 727	143·758	106·348
1953	−22·4 058	85·1 812	−55·7 851	−2·2 195	7·6 198	3·1 752	−7·8 487	53·1 962	−36·5 884
1954	−15·6 208	−43·3 871	−58·3 707	17·955	19·511	−4·5 264	−9·8 457	−354·147	−112·239
1955	0·2 649	68·5 572	−13·772	74·0 418	12·5 979	1·4 103	1·1 257	−384·8 256	−64·1 407
1956	−11·0 116	2·7 099	55·4 424	27·0 726	6·0 157	87·5 013	7·9 411	300·1 571	47·0 133
1957	−54·2 231	−2·6 858	−28·2 463	−8·5 215	3·6 717	−11·4 206	18·557	−443·924	−47·0 606
1958	−28·2 573	−57·8 244	−77·8 087	−12·2 841	−29·8 504	−12·9 472	6·9 879	−1 116·4 496	−200·7 784
1959	6·2 803	37·5 867	−42·6 524	5·8 550	−2·0 402	−13·4 393	−6·4 025	−502·7 509	−85·9 274
1960	80·5 654	150·9 852	−23·5 943	83·2 664	32·6 246	−3·2 259	5·2 739	327·3 173	77·9 684
1961	1·3 342	97·204	−9·8 145	96·7 829	22·5 278	−13·2 993	0·6 456	716·3 783	192·9 713
1962	−43·0 716	−4·5 161	−92·1 299	19·3 819	−19·2 166	1·4 718	−1·7 117	−6·7 455	−80·6 829
1963	10·8 475	85·3 619	−34·8 935	72·5 099	29·6 478	35·7 644	8·7 986	−231·4 437	15·7 486
1964	88·7 903	207·0 309	67·7 035	18·0 854	67·8 819	33·8 505	−12·1 084	430·5 595	199·4 975
1965	67·7 472	72·5 641	32·0 962	−14·6 514	44·0 753	−63·1 924	−7·3 841	998·7 620	−46·9 952
1966	−10·7 502	−39·6 969	4·3 640	−33·3 417	−114·060	−20·6 571	16·3 573	306·8 756	−112·1 003

is approximately 0·65. Thus, the larger average for U in the conditional forecast as compared with the unconditional forecast may be attributed, to some extent, to relatively larger errors of predictions in the years 1960, 1961, 1964, 1965 and 1966 where the standardised prediction errors are close to or greater than one.

7.2.3 THE TWO AGGREGATE MODELS: ONCE AGAIN

In the previous chapter two models of aggregate personal saving were discussed and compared with reference to their derivation and possible analytical applications. These two models were:

1. The Conventional model where saving was measured as a residual from the income account of the personal sector, and

2. The Alternative model where saving was measured from the balance sheet of the personal sector.

With respect to the conventional model, a distinction was also made between the single-equation and the simultaneous-equation conventional model.

In this sub-section, the conditional and unconditional forecasting performance of the conventional and the alternative models are examined. A bird's-eye-view and estimates of Theil's Inequality coefficient and its decompositions are presented in *Table P. 4*.

Table P. 4 THE FORECASTING PERFORMANCE OF THE AGGREGATE MODELS

Type of prediction	Unconditional		Conditional	
Index	$\hat{S}^C$	$\hat{S}^A$	$\hat{S}^C$	$\hat{S}^A$
Overestimation	47·05%	50·0%	35·71%	57·13
Underestimation	47·05%	35·71%	50·00%	28·58
Turning points	5·90%	14·29%	14·29%	14·29
U	0·3734	1·1556	0·5552	2·6601
U^M	0·0041	0·0840	0·0262	0
U^V	0·0557	0·1908	0·2120	0·4610
U^C	0·9402	0·7252	0·7617	0·5390
U^R	0·0007	0·5738	0·0097	0·9024
U^D	0·9952	0·3421	0·9641	0·0976
R	0·9159	0·5376	0·7606	0·1416
α	−5·4016	57·566	−30·0152	104·371
β	1·0120	0·3299	1·0936	0·045

Notes
1. Broad definitions of saving
2. $\hat{S}^C$ and $\hat{S}^A$ refer to the conventional and the alternative models respectively.

From the table it is easy to observe the forecasting superiority of: (1) the unconditional over the conditional approach, and (2) the conventional over the alternative approach. Does this mean that, for forecasting purposes, the forecaster should rely on the single-equation conventional model? The answer, in the author's opinion, is yes and no, depending on the purpose which the forecast is to serve. Suppose, for example, that the purpose of the forecast is to examine the effects on aggregate personal saving of changing both the rates of interest and the tax provisions regarding investment in owner-occupied housing and life assurance and superannuation saving. Obviously, it is not possible to carry out such a forecast with the single-equation conventional model, unless one uses another model which links the explanatory variables in the single equation with these instruments of economic policy. It is necessary to construct a 'data-generating model' *which links interest rates and the relevant tax provisions with income and the stock of liquid assets, and then to use the predicted values for Y_t^d and L_t in forecasting aggregate saving from the single equation. In other words, a policy-motivated forecast cannot be carried out unless a more-than-one-equation model is specified and estimated.*

Thus, in a policy-motivated forecast the problem is reduced to that of the choice between the conditional-conventional-model and the conditional-alternative-model. To begin with, it was pointed out in Chapter 6 that certain policy questions cannot be examined using the conventional-simultaneous-equation model of aggregate personal saving. One example is the effects of the tax discrimination in favour of life assurance and superannuation saving. Secondly, even for those policy questions which can be examined using either model, the alternative model is likely, in principle, to be more appropriate than the conventional model since more factors are taken into account in the former. The following policy example helps to illustrate the difference between the two models with respect to a policy-motivated forecast.

Assume that early in 1966 the British Government had adopted a policy similar to the Barber policy package. More precisely, such a policy would have involved the following measures:

1. A reduction in the standard income tax rate by $2\frac{1}{2}$ pence in the £, i.e. $G^{10} = 0.3875$.
2. A reduction in outlay taxation of the order of £300, i.e. $G^{EX} = 1.0765$.
3. A reduction in bank rate by 1%: i.e. $BR = 5.46$.
4. The abolition of hire purchase restrictions, i.e. $HPC = -33\frac{1}{3}$.
5. An increase in the tax concessions to owner-occupiers; i.e. $\delta = 1$.

The problem to be investigated is: what would the effect have been on aggregate personal saving? These policy changes were simulated in the computer using the conventional-simultaneous-equation model and the alternative model. The results obtained are shown in *Table P. 5,* which shows an increase of: more than 9% in aggregate personal saving according to the alternative model, and only 4% approximately according to the conventional model. The discrepancy may be explained partly by the tendency to overestimate by the alternative model and to underestimate by the conventional model which was noted earlier, and partly because the conventional model accounts for the adjustment in the holdings of ΔFA_3, ΔFA_4 and ΔFA_5 only.

It emerges from the previous discussion that while the conventional model is superior to the alternative model on purely forecasting grounds, the latter is more useful when certain policy changes are envisaged. In this situation one cannot discard one model completely, since each model contains some useful

Table P. 5 EFFECTS OF VARIATIONS IN POLICY INSTRUMENTS ON AGGREGATE PERSONAL SAVING AND ITS COMPOSITION (1966)

Variable	Case A (£m)	Case B (£m)	$(B-A)$ (£m)	$(B-A)/A$ (%)
ΔFA_{1t}	66·6	66·6	0	0
ΔFA_{2t}	386·5	385·0	−1·5	−0·38
ΔFA_{3t}	871·4	1 019·1	147·7	16·94
ΔFA_{4t}	−26·3	−62·9	−36·6	−139·16
ΔFA_{5t}	−4·7	31·9	36·6	778·72
ΔFA_{6t}	−226·2	−91·0	135·2	59·77
ΔFA_{7t}	167·9	187·4	19·5	11·61
ΔFA_{8+9t}	−761·4	−761·4	0	0
ΔHL_t	715·5	718·7	3·2	0·44
ΔBL_t	−44·8	82·4	127·2	−283·92
$(\Delta HP + \Delta OL)_t$	−18·24	183·5	201·74	−1 106·03
RS_{1t}	238·6	392·2	153·60	64·37
RS_{2t}	644·6	647·7	3·10	0·48
RS_{3t}	300·3	341·3	41·00	13·65
RS_{4t}	30·4	37·3	7·1	23·35
NIF_t	1 140·2	1 132·7	−7·5	−0·66
$\hat{S}_t^A$	1 771·0	1 936·3	165·3	9·33
$\hat{S}_t^C$	2 190·0	2 269·1	79·1	3·61

Case A: Predictions for the year 1966, given the economic policy actually adopted.
Case B: Predictions for the year 1966, assuming the policy changes described in the text.

independent information. Instead, an attempt should be made to form a *combined forecast* based on the two conditional models.

Following Bates and Granger,[10] let the variance of errors for the two forecasts be denoted by σ_1^2 and σ_2^2 for all values of t, and assuming that both forecasts are serially independent, the combined forecast may be obtained by a linear combination of the two sets of forecasts, giving a weight K to the first set of forecasts and a weight $(1 - K)$ to the second set. The variance of errors in the combined forecast σ_C^2 can be written as:

$$\sigma_C^2 = K^2 \sigma_1^2 + (1 - K)^2 \sigma_2^2 + 2rK\sigma_1(1 - K)\sigma_2 \tag{i}$$

where r is the correlation coefficient between the errors in the first set of forecasts and those in the second set. K is selected so that σ_2^2 is a minimum. Differentiating (i) with respect to K, and equating to zero, the minimum of σ_2^2 occurs when:

$$K = (\sigma_2^2 - r\sigma_1\sigma_2)/(\sigma_1^2 + \sigma_2^2 - 2r\sigma_1\sigma_2) \tag{ii}*$$

The combined forecast for a time period t is given by:

$$f_{c.t} = K_t f_{1.t} + (1 - K_t)f_{2.t} \tag{iii}$$

where f_1, f_2, f_c are: first set of forecasts, second set of forecasts and combined forecast respectively.

* In Bates and Granger (ii) appears as:

$$K = (\sigma_2^2 - r\sigma_1\sigma_2)/(\sigma_1^2 \ominus \sigma_2^2 - 2r\sigma_1\sigma_2)$$

The circled sign is wrong; it is an obvious typing error.

Table P. 6 THE COMBINED CONDITIONAL FORECAST

Year	$\hat{S}^A$ (£m)	$\hat{S}^C$ (£m)	Actual (£m)	Combined	K	r
1952	403·5	440·9	547·3	547·3	−2·8 428	1*
1953	751·7	735·1	698·5	689·3	−2·7 553	1*
1954	1 069·8	827·9	715·7	854·1	0·1 080	0·1 339
1955	1 219·7	899·0	834·9	940·5	0·1 292	−0·1 847
1956	677·7	930·9	977·9	893·6	0·1 474	−0·3 866
1957	1 456·7	1 059·9	1 012·8	1 116·9	0·1 437	−0·5 495
1958	2 104·3	1 188·7	987·9	1 167·5	−0·0 231	0·3 064
1959	1 746·6	1 329·8	1 243·9	1 306·2	−·0 566	0·4 448
1960	1 318·5	1 567·8	1 645·8	1 585·0	−0·0 688	0·4 904
1961	1 191·7	1 715·1	1 908·1	1 771·1	−0·1 070	0·6 062
1962	1 725·0	1 798·9	1 718·3	1 808·2	−0·1 243	0·6 502
1963	2 121·5	1 874·4	1 890·1	1 842·2	−0·1 299	0·6 680
1964	1 817·4	2 048·5	2 248·0	2 081·6	−0·1 431	0·6 756
1965	1 206·6	2 252·4	2 205·4	2 397·9	−0·1 392	0·7 057
1966	1 771·0	2 190·0	2 077·9	2 252·5	−0·1 493	0·7 254

Notes

$\hat{S}^C$ Predicted aggregate personal saving (broad definition) as derived from the conventional model (6.1b).
$\hat{S}^A$ Predicted aggregate personal saving (broad definition) as derived from the alternative model (6.1).
* Assumed arbitrarily.

This method was used in deriving a combined forecast of aggregate personal saving in the United Kingdom (1952–66) on the basis of both the conditional conventional and alternative models. The results are presented in *Table P. 6*.

7.3 CONCLUDING REMARKS AND SUGGESTIONS FOR FURTHER RESEARCH

The aim of this study has been to explore the possibilities of extending the conventional treatment of the aggregate saving function towards the policy sphere. Several interesting conclusions and topics for further research have emerged.

The results obtained indicate that both monetary and tax policy influence aggregate personal saving and its composition. With respect to monetary policy, it has been found that savings depend upon the stock of liquid assets and that variations in interest rates not only influence the composition of personal saving, but also lead to a net faviourable effect on the aggregate level. Concerning tax policy, the analysis of the incidental, incentive, and switching effects of taxation on saving has been most revealing, particularly with reference to tax discriminations.

In Chapters 6 and 7 the limitations of the conventional aggregate saving function have been outlined in the context of policy formulation. An alternative approach, based on the net worth definition of personal saving, has been advocated but unfortunately it proved unsatisfactory in terms of forecasting.

Nevertheless, its superiority as a policy-making framework is a suitable justification for further research. This would involve an improvement in the specification of the model, as well as the application of more sophisticated techniques of estimation. In addition, unless a serious attempt is made to improve the quality of the Balance Sheet statistics and to explain the mysteries surrounding the unidentified items in the Flows of Funds accounts, progress in this important field will only proceed at a very slow rate.

Data Appendix

Table A TRANSACTIONS IN ASSETS AND LIABILITIES BY THE PERSONAL SECTOR (£m)

Year	ΔFA_{1t}	ΔFA_{2t}	ΔFA_{3t}	ΔFA_{4t}	ΔFA_{5t}	ΔFA_{6t}	ΔFA_{7t}	ΔFA_{8t}	ΔFA_{9t}	ΔHL_t	ΔBL_t	ΔHP_t	ΔOL_t	RS_{1t}	RS_{2t}
1952	36	70	93	11	−68	286	−8	−37	—	139	−103	18	13	99	181·3
1953	55	120	133	29	−50	110	21	−104	—	168	−7	31	10	167	258·5
1954	64	149	253	35	5	−87	34	−100	—	236	72	96	19	221	300·7
1955	48	−130	221	31	−11	452	47	8	—	278	−1	72	12	260	309·9
1956	37	25	180	56	14	92	133	−102	—	215	5	−63	5	289	188·9
1957	27	198	195	11	47	−181	126	−67	5	229	3	37	4	296	246·8
1958	25	188	186	94	149	121	108	−165	15	227	193	82	15	314	332·9
1959	67	384	390	85	206	−56	92	−377	30	362	339	224	−4	382	426·9
1960	51	197	338	57	173	302	144	−376	13	380	257	22	20	466	355·8
1961	49	189	343	−7	110	−94	241	−305	7	369	61	−21	25	520	239·1
1962	3	301	553	5	58	−40	289	−396	34	414	221	−1	−8	522	245·3
1963	46	356	743	−7	82	−246	205	−572	60	572	90	69	−2	541	369·1
1964	75	454	776	−26	140	−67	130	−649	77	758	129	109	27	669	422·0
1965	77	512	844	−124	54	−75	268	−751	59	695	−33	63	30	688	310·4
1966	37	253	797	10	−80	−4	233	−600	105	721	−60	−102	73	649	198·9

Table A TRANSACTIONS IN ASSETS AND LIABILITIES BY THE PERSONAL SECTOR (£m) (cont.)

Asset / Year	RS_{3t}	RS_{4t}	STA_t	PR_{1+2t}	PR_t^R	II_{1t}	II_{2t}	OUP_{1+2t}	ADM_t	$UNIP_t$	ΔBSS_t	ΔBSD_t	ΔTSB_t	$RS_{3.1t}$	IDM_t
1952	197	−15	10	390	317	110·623	62·377	424	105	−689	129·4	−10·7	7	151	36·99
1953	193	33	7	422	341	122·834	71·166	453	111	−583	151·9	5·3	30	150	68·3
1954	233	44	20	449	364	149·988	66·012	472	120	−613	196·7	19·5	44	168	68·8
1955	262	41	44	487	399	160·215	83·785	514	139	−981	196·8	−5·4	37	189	89·2
1956	209	32	39	523	442	171·501	102·499	574	150	−662	177·6	−23·0	54	165	86·4
1957	200	30	31	572	497	191·671	114·329	629	167	−580	175·6	−4·4	31	185	44·9
1958	238	14	15	621	542	218·368	124·632	688	169	−907	183·6	9·5	26	217	98·4
1959	237	39	24	664	575	254·893	140·107	727	190	−634	254·1	15·2	39	230	107·6
1960	274	68	29	722	621	284·086	164·914	778	198	−753	197·7	8·3	55	242	98·6
1961	293	51	44	775	664	331·619	183·381	872	213	−378	200·3	3·5	66	260	113·0
1962	255	17	46	852	706	348·180	224·820	944	246	−658	344·1	16·8	107	242	44·9
1963	288	59	36	953	760	399·629	234·371	1 017	264	−615	467·5	29·2	133	273	141·0
1964	233	99	58	1 046	795	465·642	246·358	1 107	290	−461	486·9	22·2	149	307	149·7
1965	274	61	69	1 044	836	536·364	261·636	1 194	318	−609	629·7	1·6	102	319	42·99
1966	267	19	72	1 121	902	553·544	316·456	1 340	355	−605	749·0	4·5	114	333	2·8

Sources

1. Columns 1–13 and 25, Bank of England *Quarterly Bulletin*[9b] (Dec. 1967)
2. Columns 14–18 and 26–30, *National Income and Expenditure* [25b]
3. Columns 19–24, *Annual Abstract of Statistics* [25a]
Increase in assets and liabilities +
Decrease in assets and liabilities −

Notes

1. In the Bank of England Sector Financing Tables, Non-Marketable Government Debt includes deposits with Trustee Savings Banks and Post Office Savings Banks (Ordinary Departments), in addition to interest accrued on National Savings Certificates. In this study these items are included with deposits with Non-Bank Financial Institutions
2. The method of estimating investment in motor cars and in consumer durables is described in detail in Chapter 2, section 2.2.1.
3. The *Annual Abstract of Statistics* estimates of individual premiums to Life Assurance Companies were adjusted by deducting from the total amount of premiums paid the estimated amount of employers' contributions to superannuation schemes with Life Assurance Companies. The adjustment was made on the basis of information provided in the National Accounts Statistics: *Sources and Methods*[153] (p. 128).

Table B STOCKS OF ASSETS AND LIABILITIES (£m)

Year	FA_{2t-1}	FA_{3t-1}	FA_{4t-1}	FA_{5t-1}	FA_{6t-1}	FA_{7t-1}	BL_{t-1}	HP_{t-1}	DU_{t-1}	$OFCF_{t-1}$
1952	4 101	4 765·0	1 709·9	1 120·5	2 917	405	622	298	1 266·8	2 204
1953	4 207	4 912·6	1 725·7	1 067·8	3 183	397	519	316	1 448·0	2 401
1954	4 382	5 123·1	1 748·6	1 012·5	3 293	418	512	347	1 706·5	2 594
1955	4 595	5 393·0	1 767·6	973·1	3 206	452	584	443	2 007·2	2 827
1956	4 513	5 644·5	1 813·6	991·1	3 658	499	583	515	2 317·1	3 089
1957	4 575	5 827·9	1 833·3	966·4	3 750	622	588	452	2 506·0	3 298
1958	4 800	6 017·8	1 907·4	998·4	3 569	748	591	489	2 752·9	3 498
1959	5 013	6 230·3	1 887·3	1 040·7	3 690	856	784	571	3 085·8	3 736
1960	5 464	6 552·6	2 017·5	1 211·7	3 634	948	1 123	795	3 512·7	3 973
1961	5 721	6 838·7	2 084·0	1 390·3	3 936	1 092	1 380	817	3 868·5	4 247
1962	5 950	7 135·8	2 138·7	1 551·0	3 842	1 333	1 441	796	4 107·6	4 540
1963	6 254	7 652·3	2 122·6	1 611·7	3 802	1 622	1 662	795	4 352·9	4 795
1964	6 656	8 324·2	2 133·8	1 697·2	3 556	1 827	1 752	864	4 722·0	5 083
1965	7 185	9 029·4	2 110·2	1 757·6	3 489	1 957	1 881	973	5 144·0	5 316
1966	7 774	9 818·0	2 076·4	1 891·7	3 414	2 225	1 848	1 036	5 454·0	5 590

Notes

1. Columns 1, 2, 5−8 and 10 are based on J. Revell[174]
2. Columns 3, 4, 12, 14−16 and 19 are based on the *Annual Abstract of Statistics*[25a]
3. Columns 9, 11, 17 and 18 are based on Blue Book figures[25b]
4. Column 13 is based on estimates by the Radcliffe Committee[32a]

Table B STOCKS OF ASSETS AND LIABILITIES (£m) *(cont.)*

Year	NV_{t-1}	$SLIF_t$	$SSUP_t$	BSS_{t-1}	BSD_{t-1}	TSB_{t-1}	DM_{t-1}	BI_{t-1}	L_t
1952	1 510	2 865·75	1 106·89	1 057	208·2	115·7	94·8	207	7 395·9
1953	1 495	3 082·66	1 282·98	1 186·1	197·5	122·4	131·8	358	7 477·9
1954	1 700	3 345·25	1 457·39	1 338·4	202·7	143·7	200·1	508	7 562·0
1955	1 777	3 618·24	1 661·40	1 535·1	222·1	192·6	268·8	676	7 765·9
1956	1 912	3 874·32	1 920·32	1 732·3	216·5	226·2	358·0	885	8 075·0
1957	1 840	4 149·76	2 223·88	1 909·3	193·5	282·8	371·8	1 030	8 226·4
1958	1 768	4 522·64	2 500·0	2 085·0	189·0	316·8	416·4	1 215	8 527·7
1959	1 748	4 947·80	2 791·84	2 268·6	198·5	342·6	514·8	1 432	8 740·4
1960	1 956	5 431·67	3 123·97	2 523·0	213·8	380·5	622·2	1 662	9 322·6
1961	2 046	5 944·46	3 480·18	2 720·9	222·1	434·0	720·5	1 904	9 907·5
1962	2 001	6 496·49	3 889·15	2 920·9	225·5	499·0	731·2	2 164	10 436·7
1963	2 219	7 135·91	4 295·72	3 264·9	242·4	603·5	775·5	2 406	10 978·3
1964	2 358	7 883·50	4 704·14	3 732·8	271·1	733·4	916·9	2 679	11 770·5
1965	2 495	8 640·35	5 113·28	4 218·6	193·1	885·1	1 066·9	2 986	12 577·5
1966	2 625	9 371·47	5 580·16	4 848·6	294·8	994·0	1 109·8	3 305	13 529·2

Sources

1. Annual estimates for FA_2, FA_3, FA_6, FA_7, BL, HP, and $OFCF$ were obtained by simple linear extrapolation on the basis of J. Revell's 1957 estimates[174]
2. Annual estimates for $SSUP$ were obtained by simple linear extrapolation using the Radcliffe Report estimate[32a] for 1958

Table C RATES OF INTEREST (%)

Year	R_t^L	R_t^S	R_t^O	RBS_t	RBD_t	$RTSB_t$	RSD_t	$RNSC_t$	BR_t	RTB_t	RM_t	$RN1_t$	$RN2_t$	$RN3_t$	R_t^{LA}
1952	4·25	2·98	6·46	2·38	1·79	2·75	2·30	3·0	4·0	0·98	4·32	4·24	3·95	3·95	8·625
1953	3·95	3·03	6·06	2·45	1·86	2·92	2·39	3·0	3·5	2·4	4·55	3·97	4·03	4·24	7·851
1954	3·55	2·61	5·40	2·45	1·88	2·94	2·40	3·05	3·0	2·108	4·58	3·59	3·67	3·88	7·267
1955	4·24	3·81	5·43	2·61	2·01	3·15	2·56	3·05	4·5	1·786	4·66	4·14	3·98	4·63	7·627
1956	5·13	4·67	6·25	3·08	2·44	3·61	3·02	3·625	5·5	4·087	5·32	5·07	4·88	4·43	8·434
1957	5·49	4·48	6·27	3·45	2·83	3·81	3·37	4·20	7·0	4·934	5·98	5·44	5·35	5·04	8·814
1958	5·47	4·7	6·23	3·48	2·9	3·95	3·43	4·20	4·0	6·43	6·13	5·50	5·51	5·38	8·793
1959	5·19	4·54	4·83	3·43	2·87	4·00	3·41	4·20	4·0	3·164	5·98	5·21	5·37	5·37	7·909
1960	5·77	5·66	4·60	3·37	2·94	4·20	3·44	4·20	5·0	3·613	5·89	5·7	5·96	5·45	8·310
1961	6·29	5·98	5·12	3·54	3·11	4·49	3·64	4·20	6·0	4·436	6·28	6·26	6·16	5·88	8·818
1962	5·96	5·31	5·57	3·70	3·26	4·75	3·82	4·20	4·5	5·354	6·61	6·04	6·20	6·38	8·429
1963	5·43	4·83	4·40	3·56	3·15	4·79	3·72	3·89	4·0	3·644	6·27	5·44	5·50	5·70	7·961
1964	5·98	5·54	4·63	3·50	3·11	4·91	3·70	3·79	7·0	3·738	8·16	5·92	5·81	5·70	8·509
1965	6·56	6·57	5·54	3·78	3·39	4·99	3·94	3·79	6·0	6·623	6·63	6·52	6·40	6·07	9·497
1966	6·94	6·77	5·67	4·01	3·62	4·39	4·20	4·36	7·0	5·481	6·95	6·89	6·77	6·48	10·043

Notes

1. Estimates for *RN1*, *RN2* and *RN3* were obtained by means of De Leeuw's distributed lag function[40c] on the basis of Quarterly Data for interest rates. See Chapter 3, section 3.2.1 *F*, the number of lags, was assumed to be equal to 11.
2. Annual estimates of R^{LA} were obtained using formula (8) in Chapter 5, section 5.2.1.

Sources

1. Columns 1–7, 9–11 and 15 the *Annual Abstract of Statistics*[25a]
2. Column 8, *Financial Statistics*[25d]
3. Columns 12–14, Bank of England *Quarterly Bulletin*[9b]

Table D PERSONAL INCOME, EXPENDITURE AND TAXATION

Year	Y_t	T_t^P	W_t	OY_t	$Y_{2.t}$	$T_{2.t}$	Y_t^P	C_t	S_t	ATR_t	NIC_t	G_t^{10}	G_t^{EX}
1952	12 793	1 177	9 107	911	2 775	596	12 176	10 766	380	−14	476	0·475	1·1 615
1953	13 568	1 134	9 634	1 002	2 932	600	12 918	11 475	431	9	525	0·4 565	1·1 512
1954	14 343	1 236	10 284	1 021	3 029	651	13 613	12 164	382	33	532	0·45	1·1 385
1955	15 571	1 330	11 244	1 115	3 203	656	14 630	13 113	490	35	594	0·4 315	1·1 353
1956	16 738	1 452	12 262	1 193	3 272	678	15 760	13 829	769	20	642	0·425	1·143
1957	17 652	1 602	12 958	1 252	3 420	707	16 821	14 599	766	0	657	0·425	1·1 365
1958	18 600	1 696	13 465	1 484	3 633	729	17 824	15 386	605	50	859	0·425	1·005
1959	19 694	1 776	14 102	1 636	3 946	775	18 800	16 196	802	15	897	0·397	1·046
1960	21 205	1 991	15 164	1 653	4 376	850	20 013	17 006	1 195	95	913	0·3 875	1·0 374
1961	22 908	2 249	16 397	1 802	4 700	947	21 532	17 917	1 649	20	1 072	0·3 875	1·0 635
1962	24 102	2 458	17 289	1 981	4 826	1 022	22 984	18 966	1 503	−30	1 197	0·3 875	1·0 758
1963	25 497	2 510	18 160	2 234	5 094	1 041	24 353	20 141	1 504	17	1 303	0·3 875	1·0 638
1964	27 594	2 801	19 662	2 369	5 582	1 147	25 996	21 492	1 731	95	1 444	0·3 875	1·0 846
1955	29 846	3 373	21 218	2 729	6 000	1 345	27 953	22 851	1 745	150	1 685	0·406	1·2 017
1966	31 508	3 646	22 690	2 973	6 068	1 363	30 055	24 116	1 844	35	1 797	0·4 125	1·1 587

Notes

1. Annual Estimates of Y^P were obtained by applying formula (5) of Chapter 3 to quarterly figures of personal income, for $F = 11$, and $\lambda = 0.9$.
2. The method of calculating G^{EX} was described in Chapter 6.
3. Y_t is total personal income and is equal to $W_t + OY_t + Y_{2.t}$.
4. $T_{2.t}$ is taxes on non-wage income.

Sources

1. Columns 1–6, and 8–11 are based on Blue Books[25b]
2. Column 7 is based on *Economic Trends*[25c] estimates
3. Columns 12 and 13 are based on estimates of the Budget Financial Statements.

Table E PRICES

Year	PX_t	PD_t	PM_t	PN_t	RP_t
1952	0·837	0·9 650	0·9 435	0·7 540	0·6 868
1953	0·854	0·9 213	0·8 651	0·8 005	0·7 791
1954	0·870	0·9 058	0·8 635	0·8 323	0·8 270
1955	0·901	0·9 185	0·8 757	0·8 561	0·8 508
1956	0·942	0·9 856	0·7 016	0·8 822	0·8 321
1957	0·973	1·000	0·9 846	0·9 156	0·8 898
1958	1·000	1·000	1·000	0·9 483	1·000
1959	1·006	0·9 787	0·9 693	0·9 785	1·0 719
1960	1·015	0·9 693	0·9 467	0·9 957	1·0 765
1961	1·044	0·9 782	0·94 322	1·0 078	1·0 499
1962	1·082	0·9 754	0·9 177	1·0 283	1·0 602
1963	1·096	0·9 149	0·8 227	1·0 579	1·0 933
1964	1·127	0·9 215	0·8 169	1·0 799	1·0 939
1965	1·177	0·9 411	0·8 188	1·1 072	1·0 953
1966	1·223	0·9 559	0·8 267	1·1 465	1·1 311

Notes

1. *PX*, *PD* and *PM* were derived from the estimates of total consumers' expenditure, and consumers' expenditure on durable goods, and motor cars and motor cycles at current and constant prices.
2. *PN* was estimated by applying formula (5) of Chapter 3 on annual figures of *PX*, for $F = 3$ and $\lambda = 0·5$.

Source

Blue Book[25b]

Table F MISCELLANEOUS

Year	HPC_t	ALA_t	O_t	A_1	A_2	Male A_{3t}	Female A_{3t}	b_t^S	b_t^M	$SWLA_t$
1952	21·5	10	−0·0049	4·5939	6·3056	7·5386	10·2642	79·75	132·8	72·11
1953	1·8	20	0·0016	4·7960	6·3932	7·6604	10·4789	84·50	140·4	74·61
1954	−10·7	50	0·0177	4·8870	6·4829	7·7856	10·7011	84·50	140·4	73·86
1955	−0·6	60	0·0316	5·0430	6·5748	7·9144	10·9312	97·875	160·367	72·99
1956	25·8	26·6	0·0131	5·2059	6·6690	8·0468	11·1697	104·00	169·0	71·76
1957	2·2	20	−0·0026	5·3759	6·7656	8·1830	11·4169	104·00	169·0	70·31
1958	−8·8	27·5	−0·0361	5·5534	6·8845	8·3232	11·6732	128·5	205·75	69·07
1959	−31·2	60	−0·0284	5·7389	6·9660	8·4675	11·9390	130·0	208·0	66·53
1960	6·7	60	0·0099	5·9327	7·0700	8·6160	12·2149	130·0	208·0	64·29
1961	3·3	60	0·0021	6·1354	7·1766	8·7690	12·5013	144·625	232·375	62·08
1962	0	60	−0·0234	6·3474	7·2861	8·9266	12·7987	149·50	240·5	59·15
1963	0	75	−0·0132	6·5693	7·3985	9·0890	13·1076	165·167	266·355	56·54
1964	0	80	0·0187	6·8016	7·5139	9·2563	13·4288	175·5	283·40	55·73
1965	2·5	80	0·0221	7·0449	7·6323	9·4288	13·7627	199·875	324·35	53·28
1966	10·0	80	−0·0044	−	−	−	−	−	−	51·23

Notes

1. The method of estimating ALA_t was described in Chapter 4, section 4.2.1.
2. Methods of estimating A_1, A_2, A_{3t} (male), and A_{3t} (female) were described in Chapter 5, section 5.2.1.

Sources

1. Column 1, Stone and Rowe[196]
2. Column 2, Balopoulos[8]
3. Column 3 is based on estimates made by Bain and El-Mokadem[3d]
4. Columns 4−7 are based on the 1952 Life Table
5. Columns 8 and 9 are based on the figures of the Budget Financial Statements
6. Column 10 the *Annual Abstract of Statistics*[25a]

Bibliography

1. AGARWALA, R., *An Econometric Model of India, 1948–1961*, F. Cass & Co., London (1970).
2. BAIN, C., 'Monetary–Fiscal Policy Reconsidered', *Journal of Political Economy*, London (Oct. 1949).
3a. BAIN, A. D., *Growth of Television Ownership in U.K. Since the War*, Department of Applied Economics, Monograph 12., Cambridge (1964).
3b. BAIN, A. D., 'The Treasury Bill Tender in the United Kingdom', *Journal of Economic Studies* (1965).
3c. BAIN, A. D., *The Control of the Money Supply*, Penguin, London (1970).
3d. BAIN, A. D. and EL-MOKADEM, A. M., 'Short-Term Forecasting of Profits in the U.K. – An Econometric Approach', *The Manchester School* (Sept. 1971).
4a. BALL, R. J., 'The Prediction of the Wage-Rate Changes in the United Kingdom Economy 1957–60', *Economic Journal*, 72 (March 1962).
4b. BALL, R. J., 'The Significance of Simultaneous Methods of Parameter Estimation in Econometric Models', *Applied Statistics*, No. 1 (1963).
4c. BALL, R. J., *Inflation and the Theory of Money*, Allen and Unwin, London (1964).
4d. BALL, R. J., 'Some Econometric Analysis of the Long Term Rate of Interest in the United Kingdom 1921–61', *The Manchester School*, 45–96 (1965).
5a. BALL, R. J. and BURNS, T., 'An Econometric Approach to Short-run Analysis of the U.K. Economy 1955–66', *Operational Research Quarterly*, 19 (Sept. 1968).
5b. BALL, R. J. and BURNS, T., 'An Interim Report on a Quarterly Statistical Model of the U.K. Economy', Unpublished Paper, *Southampton Econometric Conference* (1969).
6a. BALL, R. J. and DRAKE, P. S., Stock Adjustment Inventory Models of the U.K. Economy', *The Manchester School*, XXXI (May 1963).
6b. BALL, R. J. and DRAKE, P. S., 'The Impact of Credit Control on Consumer Durable Spending in the U.K., 1957–61', *Review of Economic Studies* (Oct. 1963).
6c. BALL, R. J. and DRAKE, P. S., 'The Relationship between Aggregate Consumption and Wealth', *International Economic Review* (Jan. 1964).
6d. BALL, R. J. and DRAKE, P. S., 'Investment Intentions and the Prediction of Private Gross Capital Formation', *Economica* (May 1964).
7. BALL, R. J. and ST. CYR, E. B. A., 'Short Term Employment Functions in British Manufacturing Industry', *Review of Economic Studies*, 33, 179–208 (1966).
8. BALOPOULOS, E. T., *Fiscal Policy Models of the British Economy*, North-Holland Publishing Co., Amsterdam (1967).
9a. BANK OF ENGLAND., *Annual Report*.
9b. BANK OF ENGLAND, *Quarterly Bulletin*.
10. BATES, J. M. and GRANGER, C. W. J., 'The Combination of Forecasts', *Operational Research Quarterly*, 20, No. 4, 451–468 (1969).
11. BERMAN, L. S., 'The Flows of Funds in the U.K.', *Journal of the Royal Statistical Society*, 128, 321–360 (1965).
12a. BODKIN, R., 'Windfall Income and Consumption', *Proceedings of the Conference on Consumption and Saving*, II (eds. I. FRIEND and R. JONES), Philadelphia, 175–87 (1960).
12b. BODKIN, R., Rejoinder (*op. cit.* 12a), p. 206.

182   Bibliography

13. BOWEN, W. G., *The Wage-Price Issue: A Theoretical Analysis*, Princeton University Press, Princeton, N.J. (1960).
14. BRADY, D. S., 'Family Saving in Relation to Changes in the Level and Distribution of Income', *Studies in Income and Wealth*, N.B.E.R., New York (1952).
15. BRITTAIN, Sir H., *The British Budgetary System*, Allen and Unwin, London (1959).
16. BRONFENBRENNER, M. and MAYER, T., 'Liquidity Functions in the American Economy', *Econometrica* (1960).
17. BROWN, E. C., 'Analysis of Consumption Taxes in Terms of the Theory of Income Determination', *The American Economic Review* (May 1950).
18. BRUNDO, W. W. and BOWER, F., *Taxation in the United Kingdom*, World Tax Series, Harvard Law School, Boston-Toronto (1957).
19. BRUNNER, K. and MELTZER, A., 'Some Further Investigations of Demand and Supply Functions for Money', *Journal of Finance*, 19 (May 1964).
20. BUDZEIKA, G., 'Commercial Banks as Suppliers of Capital Funds to Business', Essays in Money and Credit, Federal Reserve Bank of New York (1954).
21. BURKHEAD, J., 'Changes in Functional Distribution of Income', *Journal of the American Statistical Association*, 48 (1953).
22. CAGAN, P., *The Effect of Pension Plans on Aggregate Saving*, N.B.E.R., New York (1965).
23. CARTER, A. M., *Redistribution of Incomes in Post-War Britain*, Kennikat Press Inc., New Haven (1954).
24. CATT, A., 'Credit Rationing and the Keynesian Model', *Economic Journal*, 75 (1965).
25a. CENTRAL STATISTICAL OFFICE, *Annual Abstract of Statistics*, H.M.S.O., London.
25b. CENTRAL STATISTICAL OFFICE, *National Income and Expenditure*, Annual 'Blue Book', H.M.S.O., London
25c. CENTRAL STATISTICAL OFFICE, *Economic Trends*, H.M.S.O., London (monthly).
25d. CENTRAL STATISTICAL OFFICE, *Financial Statistics*, H.M.S.O., London (monthly).
25e. CENTRAL STATISTICAL OFFICE., *Monthly Digest of Statistics*, H.M.S.O., London.
26. CHAMPERNOWRNE, D. G., 'A Model of Income Distribution', *Economic Journal*, 63 (1953).
26a. CHOW, G., 'On the Long-run and the Short-run Demand for Money', *Journal of Political Economy*, 74, 111–131 (1966).
27a. CHRIST, C., *A Test of an Econometric Model of the United States, 1921–1947*, Conference on Business Cycles, N.B.E.R., New York (1951).
27b. CHRIST, C., *Measurement in Economics: Studies in Mathematical Economics and Econometrics*, In memory of Yehuda Grunfeld, Stanford University Press (1963).
27c. CHRIST, C., *Econometric Models and Methods*, Wiley, New York (1966).
28. CLARK, C., 'A System of Equations Explaining the United States Trade Cycle, 1921–1941', *Econometrica*, 17 (1949).
29. CLAYCAMP, H., *The Composition of Consumer Savings Portfolios*, Unpublished Ph.D., Urbana 1963 (as reported by Ferber, *op. cit.* 56c).
30. COHEN, J., 'Integrating the Real and Financial via the Linkage of Financial Flow', *Journal of Finance*, **XXIII** (March 1968).
31. COMMISSION ON MONEY AND CREDIT, *Impacts of Monetary Policy*, Prentice-Hall, Englewood Cliffs, N.J. (1963).
32a. COMMITTEE ON THE WORKING OF THE MONETARY SYSTEM, *Report*, Chairman: Lord Radcliffe, H.M.S.O., London (1959).
32b. COMMITTEE ON THE WORKING OF THE MONETARY SYSTEM, *Principal Memoranda of Evidence*, 1, 2 and 3, H.M.S.O., London (1960).
32c. COMMITTEE ON THE WORKING OF THE MONETARY SYSTEM, *Minutes of Oral Evidence*, H.M.S.O., London (1960).
33. COPPOCK, D. J., 'The Periodicity and Stability of Inventory Cycles in the U.S.A.', *The Manchester School* (May and Sept. 1959).
34. CROCKETT, J., *Income and Asset Effect on Consumption: Aggregate and Cross Section*, Studies in Income and Wealth, 28 N.B.E.R., New York, 97–132 (1964).
35. CROCKETT, J. and FRIEND, I., 'Consumer Investment Behaviour', in FERBER, R. (ed.), *Determinants of Investment Behaviour*, N.B.E.R., New York (1967).

36. CROUCH, R. L., 'A Model of the U.K. Monetary Sector', *Econometrica*, **35**, 398–418 (1967).
37. CULLINGWORTH, J. B., *Housing Needs and Planning Policy*, Routledge and Kegan Paul, London (1960).
38. DARLING, P. G., 'Manufacturers' Inventory Investment 1947–58', *American Econometric Review*, (Dec. 1959).
39. DARLING, P. G. and LOVELL, M. C., 'Factors Influencing Investment in Inventories', *Econometrica* (Oct. 1960).
40a. DE-LEEUW, F., 'The Demand for Capital Goods by Manufacturers: A Study of Quarterly Time Series', *Econometrica*, **30** (1962).
40b. DE-LEEUW, F., 'Financial Markets in Business Cycles: A Simulation Study', *American Economic Review* (May 1964).
40c. DE-LEEUW, F., *The Brookings Quarterly Econometric Model of the United States*, North Holland Publishing Co., Amsterdam (1965).
41. DHRYMES, P. and KURZ, M., 'Investment Dividend and External Finance Behaviour of Firms', in FERBER, R. (ed.), *Determinants of Investment Behaviour*, N.B.E.R., New York (1967).
42. DICKS-MIREAUX,, L. A. and DOW, J. C. R., 'The Determinants of Wage Inflation: United Kingdom, 1946–1956', *Journal of the Royal Statistical Society, Series A (General)*, **22** (1959).
43. DOUGLAS, A., 'A Theory of Saving and Portfolio Selection', *Review of Economic Studies*, **XXV**, 453–464 (Oct. 1968).
44. DOW, J. C. R., *The Management of the British Economy 1945–60*, Cambridge University Press, London (1964).
45a. DUESENBERRY, J. S., *Income Saving and Theory of Consumer Behaviour*, Harvard University Press, Cambridge, Mass. (1949).
45b. DUESENBERRY, J. S., *Business Cycles and Economic Growth*, McGraw-Hill, New York (1958).
45c. DUESENBERRY, J. S., 'Comments on General Saving Relations', *Proceedings of the Conference on Consumption and Saving*, **II** (eds. I. FRIEND and R. JONES), Philadelphia, 188–191 (1960).
45d. DUESENBERRY, J. S., 'The Portfolio Approach to the Demand for Money and Other Assets', *Review of Economics and Statistics*, **XLV** Supp. (1963).
46. DUESENBERRY, J. S. and ECKSTEIN, O., 'A Simulation of the United States in Recession', *Econometrica* (Oct. 1960).
47. DUESENBERRY, J. S., FROMM, G., KLEIN, L. R. and KUH, E. (eds.) *The Brookings Quarterly Econometric Model of the United States*, North Holland Publishing Co., Amsterdam (1965).
48. DURBIN, J. and WATSON, G. S., 'Testing for Serial Correlation in Least-Squares Regression', *Biometrica* (1950/51).
49. THE ECONOMIST, London (weekly).
50a. EISNER, R., 'A Distributed Lag Investment Function', *Econometrica*, **28** (1960).
50b. EISNER, R. 'Another Look at Liquidity Preference', *Econometrica*, **31** (July 1963).
51. EISNER, R. and STROTZ, R. H., 'Determinants of Business Investment', in *Impacts of Monetary Policy*, Commission on Money and Credit, Prentice-Hall, Englewood-Cliffs, N.J., 60–338 (1963).
52. EL-MOKADEM, A. M. and WHITTAKER, R. A., *Further Evidence on the Speculative Demand for Money in the United Kingdom*, Unpublished paper, University of Lancaster (April 1971).
53. FAMILY EXPENDITURE SURVEY, *Report for 1957–1959*, Ministry of Labour, London.
54. FARRELL, M. J., 'The New Theories of Consumption Functions', *Economic Journal*, **69** (1959).
55a. FEIGE, E. L., *The Demand for Liquid Assets: A Temporal Cross-Section Analysis*, Prentice-Hall, Englewood-Cliffs, N.J. (1964).
55b. FEIGE, E. L., 'Expectations and Adjustment in the Monetary Sector', *American Economic Review*, Papers and Proceedings (May 1967).
56a. FERBER, R., *A Study of Aggregate Consumption Functions*, N.B.E.R. Technical Paper No. 8 (1953).

56b. FERBER, R., 'The Accuracy of Aggregate Saving Functions in Post War Years', *Review of Economic Studies*, 37 (1955).

56c. FERBER, R., *Research on Household Behaviour*, Surveys of Economic Theory, III, Macmillan, London (1966).

57a. FISHER, D., 'The Demand for Money in Britain. Quarterly results. 1951–67', *Manchester School*, 329–344 (1968).

57b. FISHER, D., 'The Objectives of British Monetary Policy 1951–1964', *Journal of Finance*, XXIII (1968).

58a. FISHER, F. M., The Place of Least Squares in Econometrics: Comment', *Econometrica*, 30, 565–567 (1962).

58b. FISHER, F. M., *The Identification Problem in Econometrics*, McGraw-Hill, New York (1966).

59. FISHER, M. R., 'Explorations in Savings Behaviour', *Bulletin of Oxford University Institute of Statistics*, 18, 201–278 (Aug. 1956).

60. FORD, P. and THOMAS, C. J., *Housing Targets*, Blackwell, Oxford (1953).

61. FOX, K. A., SENGUPTA, J. K. and THORBECKE, E., *The Theory of Quantitative Economic Policy*, North Holland Publishing Co., Amsterdam (1966).

62a. FRIEDMAN, M., *A Theory of the Consumption Function*, N.B.E.R.: Princeton University Press, Princeton, N.J. (1957).

62b. FRIEDMAN, M., 'The Demand for Money: Some Theoretical and Empirical Results', *Journal of Political Economy*, 67 (1959).

62c. FRIEDMAN, M., 'Comments on Windfall Income and Consumption', *Proceedings of the Conference on Consumption and Saving*, II, Philadelphia, 191–206 (1960).

62d. FRIEDMAN, M., 'Windfalls, the "Horizon" and Related Concepts in the Permanent Income Hypothesis', in CHRIST, C. (ed.), *Measurement in Economics*, Stanford University Press (1963).

63. FRIEDMAN, M. and MEISELMAN, D., *The Relative Stability of Monetary Velocity and Investment Multipliers in the United States, 1847–1958,* Commission on Money and Credit, Prentice-Hall, Englewood-Cliffs, N.J. (1963).

64. FRIEDMAN, M. and SCHWARTZE, A., *A Monetary History of the United States, 1867–1960*, N.B.E.R.: Princeton University Press (1963).

65. FRIEND, I., 'Determinants of the Volume and Composition of Saving with Special Reference to the Influence of Monetary Policy', in *Impacts of Monetary Policy*, Commission on Money and Credit, Prentice-Hall, Englewood-Cliffs, N.J. (1963).

66. FRIEND, I. and JONES, R., 'The Concepts of Saving', *Proceedings of the Conference on Consumption and Saving*, II, Philadelphia, 336–359 (1960).

67. FRIEND, I. and KRAVIS, I. B., 'Consumption Patterns and Permanent Income', *American Economic Review*, 47, 536–555 (1957).

68. GALLAWAY, L. E. and SMITH, P. E., 'A Quarterly Econometric Model of the United States', *Journal of American Statistical Association*, 56 (1961).

69a. GEHRELS, F. and WIGGINS, S., 'Interest Rates and Manufacturers' Fixed Investment', *American Economic Review*, 47 (March 1957).

69b. GEHRELS, F. and WIGGINS, S., 'Correction', *American Economic Review*, 47 (Sept. 1957).

70a. GIBSON, N. J., 'Money, Banking and Finance', in PREST., A. R. (ed.) *A Manual of Applied Economics*, Weidenfeld and Nicolson, London (1966).

70b. GIBSON, N. J., *Financial Intermediaries and Monetary Policy*, Institute of Economic Affairs, Hobart Paper No. 39 (1967).

71. GLAUBER, R. and MEYER, J., *Investment Decisions, Economic Forecasting and Public Policy*, Harvard University Press, Cambridge, Mass. (1964).

72a. GODLEY, W. A. H. and GILLION, C., 'What has Really Happened to Output?: A Comment', *Bulletin of Oxford Institute of Statistics*, 26 (1964).

72b. GODLEY, W. A. H. and GILLION, C., 'Measuring National Product', *National Institute Economic Review* (Feb. 1964).

73a. GOLDBERGER, A. S., *Impact Multipliers and Dynamic Properties of the Klein-Goldberger Model*, North-Holland Publishing Co., Amsterdam (1959).

73b. GOLDBERGER, A. S., *Econometric Theory*, Wiley & Sons, New York (1964).

74. GOLDBERGER, A. S., NAGAR, A. L. and ODEH, H. S., 'The Covariance Matrices

of Reduced Form Coefficients and of Forecasts for a Structural Econometric Model',
Econometrica, **29** (1961).

75. GOLDFIELD, S., *Commercial Bank Behaviour and Economic Activity,* North-Holland Publishing Co., Amsterdam (1966).

76. GOLDSMITH, R., *A Study of Saving in the United States,* (3 vols), Greenwood Press, Conn. (1953).

77a. GORMAN, W. M., 'Separable Utility and Aggregation', *Econometrica*, **27**, 469–481 (1959).

77b. GORMAN, W. M., 'The Empirical Implications of a Utility Tree: A comment', *Econometrica,* **27**, 489–490 (1959).

78. GREBLER, L. and MAISEL, S., 'Determinants of Residential Construction: A Review of Present Knowledge', in *Impacts of Monetary Policy*, Commission on Money and Credit, Prentice-Hall, Englewood-Cliffs N.J. (1963).

79a. GURLEY, J. and SHAW, E., 'Financial Aspects of Economic Development', *American Economic Review,* **45** (1955).

79b. GURLEY, J. and SHAW, E., 'Financial Intermediaries and the Saving Investment Process', *Journal of Finance,* **11** (May 1956).

79c. GURLEY, J. and SHAW, E., 'Intermediaries as Monetary Policy: Reply', *American Economic Review* (March 1958).

79d. GURLEY, J. and SHAW, E., *Money in a Theory of Finance,* Brookings Institute, Washington D.C. (1960).

80. GUTTENTAG, J.,'Credit Availability, Interest Rates and Monetary Policy', *Southern Economic Journal* (Jan. 1960).

81a. HAAVELMO, T., 'The Effect of the Rate of Interest on Investment: a Note', *Review of Economics and Statistics* (Feb. 1941).

81b. HAAVELMO, T., 'Methods of Measuring the Marginal Propensity to Consume', *Journal of American Statistical Association,* **42** (1947).

82a. HAMBURGER, M., 'The Demand for Money by Households, Money Substitutes and Monetary Policy', *Journal of Political Economy,* **74** (1968).

82b. HAMBURGER, M., 'Household Demand for Financial Assets', *Econometrica,* **36**, No. 1 (1968).

83. HANSEN, M. H., HURWICZ, W. N. and MADOW, W. G., *Sample Survey: Methods and Theory,* Wiley & Sons, New York (1953).

84. HARBURGER, A. C., *The Demand for Durable Goods,* University of Chicago (1960).

85. HART, A. G., 'Model-Building and Fiscal Policy', *American Economic Review* (Sept. 1945).

86. HELLER, H. R., 'The Demand for Money: The Evidence from the Short-Run Data', *Quarterly Journal of Economics* (May 1965).

87. H.M. CUSTOMS AND EXCISE DUTIES, Annual Reports of the Commissioners, H.M.S.O., London.

88. H.M. INLAND REVENUE, Annual Reports of the Commissioners, H.M.S.O., London.

89. H.M. OCCUPATIONAL PENSION SCHEMES, A Survey by the Government Actuary, H.M.S.O., London (1958).

90. H.M. CENTRAL OFFICE OF INFORMATION, *The British System of Taxation,* Pamphlet 10, H.M.S.O., London (1966).

91a. HICKS, J. R., *Value and Capital* (2nd ed.), Clarendon Press, Oxford (1946).

91b. HICK, J. R., 'Future of the Rate of Interest', *Manchester Statistical Society* (1958).

91c. HICKS, J. R., 'A World Inflation?', in *Essays in World Economics*, Oxford University Press (1959).

92. HODGMAN, D., 'The Deposit Relationship and Commercial Bank Investment Behaviour', *Review of Economics and Statistics,* 257–268 (Aug. 1961).

93. HOOD, W. C. and KOOPMANS, T. C. (eds.), *Studies in Econometric Methods,* Wiley & Sons, New York (1952).

94. HOUTHAKKER, H. S. and HALDI, J., 'Household Investment in Automobiles', *Proceedings of the Conference on Consumption and Saving,* **1**, Philadelphia, 175–225 (1960).

95. HOUTHAKKER, H. S. and TAYLOR, L. D., *Consumer Demand in the United States, 1929–70,* Harvard University Press, Cambridge, Mass. (1966).

96.   HUANG, D. S., 'The Short-run Flows of Non-Farm Residential Mortgage Credit',
      Econometrica, 34, 433–459 (1966).
97.   HURWICZ, L., 'Least Squares Bias in Time Series', in KOOPMANS, T. C. (ed.),
      Statistical Inference in Dynamic Economic Models, Wiley & Sons, New York (1950).
98a. JOHNSON, H. G., 'Monetary Theory and Policy', *American Economic Review*,
      335–384 (June 1962).
98b. JOHNSON, H. G., *Essays in Monetary Economics*, Allen and Unwin, London (1967).
99a. JOHNSTON, J., *Statistical Cost Analysis*, McGraw-Hill, New York (1960).
99b. JOHNSTON, J., 'An Econometric Study of the Production Decision', *Quarterly
      Journal of Economics*, 75 (1961).
99c. JOHNSTON, J., 'An Econometric Model of the U.K.', *Review of Economic Studies*
      (Feb. 1962).
99d. JOHNSTON, J., *Econometric Methods*, McGraw-Hill, London (1963).
100. JONES, D. M., 'The Demand for Money: A Review of the Empirical Literature',
      Staff Economic Studies, Board of Governors of the Federal Reserve System (1965).
101. KALDOR, N., *An Expenditure Tax*, Allen & Unwin, London (1965).
102. KALECKI, M., *The Distribution of the National Income*, A.E.A. Readings in the
      Theory of Income Distribution, Allen & Unwin, London (1946).
103. KANE, E. and MALKIEL, B. G., 'Bank Portfolio Allocation, Deposit Variability and
      the Availability Doctrine', *Quarterly Journal of Economics* (Feb. 1965).
104. KATONA, G., *The Powerful Consumer*, New York, McGraw-Hill (1960).
105. KAVANAGH, N. J. and WALTERS, A. A., 'Demand for Money in the U.K.
      1877–1961: Some Preliminary Findings', *Bulletin of Oxford University Institute of
      Statistics*, 28 (1966).
106. KEITH, G., 'The Impact of Federal Taxation on the Flow of Personal Savings
      Through Investment Intermediaries', in *Private Financial Institutions*, Prentice-
      Hall, Englewood-Clitts N.J. (1963).
107. KENDALL, M. G. and STUART, A., *The Advanced Theory of Statistics*, Griffin,
      London (1967, 1968 and 1969).
108a. KEYNES, J. M., *A Treatise on Money*, Macmillan, London (1933).
108b. KEYNES, J. M., *The General Theory of Employment, Interest and Money*,
      Macmillan, New York (1936).
109a. KLEIN, L. R., 'Remarks on the Theory of Aggregation', *Econometrica* (1946).
109b. KLEIN, L. R., 'The Use of Econometric Models as a Guide to Policy', *Econometrica*
      15 (1947).
109c. KLEIN, L. R., 'Notes on the Theory of Investment', *Kyclos*, 1 (1948).
109d. KLEIN, L. R., *Economic Fluctuations in the United States 1921–1941*, Wiley &
      Sons, New York (1950).
109e. KLEIN, L. R., 'Estimating Patterns of Savings Behaviour from Sample Survey Data',
      Econometrica, 19 (1951).
109f. KLEIN, L. R., 'Studies in Investment Behaviour', *N.B.E.R. Conference on Business
      Cycles*, New York (1951).
109g. KLEIN, L. R., *A Textbook of Econometrics*, Row-Paterson, Evanston, III (1953).
109h. KLEIN, L. R. (ed.), *Contributions of Survey Methods to Economics*, Columbia
      University Press, New York (1954).
109i. KLEIN, L. R., 'Empirical Foundations of Keynesian Economics', in: KURIHAR
      (ed.) *Post-Keynesian Economics*, North-Holland, New Brunswick N.J. (1954).
109j. KLEIN, L. R., 'Patterns of Savings: The Surveys of 1953 and 1954', *Bulletin of
      Oxford University Institute of Statistics* (May 1955).
109k. KLEIN, L. R., 'The Estimation of Distributed Lags', *Econometrica*, 26 (1958).
109l. KLEIN, L. R., 'The Friedman–Becker Illusion', *Journal of Political Economy*, 66
      (1958).
109m. KLEIN, L. R., 'Some Theoretical Issues in the Measurement of Capacity',
      Econometrica (1960).
109n. KLEIN, L. R., 'Entrepreneurial Saving', *Proceedings of the Conference on
      Consumption and Saving*, Philadelphia, 297–335 (1960).
109o. KLEIN, L. R., *An Introduction to Econometrics*, Prentice-Hall International (1962).
109p. KLEIN, L. R., 'A Post-War Quarterly Model', in *Studies in Income and Wealth*, 28,

Models of Income Determination, N.B.E.R.: Princeton University Press, 11–58 (1964).

110. KLEIN, L. R. and BALL, R. J., 'Some Econometrics of Determination of Prices', *Economic Journal*, **69** (1952).

111. KLEIN, L. R. and GOLDBERGER, A. S., *An Econometric Model of the United States, 1929–1952*, North-Holland Publishing Co., Amsterdam (1955).

112. KLEIN, L. R., BALL, R. J., *et al.*, *An Econometric Model of the United Kingdom*, Blackwell, Oxford (1961).

113. KLEIN, L. R. and LIVIATAN, N., 'The Significance of Income Variability on Savings Behaviour', *Bulletin of Oxford University Institute of Statistics*, **19**, 151–160 (1957).

114. KOOPMANS, T. C. (ed.), *Statistical Inference in Dynamic Economic Models*, Wiley & Sons, New York (1950).

115. KOYCK, L. M., *Distributed Lags and Investment Analysis*, North-Holland Publishing Co., Amsterdam (1954).

116. KREININ, M. E., 'Windfall Income and Consumption', *American Economic Review*, **51**, 388–390 (June 1961).

117a. KUH, E., 'The Validity of Cross-Sectionally Estimated Behaviour Equations in Time Series Applications', *Econometrica*, **27** (1959).

117b. KUH, E., 'Income Distribution and Employment Over the Business Cycle', Ch. 8 in the *Brookings–S.S.R.C. Quarterly Model of the United States*, North-Holland Publishing Co., Amsterdam (1965).

118a. KUH, E. and MEYER, J. R., 'How Extraneous are Extraneous Estimates', *Review of Economics and Statistics*, **39** (1957).

118b. KUH, E. and MEYER, J. R., 'Investment Liquidity and Monetary Policy', in *Impacts of Monetary Policy*, Commission on Money and Credit, Prentice-Hall, Englewood-Cliffs N.J. (1963).

119. KURIHARA, K. K., 'Growth Models and Fiscal Policy Parameters', *Public Finance* (1956).

120a. LAIDLER, D., 'Some Evidence on the Demand for Money', *Journal of Political Economy*, **74** (Feb. 1966).

120b. LAIDLER, D., 'The Rate of Interest and the Demand for Money: Some Empirical Evidence', *Journal of Political Economy*, **74** (Dec. 1966).

121a. LATANÉ, H., 'Cash Balances and the Interest Rate. A Pragmatic Approach', *Review of Economics and Statistics*, **36** (Nov. 1954).

121b. LATANÉ, H., 'Income Velocity and Interest Rates: A Pragmatic Approach', *Review of Economics and Statistics*, **42** (Nov. 1960).

122. LEE, T., 'Substitutability of Non-Bank Intermediaries Liabilities for Money: the Empirical Evidence', *Journal of Finance*, **21** (Sept. 1968).

123. LEIJONHUFVUD, A., *On Keynesian Economics and the Economics of Keynes*, Oxford University Press, New York (1968).

124. LEPPER, S., 'Effects of Alternative Tax Structures on Individuals' Holdings of Financial Assets', in *Risk Aversion and Portfolio choice*, Wiley & Sons, New York (1967).

125. LIFE INSURANCE ASSOCIATION OF AMERICA, *Life Insurance Companies as Financial Institutions*, in Commission on Money and Credit, Prentice-Hall, Englewood-Cliffs N.J. (1965).

126. LINDBLOM, C. E., 'Decision Making in Taxation and Expenditure', in *Public Finances: Needs, Sources and Utilization*, N.B.E.R.: Princeton University Press, N.J. (1961).

127a. LOVELL, M. C., 'Manufacturers' Inventories Sales Expectations and the Acceleration Principle', *Econometrica* (July 1961).

127b. LOVELL, M. C., 'Determinants of Inventory Investment', in *Studies in Income and Wealth*, **28**, *Models of Income Determination*, N.B.E.R.: Princeton University Press (1964).

128a. LUBELL, H., 'Effects of Income Redistribution on Consumers' Expenditures', *American Economic Review*, **XXXVII**, 157–170 (1947).

128b. LUBELL, H., 'Effects of Income Redistribution on Consumers' Expenditures: A

Correction', *American Economic Review*, **XXXVII**, 930–931 (1947).
129a. LYDALL, H. F., *British Incomes and Savings*, Oxford University Press (1955).
129b. LYDALL, H. F., 'The Impact of the Credit Squeeze on Small and Medium Sized Manufacturing Firms', *Economic Journal*, **LXVII**, 415–431 (1957).
129c. LYDALL, H. F., 'Income Assets and the Demand for Money', *Review of Economics and Statistics*, **XL** (1958).
129d. LYDALL, H. F., 'The Distribution of Employment Incomes', *Econometrica*, **27** (1959).
130. MACK, R. P., 'The Direction of Change in Incomes and the Consumption Function', *Review of Economics and Statistics*, **30** (Nov. 1948).
131. MAISEL, S., 'Non-Business Construction', *The Brookings Quarterly Econometric Model of the United States*, Rand-McNally & Co., Chicago (1965).
132a. MALINVAUD, E., 'Estimation et Prevision dans les Modeles Economiques Autoregressifs', *Revue de l'Institut International de Statistique*, **29** (1961).
132b. MALINVAUD, E., *Statistical Methods of Econometrics*, North-Holland Publishing Co., Amsterdam (1966).
133. MALKIEL, B. G., *The Term Structure of Interest Rates*, Princeton University Press, Princeton, N.J. (1966).
134. MARKOWITZ, H., *Portfolio Selection*, Wiley & Sons, New York (1959).
135. MEIGS, A., *Free Reserves and the Money Supply*, University of Chicago Press (1962).
136. MERRETT, A. J., 'Owner-Occupation, Interest Rates and Taxation', *District Bank Review* (1964).
137. METZLER, L. A., 'Effects of Income Redistribution', *Review of Economic Statistics*, 49–57 (Feb. 1943).
138. MEYER, J. and KUH, E., *The Investment Decision: An Empirical Study*, Harvard University Press, Cambridge, Mass. (1957).
139. MILLER, R. F. and WATTS, H. W., 'A Model of Household Investment in Financial Assets', in FERBER, R. (ed.), *Determinants of Investment Behaviour*, N.B.E.R., New York (1967).
140. MISHAN, E. J. and DICKS-MIREAUX, L. A., 'Progressive Taxation in an Inflationary Economy', *American Economic Review* (1958).
141. MODIGLIANI, F., 'Fluctuations in the Saving–Income Ratio: A Problem in Economic Forecasting', in *Studies in Income and Wealth*, **II**, N.B.E.R., New York (1949).
142a. MODIGLIANI, F. and ANDO, A., 'Tests of the Life Cycle Hypothesis of Savings', *Bulletin of Oxford Institute of Statistics*, **19**, 99–124 (May 1957).
142b. MODIGLIANI, F. and ANDO, A., 'The Permanent Income and the Life Cycle Hypothesis of Saving Behaviour: Comparison and Tests', *Proceedings of the Conference on Consumption and Saving*, **II**, Philadelphia, 49–174 (1960).
143. MODIGLIANI, F. and BRUMBERG, R. E., 'Utility Analysis and the Consumption Function: An Interpretation of Cross-Section Data', in KURIHARA (ed.), *Post-Keynesian Economics*, North-Holland, New Brunswick N.J., 388–436 (1954).
144. MODIGLIANI, F. and SUTCH, P., 'Innovations in Interest Rate Policy', *American Economic Review*, Papers and Proceedings (May 1966).
145a. MORGAN, J., 'Factors Relating to Consumer Saving, when it is Defined as a Net-Worth Concept', in KLEIN, L. R. (ed.), *Contributions of Survey Methods to Economics*, Columbia University Press, New York (1954).
145b. MORGAN, J., 'A Comment on Miller and Watts Paper' (*op. cit.* 139).
146a. MORGAN, V. E., *The Structure of Property Ownership in Great Britain*, Clarendon Press, Oxford (1960).
146b. MORGAN, V. E., 'Personal Saving and the Capital Market', *District Bank Review* (1967).
147. MURRAY, R. F., *Economic Aspects of Pensions: A Summary Report*, N.B.E.R., New York (1968).
148. MUSGRAVE, R. A., *The Theory of Public Finance*, McGraw-Hill, New York (1959).
149. MUSGRAVE, R. A. and DOMAR, E., 'Proportional Income Taxation and Risk-Taking', *Quarterly Journal of Economics*, **LVIII**, 388–422 (1944).
150. MUSGRAVE, R. A. and PAINTER, M. S., 'The Impact of Alternative Tax

Structures on Personal Consumption and Saving', *Quarterly Journal of Economics*, **LXII**, 475–500 (1947–48).

151. MUTH, R. F., 'The Demand for Non-Farm Housing', in HARBURGER, A. C..(ed.), *The Demand for Durable Goods*, University of Chicago Press, 29–96 (1960).

152. NASULAND, B., 'Some Effects of Taxes on Risk Taking', *Review of Economic Studies*, **XXXV**, 289–306 (July 1968).

153. NATIONAL ACCOUNT STATISTICS, *Sources and Methods* (ed. R. MAURICE), H.M.S.O., London, 99–201 (1968).

154. NATIONAL BUREAU OF ECONOMIC RESEARCH, 'The Behaviour of Income Shares – Selected Theoretical and Empirical Issues', *Studies in Income and Wealth*, **XXVII**, Princeton University Press, N.J. (1964).

155. NATIONAL AND SCOTTISH SAVINGS COMMITTEES, *Evidence in Committee on the Working of the Monetary System*, H.M.S.O., London (1960).

156. NATIONAL INSTITUTE OF ECONOMIC AND SOCIAL RESEARCH, *Short-run Forecasting of Motor Cars* (1968).

157a. NERLOVE, M., 'The Market Demand for Durable Goods: A Comment', *Econometrica*, **28** (1960).

157b. NERLOVE, M. and WALLIS, K. F., 'Use of the Durbin–Watson Statistic in Inappropriate Situations', *Econometrica*, **34**, 235–238 (1966).

158. NEVITT, A. A., *Housing, Taxation and Subsidies*, Nelson and Sons, London (1966).

159. NICHOLSON, J., 'The 1955 Savings Survey', *Bulletin of Oxford University Institute of Statistics* (1958)

160. NORTON, W., *An Econometric Model of the Monetary Sector in the U.K.*, Unpublished Ph.D. Thesis, University of Manchester (1967).

161. O.E.C.D., *Capital Markets Study*, **II, III** and **IV**, O.E.C.D. (1968, 1969 and 1967).

162a. ODLING-SMEE, J. C., 'The Rise in the United Kingdom Personal Saving Ratio', *Bulletin of Oxford Institute of Statistics*, **29**, No. 3, 281–287 (Aug. 1967).

162b. ODLING-SMEE, J. C., 'The Private Short-term Demand for Vehicles in the United Kingdom, 1955–66: A Preliminary Investigation', *Bulletin of Oxford University Institute of Statistics*, **30**, 189–200 (1968).

163. O'HERLICHY, C. ST. J., 'Demand for Cars in Great Britain', *Applied Statistics*. **14**, 162–195 (1965).

164a. OKUN, A. M., 'Comments on "The Concepts of Saving" ', *Proceedings of the Conference on Consumption and Saving*, Philadelphia (1960).

164b. OKUN, A. M. 'Monetary Policy, Debt Management and Interest Rates: A Quantitative Approach', in *Impacts of Monetary Policy*, Commission on Money and Credit, Prentice-Hall, Englewood-Cliffs N.J. (1963).

165. OXFORD INSTITUTE OF STATISTICS, Bulletins 1955, 1956 and 1957. Articles on Saving Surveys and related topics.

166. PATINKIN, D., *Money, Interest and Prices*, Harper and Row, Evanston, Ill. (1956).

167. PAVLOPOULOS, P., *A Statistical Model for the Greek Economy, 1949–1959*, North-Holland Publishing Co., Amsterdam (1966).

168. PEARCE, I. F., *A Contribution to Demand Analysis*, Clarendon Press, Oxford (1964).

169. PEARSE, P. H., 'Automatic Stabilization of the British Taxes on Income', *Review of Economic Studies* (Feb. 1962).

170. PECHMAN, J. A., 'Yield of the Individual Income Tax During a Recession', in: *Policies to Combat Depression*, N.B.E.R.: Princeton University Press, N.J. (1956).

171. PETERS, W., 'Notes on the Theory of Replacement', *Manchester School*, **24**, 270–288 (1956).

172. POLLACK, J. J., 'Fluctuations in the United States Consumption 1919–32', *Review of Economic Studies*, **19**, 133–143 (1937).

173a. PREST, A. R., *Public Finance in Theory and Practice*, Weidenfeld and Nicolson, London (1960).

173b. PREST, A. R., 'The Sensitivity of the Yield of Personal Income Tax in the United Kingdom', *Economic Journal* (Sept. 1962).

174. REVELL, J. (Assisted by G. HOCKLEY and J. MOYLE), *The Wealth of the Nation: The National Balance Sheet of the United Kingdom, 1957–1961*, Cambridge University Department of Applied Economics (1967).

175. RICHTER, M. K., 'Cardinal Utility, Portfolio Selection and Taxation', *Review of Economic Studies* (1960).

176. RIFLER, W., *Evidence to the Radcliffe Committee on the Working of the Monetary System*, Memo. I, H.M.S.O., London (1960).

177. ROBINSON, N. Y., 'The Acceleration Principle: Department Store Inventories 1920–56', *American Economic Review* (June 1959).

178. ROOSA, R., 'Interest Rates and the Central Bank', in *Money, Trade and Economic Growth*, in honour of J. H. Williams, Harvard University Press, New York (1951).

179. ROSS, C. R., 'What Has Really Happened to Output?', *Bulletin of Oxford Institute of Statistics*, (Feb. 1964).

180. ROY, A. D., 'Safety First and the Holding of Assets', *Econometrica* (July 1952).

181. SAUNDERS, D., 'Some Problems in the Estimation of Personal Savings and Investment', *Manchester Statistical* Society (Nov. 1954).

182. SCHULTZE, C. L. and TRYON, J. L., 'Prices and Wages', in *The Brookings Quarterly Econometric Model of the United States*, North-Holland Publishing Co., Amsterdam (1965).

183. SHAPIRO, R., 'Financial Intermediaries, Credit Availability and Aggregate Demand', *Journal of Finance*, **XXI**, (Sept. 1966).

184. SILBER, W., 'Portfolio Substitutability Regulations and Monetary Policy', *Quarterly Journal of Economics*, **LXXXIII**, 197–219 (1969).

185a. SMITH, P. E., 'Individual Income Tax Rate Progression and the Saving Function', *Quarterly Journal of Economics*, **LXXVIII** (1964).

185b. SMITH, P. E., 'Taxes, Transfers and Economic Stability', *Southern Economic Journal*, **XXXV**, 157–166 (1968).

186. SMITHIES, A. and BUTTERS, S. K. (eds.), *Readings in Fiscal Policy*, Allen and Unwin, London (1950).

187. SMYTH, D. J. 'Saving and the Residual Error', *Bulletin of Oxford University Institute of Statistics*, **26** (1964).

188. SNOWBARGER, M. and SUITS, D. B., 'Consumer Expenditures for Durable Goods', in FERBER, R. (ed.), *Determinants of Investment Behaviour*, N.B.E.R., New York (1967).

189. SPARKS, G. R., 'An Econometric Analysis of the Role of Financial Intermediaries in Post-War Residential Business-Cycles', in *Determinants of Investment Behaviour*, N.B.E.R., New York, 301–332 (1967).

190. ST. CYR, E. B. A., 'The Cyclical Behaviour of Employment and Factor Income Shares in British Manufacturing Industry, 1955–1964', Unpublished Ph.D. Thesis, Manchester University (1966).

191. STAEHL, H., 'Short-period Variations in the Distribution of Income', *Review of Economic Studies*, **19**, 133–143 (1937).

192. STARLEAF, D. R. and REIMER, R., 'The Keynesian Demand Function for Money: Some Statistical Tests', *Journal of Finance*, **22**, 71–76 (1967).

193. STIGLITZ, J. E., 'The Effects of Income, Wealth and Capital Gains Taxation on Risk-Taking', *Quarterly Journal of Economics*, **LXXXIII**, 263–83 (1969).

194a. STONE, R., *Measurement of Consumers' Expenditure and Behaviour in the U.K. 1920–1938*, Columbia University Press, New York (1954).

194b. STONE, R., 'Private Saving in Britain, Past, Present and Future', *The Manchester School*, **32**, No. 2, 79–112 (1964).

195. STONE, R. and ROWE, D. A., 'The Market Demand for Durable Goods', *Econometrica*, **25**, 423–443 (1957).

196. STONE, R. and ROWE, D. A., 'A Post-War Expenditure Function', *The Manchester School*, **30**, 187–201 (1962).

197. STREETEN, P., 'The Effect of Taxation on Risk Taking', *Oxford Economic Papers*, V 271–287.

198a. STROTZ, R. H., 'The Empirical Implications of a Utility Tree', *Econometrica*, **25**, 269–280 (1957).

198b. STROTZ, R. H., 'The Utility Tree: A Correction and Further Appraisal', *Econometrica*, **27**, 482–488 (1959).

199a. SUITS, D. B., 'Forecasting and Analysis with an Econometric Model', *American Economic Review,* **57** (1962).

199b. SUITS, D. B., 'The Determinants of Consumer Expenditure: A Review of Present Knowledge', in *Impacts of Monetary Policy,* Commission on Money and Credit, Prentice-Hall, Englewood Cliffs N.J. (1963).

200. TAIT, A. A., *Taxation of Personal Wealth,* University of Illinois, Urbana (1967).

201. TAUBMAN, P., *A Synthesis of Saving Theory, with Special Reference to the Components of Personal Income,* Unpublished Ph.D. Thesis, University of Pensylvania (1964). Reported by J. Crockett and I. Friend in *Consumer Investment Behaviour,* N.B.E.R., New York (1967).

202. TEIGEN, R., 'Demand and Supply Functions for Money in the United States: Some Structural Estimates', *Econometrica,* **32** (Oct. 1964).

203a. THEIL, H., *Optimal Decision Rules for Government and Industry,* North-Holland Publishing Co., Amsterdam (1964).

203b. THEIL, H., *Linear Aggregation of Economic Relations,* North-Holland Publishing Co., Amsterdam (1965).

203c. THEIL, H., *Applied Economic Forecasting,* North-Holland Publishing Co., Amsterdam (1966).

204. THEIL, H. and ZELLNER, A., 'Three Stage Least Squares: Simultaneous Estimation of Simultaneous Equations', *Econometrica,* **30**, 54–78 (1962).

205. THOMPSON, L. E., BUTTERS, J. K. and BOLLINGER, L. L., *Effects of Taxation: Investment by Individuals,* Harvard University Press, Cambridge, Mass. (1953).

206a. TINBERGEN, J., *Statistical Testing of Business Cycle Theories,* **I.** *A Method and its Application to Investment Activity.* **II.** *Business Cycles in the United States, 1919–1932,* League of Nations Geneva (1939).

206b. TINBERGEN, J., *On the Theory of Economic Policy,* North-Holland Publishing Co., Amsterdam (1952).

206c. TINBERGEN, J., *Economic Policy: Principles and Design,* North-Holland Publishing Co., Amsterdam (1956).

207a. TOBIN, J., 'Liquidity Preference as Behaviour Towards Risks', *Review of Economic Studies* (1958–1959).

207b. TOBIN, J., 'The Theory of Portfolio Selection', in *The Theory of Interest Rates,* Macmillan, London, 3–51 (1965).

207c. TOBIN, J., 'Consumer Debt and Spending: Some Evidence from Analysis of a Survey', in HESTER, D. and TOBIN, J. (eds.), *Studies of Portfolio Behaviour,* Wiley & Sons, New York (1967).

208. TUSSING, A., 'Can Monetary Policy Influence the Availability of Credit', *Journal of Finance,* **XXI** (March 1966).

209. UNIVERSITY OF MICHIGAN, (SURVEY RESEARCH CENTER) *Life Assurance Ownership Among American Families,* University of Michigan (1957).

210. VALAVANIS, S., *Econometrics,* McGraw-Hill, New York (1959).

211. WATTS, H. and TOBIN, J., 'Consumer Expenditure and the Capital Account', in *Studies in Portfolio Behaviour,* Wiley & Sons, New York (1967).

212. WAUGH, F. V., 'The Place of Least Squares in Econometrics', *Econometrica,* **29**, 386–396 (1961).

213. WHITE, W., 'The Changing Criteria in Investment Planning', in *Variability of Private Investment,* Part II, U.S. Government Printing Office, Washington D.C. (1962).

214. WORSWICK, G. N. D. and ADY, P. H. (eds.), *The British Economy in the 1950s,* Clarendon Press, Oxford (1962).

215. ZELLNER, A., 'The Short-run Consumption Function', *Econometrica,* **25**, 552–567 (1957).

216. ZELLNER, A., HUANG, D. S. and CHAU, L. C., 'Further Analysis of the Short-run Consumption Function with Emphasis on the Role of Liquid Assets', *Econometrica* (July 1965).

Index

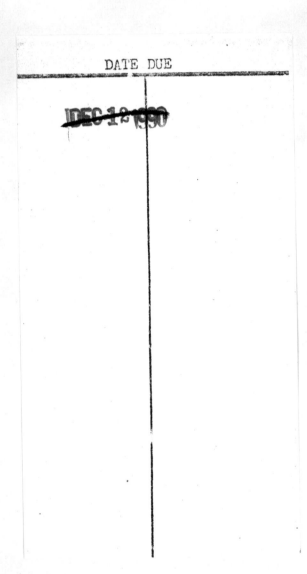